BREAKING THE IMPASSE

BREAKING

THE

IMPASSE

Consensual Approaches to
Resolving Public Disputes

LAWRENCE SUSSKIND
JEFFREY CRUIKSHANK

Basic Books., Inc., Publishers
New York

Library of Congress Cataloging-in-Publication Data

Susskind, Lawrence.
  Breaking the impasse.

  Bibliographical notes: p. 255
  Includes index.
  1. Conflict management. I. Cruikshank, Jeffrey L.
II. Title.
HD42.S87 1987   658.4   87–47511
ISBN 0–465–00751–1

For NGS and LWS

Contents

Acknowledgments

There are several of our colleagues at the Program On Negotiation at Harvard Law School to whom we owe an enormous intellectual debt. Their research and writing have been instructive and inspirational: Howard Raiffa, whose book *The Art and Science of Negotiation* provided a starting point for our work; Roger Fisher and Bill Ury, whose book *Getting to Yes* not only offered the exemplar of effective communication that we wanted to emulate but also developed the basic theoretical tenets of principled negotiation that are woven into our presentation; Bob McKersie, whose book (with Richard Walton) *A Behavioral Theory of Labor Negotiations* pointed us in the direction of integrative problem solving; Tom Schelling, whose book *The Strategy of Conflict* established one of the first frameworks within which subsequent writing on conflict management makes sense; and Jeff Rubin, whose books, particularly *Social Conflict* (with Dean Pruitt), provided us with insights into the overwhelmingly important psychological dimensions of dispute resolution. We have borrowed ideas and insights from each.

We received wise counsel at various points in the evolution of our thinking from still other colleagues and friends: Michael Wheeler, Robert Fogelson, Frank Sander, Larry Bacow, John Forester, Max Bazerman, Don Connors, Harvey Brooks, Chris Carlson, Susan Carpenter, Bob Barrett, and David Godschalk. We appreciate their detailed comments on earlier drafts of our manuscript and ask their forbearance. We have relied heavily on their suggestions, often without attribution.

A number of practitioners and close observers of public dispute resolution have challenged and stimulated us; and several, by their example, helped inform our understanding of practice: Peter Adler, Howard Bellman, Gail Bingham, Ronnie Brooks, Rich Collins, Tom Colosi, Tom Dinnell, Bruce Dotson, John Ehrmann, John Folk-Williams, Eric Green, Sam Gusman, Phil Harter, Bill Humm, Sandy Jaffee, Frank Keefe, W. J. D. Kennedy, Chris Kirtz, Jim Laue, Bill Lincoln, John McGlennon, Jim McGuire, Jonathan Marks, David O'Connor, Ric Richardson, Peter Schneider, Tom Scott, Linda Stamato, David Straus, and Joshua Stulburg.

Several graduate students and research staff members played a pivotal role in helping to document the successful mediation efforts described in this book: Eileen Babbitt, Nancy Baldwin, Heidi Burgess, Anne Cook, Norman Dale, Michael Elliott, Diane Fish, Wendy Fishbeck, David Gilmore, Kate Hildebrand, Stephen Hill, Diane Hoffman, John Horberry, Alexander Jaegerman, Karl Kim, Ron Kirtsner, Jennifer Knapp-Stumpp, Steve Konkel, David Kroninberg, Sandy Lambert, Scott McCreary, Jerry McMahon, Denise Madigan, Allan Morgan, Connie Ozawa, Maria Papalambros, Sebastian Persico, Wendy Rundle, Deborah Sanderson, Douglas Smith, Timothy Sullivan, Sylvia Watts, Alan Weinstein, Julia Wondolleck, and Karita Zimmerman.

The Kendall Foundation, the William and Flora Hewlett

Acknowledgments

Foundation, and the General Electric Foundation provided essential financial backing and encouragement at crucial junctures.

We thank everyone listed here, as well as all our other colleagues, friends, and family who offered encouragement and advice. Any flaws, errors, and weaknesses in our argument are of our own making.

BREAKING THE IMPASSE

All of the dispute resolution efforts described in this book are true, although all names and locations have been changed. At times, we have combined features of several cases to reduce the number of stories needed to make key points.

CHAPTER 1

Introduction

In the United States, we are at an impasse. Public officials are unable to take action, even when everyone agrees that something needs to be done. Consider the following:

- Almost every effort to build prisons, highways, power plants, mental health facilities, or housing for low-income families is stymied by nearby residents. There has not been a single hazardous waste treatment facility built in this country since 1975, even though everyone agrees that such plants are needed to avoid "midnight dumping" of dangerous chemicals.[1] Public officials find that even substantial electoral victories do not translate into the power needed to build such facilities.

- Four out of every five times the Environmental Protection Agency (EPA) issues new regulations, its lawyers wind up in court fending off industry's claims that the agency is being too tough on them, or fighting environmentalists' charges that it is not being tough enough. Other agencies also find that their judgments are constantly challenged, in many instances by groups with minimal technical capacity.[2]

· Every effort by public agencies to shift priorities in response to new problems is met by fierce resistance from organizations that are content with the status quo. Media campaigns, intensive lobbying, referendums, and similar strategies give these groups substantial leverage.

· The courts find it difficult to impose their will. Groups unhappy with court decisions press their legislators to change the relevant laws. Cases come back again and again on appeal as single-minded groups seek to have things their way.

Let us look at a specific situation to see just how this paralysis sets in. We will call the city Middletown, although the facts are a composite of real events in more than a dozen American cities.[3]

Almost everyone in Middletown agreed that something needed to be done to help the homeless. The rapid rise in housing costs (as well as cutbacks in spending for public housing) had increased the number of families without shelter, as well as those living in terribly overcrowded conditions. In addition, the deinstitutionalization of mental patients and cutbacks in funds for mental health care dramatically increased the number of people with severe disabilities on the street. Crime levels had risen, both public and private social service agencies were overburdened, and a great many groups were clamoring for the city to take action.

A task force appointed by the mayor completed a quick survey that confirmed the scope of the problem. The task force report called on the city to make additional community development funds available to build and operate temporary shelters for the homeless. Next, the city's housing department identified fifteen possible sites for such shelters. The city welfare department then proposed an innovative design for inexpensive communal shelters. The local press supported the findings and recommendations of the task force, and editorialized in favor of quick action.

Nevertheless, as soon as the housing department's suggested list of sites was published, the city council was overwhelmed with calls from community groups and business organizations opposed to the construction of temporary shelters in their own neighborhoods. A new organization—Real Help for the Homeless (RHH)—began a media blitz against the idea of temporary shelters. They claimed that the people on the street were in need of permanent housing, as well as a wide range of support services—job training, better nutrition, family counseling, day care, and help in dealing with a range of alcohol and drug-related abuse problems. Moreover, RHH criticized the mayor for failing to appoint one of its members to the task force, and charged that the whole idea of temporary communal shelters was simply window dressing, designed to keep costs to a minimum and to salve the consciences of middle-class do-gooders.

A third group, the Coalition for the Homeless (CFH)—spearheaded by church groups and well-established social service organizations—went to court to press the city to act on the recommendations of the mayor's task force. CFH charged that the city was in violation of its own laws, as well as regulations governing the use of federal and state community development grants. These grants, they pointed out, were intended to benefit *all* citizens, especially the poor and the homeless.

Meanwhile, the city buildings department issued a statement indicating that the proposed temporary shelters would have to meet regular city building codes for residences or they would not be allowed to open. The state social service agency informed the mayor and the local welfare department that federal and state housing assistance funds had to be used to provide real housing, not simply temporary communal shelter. Without access to these funds, the city was going to have insufficient resources to tackle the problem of the homeless. Moreover, the social service agency expressed its opposition to temporary communal shelters as a solution to the problems of the homeless.

One member of the city council proposed that a referendum be placed on the ballot in the upcoming city council election so that the public could vote on whether or not to build temporary communal shelters. Several council members, each of whom opposed the idea of temporary shelters for different reasons, stated publicly that nothing should be done until the results of the next general election provided a mandate on how to handle the homelessness question.

Groups in favor of very different referendum articles emerged. In one neighborhood, for example, a group of residents drew up a referendum designed to exempt their community from consideration as a shelter site. They already had a jail, they argued; why should they also be stuck with a shelter?

In the first eighteen months after the task force issued its report, nothing was done. CFH's legal challenge was rejected by the court; it promptly filed an appeal. The results of the city council elections were inconclusive, as several incumbents on different sides of the homelessness question were reelected. A majority of voters failed to register a vote on the competing referendum questions. Unexpectedly, the city's lawyer charged that at least two of the referendum questions that passed were illegal, and the city went to court to challenge them.

The mayor and the governor—who each represented different political parties—transformed the question of whether state housing assistance funds could be used for temporary shelter into a battle over local versus state control. Concurrently, bills introduced by Middletown's legislative delegation were bottled up in a subcommittee headed by a rural legislator, who cast the problem of homelessness as something each city should handle on its own. In various public forums and on talk shows, RHH and CFH engaged in increasingly acrimonious debates about the elusive distinction between the types of public assistance that would solve the problems of the homeless and those that would create dependency.

Winter came and went. Newspaper accounts of families suffering from exposure began to dwindle. As the public gradually lost interest, the city council and the mayor turned their attention to other issues. The municipal and state agencies involved with the problems of the homeless continued to meet and discuss alternative courses of action. The RHH members staged several dramatic confrontations, occupying an abandoned building that they claimed should be turned over to advocates for the homeless. The city council decided to hold still another round of hearings, but nothing came of them. During the summer and early fall, the city threatened police action to evict the squatters from the abandoned building, but again, nothing happened.

As the next Thanksgiving approached, the mayor announced that the city was about to begin construction of two temporary shelters. As soon as that announcement was made, angry residents in the two targeted neighborhoods went to court, charging that the proposed temporary structures would violate the city's zoning code and also that the city had failed to complete the necessary environmental impact studies. The RHH organized a demonstration by "street people" who announced that they would refuse to live in temporary communal shelters. Then, RHH insisted that it should be given funds to build real housing and provide social services for the homeless.

The Middletown Chamber of Commerce announced that it had identified a team of experienced business executives prepared to work with the city to find ways of operating the two existing shelters more effectively. This turn of events suggested that the problems of the homeless had once again percolated to the top of the city's agenda. This time, though, there were differences. In general, the key players had a lot less patience. The mayor was rebuffed when he sought further support from the business community. Several neighborhood leaders who were energetic and respected participants the previous winter now dropped out of sight. On other fronts, people who could have been helpful apparently decided to throw in the towel.

Why is it that the duly elected officials in Middletown reached this impasse, even though almost everyone agreed that something should be done?

Why is it that the existing administrative procedures for setting standards, fashioning policy, and allocating public resources did not produce results?

Why is it that going to court failed to resolve the conflicts that emerged?

Was there something special about the circumstances faced by elected officials, action groups, and business leaders in Middletown—or were they in fact facing the types of problems now plaguing many communities?

What else might the residents and leaders of Middletown have tried? What should they do differently the next time?

In fact, Middletown was not unique. Nor is the kind of stalemate we have described limited to policy disputes concerning the homeless. Whenever community leaders try to set standards, allocate resources, or make policy in contemporary society, we can expect a fight. And, as the Middletown case suggests, these disputes are neither quiet nor limited. Most often they involve intense confrontations that move from arena to arena.

Middletown's deadlock raised cries for "greater leadership." This is often the reaction when a community is unable to act. But the best alternative to deadlock is not tougher decision making by elected or appointed officials. In fact, when frustrated officials try even harder to impose their wills, more intense versions of the same disputes are likely to erupt.

The "laws" of public policymaking tend to parallel the laws of physics: for every imposed action, there is an equal and opposite reaction. Thus, the act of imposing a decision can trigger a more heated and protracted dispute than the content of the decision originally merited. Preemptive authoritarian actions usually generate strong opposition.

Nor is compromise the answer—at least not in the familiar sense of that word. Compromise requires each party to make concessions, to "give up" something. But why should anyone offer to make concessions if everyone has been honest about their real wants and needs? Compromise suggests an outcome that just barely meets everyone's acceptable minimum. Why should this be satisfactory? Why not strive for an agreement that comes as close as possible to everyone's highest aspirations?

By definition, political compromise offers a lot less than what each side hoped to achieve. Thus, it is not likely that the parties will be enthusiastic about implementing agreements achieved through compromise.

Important public policy disputes often wind up in court. This may be because the parties involved are mired in indecision, as in Middletown; or because preemptive actions by public officials are challenged; or because political compromise has broken down. Litigation generally costs a lot of money and takes a lot of time, but it often seems the only option left to an aggrieved group. Unfortunately, the courts are often unwilling (and in many instances, unable) to fashion remedies that meet the needs of all sides.[4] Simply put, the court's purpose is to interpret the law, not to reconcile conflicting interests.

Elections are no more effective at settling policy disputes. Candidates tend to stress personality as much as issues, and even the most conscientious politicians have to balance numerous considerations. Many important public policy issues cross political boundaries, and therefore require the cooperation of local, regional, state, and federal officials. No single officeholder can deliver solutions, even from the top! Mandates are rarely clear. An electoral victory for a given candidate is hard to interpret as a statement of the public's will on a specific controversy.

Referendums are equally problematic as they usually present complex questions in overly simplified yes-or-no terms. In addition, they loom like a sword over the heads of public officials, and discourage them from acting decisively when disputes arise. Finally, because those with the money to shape public perceptions often seem to control the outcome of the electoral process, neither elections nor referendums seem to be a fair indicator of how the public wants a particular policy dispute settled.

It is unrealistic for us to expect administrative agencies (like the EPA or the Federal Trade Commission [FTC]) to rescue us when other mechanisms fail.[5] Most administrative procedures, such as hearings, are too formal to be of much help. The rules tend to get in the way of working things out. Furthermore, administrative agencies are not expected to find ways of resolving disputes. They are supposed to make sure that regulations are enforced, and that predetermined guidelines are applied uniformly. This means, of course, that unique circumstances cannot be taken into account—in most cases, it is precedent that must be observed. And administrative resolution of public disputes tends to favor those with the resources to lobby and play other behind-the-scenes political games.

Though our representative democracy—with its separate levels and branches of government—is the foundation of our political system, we need to improve the ways in which we use it to resolve public disputes. We must achieve better results at lower cost. In particular, we need to find ways of dealing with differences that will restore public confidence in government, and improve relationships among the various segments of our society.

Fortunately, new approaches to resolving public disputes have been developed and tested over the past few years. The results have been quite impressive. Indeed, there is good reason to believe that the residents and officials in Middletown, as well as those involved in many other public disputes, had tools available to them which might have proved very helpful. Those tools are *negotiated approaches to consensus building* and they have worked effectively in many situations.

Consensus building requires informal, face-to-face interaction among specially chosen representatives of all "stakeholding" groups; a voluntary effort to seek "all-gain" rather than "win-lose" solutions or watered-down political compromise; and, often, the assistance of a neutral facilitator or mediator. Such approaches must be treated as supplements—and not alternatives—to conventional decision making. Officials with statutory power must retain their authority in order to ensure accountability.

Negotiated approaches to consensus building are both deceptively simple and extraordinarily complex. What could possibly be simpler than the idea of getting everyone in a dispute together to talk things out? Yet consider the challenging questions that must be answered before anyone is likely to come to the negotiation table.

- How should the appropriate participants be identified?
- How can informal negotiations avoid violating "sunshine" (e.g. open meeting) laws and other regulations that guarantee government accountability?
- Why would those with formal authority or substantial political power agree to meet with less powerful groups?
- Do people have to give up their right to litigate if they participate in a consensus-building effort?
- How can ad hoc groups be bound by the promises they make?
- What sort of technical help must be provided to less experienced participants?
- Do informal negotiations have to take account of agreements reached in earlier situations?
- Are there people with the skills needed to mediate such disputes?

Though there are indeed satisfactory answers to these and other significant questions, it should be clear why it is no simple task to "get everyone together to talk things out." If the obstacles to consensus building were trivial, we would not have so many unresolved public disputes confronting us today.

This book offers advice to government officials, business leaders, and citizen activists interested in using negotiated approaches to consensus building to resolve public disputes. Drawing on a decade of research and experimentation in the dispute resolution field, we describe what has worked, and why. We point out the pros and cons of consensus building, and indicate the best ways of persuading others to use these approaches to resolve public disputes. We offer guidelines for selecting facilitators and mediators, and suggest appropriate remedies should negotiations go awry.

Although most of us will never hold elective office, many of us will inescapably be drawn into public disputes. For example:

- A private developer or a public agency might decide to build a structure in our neighborhood that will have a negative impact. Can we trust the regulatory system to protect our interests?
- Deep cuts may have to be made in local, state, or federal budgets. These will effect our families, employers, or other groups to which we belong. What role do we want in setting new spending priorities?
- New health and safety regulations are likely to be adopted from time to time. Some may cause our workplaces to shut down, or may otherwise transform our community. Are we willing to leave standard-setting responsibility to anonymous agency personnel?
- The water, soil, or air around us may become contaminated. Will we be forced to give up our homes? Would the government provide assistance if we were wiped out financially?
- The costs of basic utilities and public services are increasing

because so many people are taking a "not-in-my-backyard" approach to the siting of regionally necessary, but locally noxious, facilities. What can we do to make sure that siting decisions are made, and are made sensibly?

· The unavailability of liability insurance is reducing the quality and scope of services that we, our families, and our employers need. Some experts feel that this is the result of government policy. What will we do about it?

· The inappropriate management of our common resources continues to threaten the delicate ecological balance that sustains the planet. Do we want some say in such all-important resource management decisions?

We believe that ordinary citizens can use negotiated consensus building both to secure their own interests and to advance the public good.

We believe that the only way to avoid stalemate, reduce the need for litigation, and restore the credibility of government is to generate agreement on how to handle the problems that confront us. We argue not for political compromise, but for voluntary agreements that offer the wisest, fairest, most efficient, and most stable outcomes possible. This requires that all stakeholders have a chance to participate directly in any dispute resolution effort. It certainly requires substantial time and the investment of public funds. We are convinced, though, that in most cases the savings will far outweigh the additional costs.

Ours is not a nostalgic call for more direct democracy. Nor do we suggest that those with statutory authority should abdicate their rightful role as decision makers. Instead, we advocate a redefinition of both leadership and responsible citizenship. Political leaders, we argue, should take more responsibility for building consensus; citizens, public interest groups, and business leaders should participate more willingly in the search for solutions that maximize mutual gain and improve long-term relationships.

Most participants in public disputes are so accustomed to thinking in win-lose terms that they cannot imagine an approach that seeks to ensure mutual gain for all contending parties. Moreover, many sophisticated analysts of government decision making are quick to explain that face-to-face negotiation aimed at joint problem solving (rather than political compromise) is either impractical or inappropriate. It is impractical, they say, because large numbers of people simply never agree on anything—let alone on complicated matters of public policy. Further, they assert, the interests of some groups (such as generations yet unborn) are impossible to represent. They warn that it is inappropriate to seek consensus on public policy questions, because articulate and powerful groups will surely coopt or overpower their less articulate or less powerful opponents. Only the current adversarial process, they contend, adequately protects the interests of the disadvantaged.

We address these arguments later on. For now, suffice it to say that we do not agree. In our view, conventional methods of dispute resolution do a poor job of protecting the interests of the least powerful. Negotiated approaches to consensus building do demonstrably better.

This book is written primarily for the layperson, and only secondarily for students of dispute resolution. It draws heavily on the research of the Public Disputes Program at the Massachusetts Institute of Technology (part of the interuniversity Program on Negotiation based at Harvard Law School). We have spoken at length with, and also observed, elected officials, judges, and administrative personnel at every level of government. Similarly, we have worked closely with businesspeople, leaders of citizen groups, ordinary citizens, and most important, a pioneering band of professional mediators who have extended their practice from the familiar domains of collective bargaining and international diplomacy to the new arena of public disputes.

Introduction

Negotiated approaches to consensus building have worked in a wide range of difficult and politically charged situations. They are practical, appropriate, and require no new legislation. They can be tried anywhere, and at any time. Most important, they make their own friends. Once the word is out, we expect the results to speak for themselves.

CHAPTER 2

Theory and Practice of Dispute Resolution

A number of public disputes have received a great deal of attention in recent years: New York City's Westway (west side highway construction) controversy, the toxic waste clean-up efforts at Love Canal in Niagara Falls, New York; the closing of the Three Mile Island nuclear power plant in Pennsylvania, offshore oil exploration on the east and west coasts, the battle over Native American fishing rights in the Great Lakes, various efforts to combat acid rain by restricting coal burning in the midwest, numerous attempts nationwide to build low-income housing in mixed-income areas, failed efforts in many states to build new prisons, the federal debate over the siting of radioactive waste dumps, experiments with genetically engineered crops and drugs, the use of untested pesticides in emergency situations, the reallocation of water rights (and the diversion of water) in arid sections of the country, the construction of the trans-Alaska pipeline, and changes in farm credit policy. All have involved drawn-out battles in which at least one group has challenged legislative, administrative, or judicial decisions it has found unacceptable.

All of these controversies fall into a category that we call distributional disputes. They differ markedly from a second category of disputes that center primarily on the definition of constitutional or legal rights. Distributional disputes focus on the allocation of funds, the setting of standards, or the siting of facilities (including how we use our land and water). Constitutional disputes, such as those surrounding school desegregation, abortion, prayer in the schools, homosexual rights, the teaching of creationism, affirmative action, and the right to die, hinge primarily on interpretations by the courts of constitutionally guaranteed rights.

When fundamental constitutional rights are at stake, we properly turn to our judicial system. It is certainly conceivable that after the courts have defined these rights, some form of consensus building might assist in protecting them, or in reconciling them with other valid interests. We leave it to others to decide whether consensual approaches to dispute resolution can (or should) be used in resolving constitutional questions. However, when the focus is on the distribution of tangible gains and losses, and not on whether something is legal or illegal, we are firmly convinced that consensus-building strategies can help.

The distinction between these two categories of disputes is sometimes clear and sometimes less clear. First, let us look at situations in which the distinction is clear. Most disputes over environmental standard setting and utility rate setting involve the allocation of tangible benefits and costs, rather than inherent constitutional guarantees. This does not minimize the seriousness of these disputes. When higher environmental standards translate into lower corporate profits, affected corporations may well object. Conversely, if lower standards promise greater profits while threatening to endanger public health and safety, this can trigger challenges from consumer advocacy organizations or public interest groups. Regardless of which interest groups are objecting, they do so in the hope of affecting the distribution of gains and losses. Neither side disputes the government's basic right to set rates or standards.

When a new jail, oil refinery, halfway house, or landfill is proposed, nearby residents consider themselves potential losers. They fear a decline in property values, increased risks to health and safety, or both. Although the region as a whole may benefit, they stand to lose. Therefore, they are willing to spend considerable amounts of time and money to reverse a particular siting decision. They may make reference to questions of legality or fundamental rights, but what they are really contesting is a specific allocation of gains and losses, and not the government's right to site facilities.

Distributional and constitutional disputes often become entangled. For example, opponents of proposed development projects may contend that a rezoning proposal exceeds constitutional limits. Likewise, industrial interests may challenge the administration of a safety or environmental regulation on due process grounds. (For example, they may contend that Congress has exceeded the powers assigned to it by the Constitution's "commerce clause.") They may contest both the proposed regulations that affect them adversely and the government's authority to regulate.

In some instances, such confusion may be unavoidable. In others, it may be more deliberate. Some challenges to the exercise of governmental authority obviously stem from sincere ideological differences; others are cynically conceived delaying tactics. In either case, every fundamental challenge—whether ideologically motivated or tactically inspired—must be considered by the courts. Thus, final distributional decisions are, in most instances, postponed until questions of fundamental rights can be resolved.

If, as is often the case, the government's power to set policy or allocate resources is ultimately reaffirmed, the protagonists may well shift the battle to another arena in which the question is no longer whether government action is permissible, but when, where, and how it will be handled. In other words, once the constitutional question is settled, the distributional dispute can begin in earnest.

COMPROMISE AS A STRATEGY FOR HANDLING DISTRIBUTIONAL DISPUTES

In most distributional disputes, the contending forces begin by concentrating all their energies on winning—by mustering a majority in a legislative body, lobbying for supportive administrative rulings, cultivating sympathetic executive action, or securing a favorable court ruling. Disputing parties may seek to "logroll" (exchange votes), build coalitions, attempt to alter public opinion through the manipulation of the mass media, initiate referendums, or promise political or financial backing to get their way. These are the classic techniques of political bargaining.

There is nothing intrinsically wrong with such wheeling and dealing. The problem is, though, that it often produces minimally acceptable results, or no results at all. Stalemates have become quite common, even when all the disputing parties agree that something ought to be done. Although the details of the Middletown case (described in the introduction) are fictitious, the dynamics of the impasse it illustrates are all too real. When contending groups are focused on winning outright, the result is frequently a deadlock. As long as stalemates persist, important problems remain unresolved. Sometimes such a delay multiplies the inherent dangers, and compounds the difficulty of implementing meaningful solutions.

All too often, when the process of political bargaining produces a compromise, one group or another later realizes that it has been bullied into making unrealistic commitments, or bluffed into accepting less than it might otherwise have deserved. Those who feel "taken" in this way often refuse to honor their commitments. Thus, disputes that seem to have been settled in this fashion remain unresolved.

The compromise solutions that emerge from the normal political hurly-burly represent the path of least resistance. Because homes, fortunes, and even lives may well be at stake, though, it seems irresponsible—almost criminal—to accept anything less than the wisest long-term response. In our society, we cling to the belief that truly important decisions should be made "on the merits," and that they should incorporate all relevant knowledge and experience. Yet we know, and daily we see more evidence, that this is not what happens.

Instead, we often settle for political compromise achieved by splitting the difference. When two or more groups are stalemated, and both recognize that they have exhausted all means of persuasion, they sometimes agree to share the pain and make equal concessions. It should be obvious, though, that a "down-the-middle" split can produce odd results in public policymaking situations. For example, the midpoint between twelve dollars an hour and ten dollars an hour in a collective bargaining dispute is clear, but there is no midpoint between a hydroelectric plant and a nuclear power plant.

Logrolling is often used to achieve political compromise, although it, too, can produce less than satisfactory agreements. Logrolling cannot occur unless those involved in one decision are also empowered to decide other issues as well. If they are, they can swap votes with other decision makers. But to prevail on one issue, a representative must forfeit his or her vote on another. What this means is that some portion of each representative's constituents will see its most fundamental concerns bargained away in the name of political expedience.

GOOD OUTCOMES OF NEGOTIATED SETTLEMENTS

Based on the research and writing of a great many experts who study the broad spectrum of disputes, we have identified four characteristics of a good negotiated settlement: fairness, efficiency, wisdom, and stability. The outcomes generated by political compromise often fail to meet these tests.

FAIRNESS

One obvious way to evaluate the fairness of a settlement is to judge the fairness of the process by which the resolution was reached. This suggests a number of questions, such as:

- Was the process open to public scrutiny?
- Were all the groups who wanted to participate given an adequate chance to do so?
- Were all parties given access to the technical information they needed?
- Was everyone given an opportunity to express his or her views?
- Were the people involved accountable to the constituencies they ostensibly represented?
- Was there a means whereby a due process complaint could be heard at the conclusion of the negotiations?

What counts most in evaluating the fairness of a negotiated outcome are the perceptions of the participants. The key question is, "Were the people who managed the process responsive to the concerns of those affected by the final decision?" A dispute resolution process open to continuous modification by the disputants is, we would argue, the approach most likely to be perceived as fair.

Some dispute resolution experts disagree with this analysis.[1]

They argue that what counts most in evaluating fairness is that the rules of the game should not change. Central to this view is the notion of "winning the game." Those who focus on the rules not changing believe that a fair process is one that allows each disputant an equal chance to obtain every objective he or she wants. This belief leads to a bias in favor of litigation, because, presumably, the administration of the law always remains the same regardless of who the disputants are. Adherents of this view believe that litigation is always preferable to ad hoc dispute resolution efforts because the rule of law is assumed to remain constant.

Let us examine these different views about fairness in the context of the homelessness debate in Middletown, as presented in the introduction. If "winning the game" is most important, then the public officials, advocate groups, business representatives, and neighborhood residents involved in the dispute will want a guarantee that the rules by which a decision is to be made will not change unexpectedly. Any shift in procedure might undercut a carefully planned strategy, and that would be unfair. Each group's goal is to control the final policy decision, so they would surely cry "foul" if new decision rules or procedures were used to overrule their claims.

On the other hand, if the satisfaction of all the stakeholding parties is the desired outcome, no one would want the rules of the game to get in the way of an ingenious solution. If the stakeholders view homelessness as a problem to be solved, then "winning" and "losing" are irrelevant. The only issue is whether the homeless can find a decent place to live. If they cannot, everyone loses.

In a problem-solving context, perceived fairness depends more on the willingness of the parties to accommodate each other's special needs than on the rules not changing. In the Middletown case, the mayor, the city council, the various local and state agencies, and the advocacy organizations might have gotten together to invent a solution which took account of each disputant's special needs. For example, a strategy that provided temporary housing in churches or local armories would have gotten the homeless off the street, and thereby would have met their short-term needs. Such a strategy could have been linked to a city or state commitment to convert at least one abandoned building in each neighborhood to longer-term housing for needy residents—a tactic that would have addressed the welfare and housing agencies' concerns. The advocacy group for the homeless, RHH, might have been given the task of designing prototype social services for the first rehabilitated housing units. If this was accomplished successfully, RHH then could have been given the long-term assignment of managing similar social services at other sites. In other words, if each stakeholding group had been given some responsibility for making a solution work (as well as part of the credit for devising a set of good ideas), they probably all would have viewed the process as fair.

An entirely different way to think about the fairness of negotiated settlements is to concentrate on the substance of agreements rather than on the process by which they are reached. What happens when we apply this point of view to the Middletown case? Assume that the participants reached agreement on a package of short- and long-term policies such as those just described. The RHH members might ask, "Does the solution take adequate account of the fact that the homeless have the least to offer and need the most help from everyone else?" In effect, RHH might use as a test of the fairness of the agreement a rule of thumb that says, "Those most able to pay should pay the most, and the neediest should receive the most."

On the other hand, some members of the city council, in assessing the substance of the same agreement, might use a different rule of thumb. For example, they might ask, "Will the gains to all the gainers outweigh the losses to all the losers if this set of policies is adopted?" In other words, they might be more concerned about the citywide balance of costs and benefits than about the specific gains or losses to any one group. By requiring every neighborhood to accept one renovated structure, their citywide test of fairness might be met.

The mayor might evaluate the substantive fairness of the proposed agreement in still another way, asking whether the majority of the voters would be satisfied. Those inclined to use the test of majority rule do so because it is often so difficult to identify gainers and losers in public disputes. They say, "I can't be sure that the gains to the gainers outweigh the losses to the losers. Everyone values gains and losses differently." So instead they ask, "Will the majority be satisfied with the outcome?" It would not be fair, in their view, to subject the majority to the will of a minority.

In short, there is no single indicator of substantive fairness that all parties to a public dispute are likely to accept. In our field work, therefore, we avoid ironclad determinations of "fairness." We simply affirm that in a public dispute, a good process produces a good outcome; and a better process, a better outcome. A process is fair if it is perceived as fair by the disputants and the community at large.

This perception of fairness can usually be evaluated by applying four tests:

1. Was the offer to participate genuine, and were all the stakeholders given a chance to be involved? Did the offer to participate come at a timely juncture (that is, before the negotiations were too far along to be affected by latecomers)? Were all parties given access to the information and technical resources they needed to express their views effectively? In the homelessness case, for example, a fair process would have afforded all groups, and not just the city council or the mayor's task force, a voice in fashioning policy.

2. Were opportunities provided for systematic review and improvement of the decision process in response to concerns of the stakeholders? Such opportunities are best provided

not in formal hearings, or behind closed doors in task force meetings, but in open problem-solving sessions at which all participants have a chance to hear each other's ideas and suggestions.

3. Was the process perceived as legitimate after it ended, as well as when it began? Did anyone feel "taken advantage of" as a result of the negotiation? By the end of the process, all participants should be able to say, "I don't feel manipulated or coopted." In Middletown, the process could have been viewed as legitimate by the stakeholders if the RHH, the Coalition for the Homeless, the business community, and others were given a direct role in framing and implementing the city's homelessness policy.

4. In the eyes of the community, was a good precedent set? "That's probably a good way to handle this sort of thing," observers should agree at the conclusion of the process. "If it comes up again, we'll know what to do." This test is tricky, of course, because the community must reserve the right to fashion brand-new solutions that break old patterns. In general, though, there must be a good rationale for departing from precedent and it must be explained carefully.

To summarize, the best way to determine the fairness of a negotiated solution is to evaluate the attitudes and perceptions of the parties most affected. This approach is certainly open to criticism, and anyone adopting this view should be prepared for the obvious complaint that they have only enhanced the perception of fairness, and not necessarily guaranteed a truly equitable outcome.

In our view, it is more important that an agreement be perceived as fair by the parties involved than by an independent analyst who applies an abstract decision rule. If the involved parties think a given process has been fair, they are more likely to abide by its outcome; if they do not, they will seek to undermine it.

EFFICIENCY

Fairness is not enough. A fair agreement is not acceptable if it takes an inordinately long time to achieve, or if it costs several times what it should have. Nor is an outcome efficient if the negotiating parties missed opportunities for "elegant trades" (that is, exchanges that would have benefited everyone without penalizing anyone).[2]

We have identified several ways of measuring the efficiency of negotiated settlements. They are relative, of course, because efficiency in an absolute sense is as difficult to define as fairness. If it takes much longer to produce an outcome that is only slightly fairer than what might have been achieved in the absence of consensus, then the process is inefficient, and probably not worth the trouble.

Our contention is that a better process produces a more efficient as well as a fairer outcome. A better process is one that first creates a climate in which side-by-side problem solving is possible. Such a climate is a prerequisite if the participants are ever to trust each other enough to divulge their true priorities. And unless they reveal their underlying interests it is almost impossible to invent the most efficient agreements. A group like RHH, for example, would never want to talk about its internal organizational needs at a city council hearing. And yet, its commitment to confrontation might reflect its concern about holding together its members rather than an unshakable political belief. If the other parties were willing to help RHH meet its organizational needs, all sides might avoid the problems caused by direct confrontation, particularly the escalation of demands and the erosion of goodwill that escalation usually causes.

The only way to transform a win-lose confrontation—such as was faced in Middletown—into an all-gain outcome is to create a climate in which the parties will listen to and try to meet each other's needs. If, for example, the city were to give RHH the responsibility and the resources to experiment with novel social service arrangements at the first new housing site for the homeless, RHH might be able to achieve its organizational objectives more effectively than through street demonstrations.

As disputants lock horns, they must choose (explicitly or implicitly) one of two strategies. They can either choose to negotiate, or they can try to act unilaterally. For those with substantial political power, it is always tempting to take the latter route, especially given the time, expense, and uncertainty associated with consensus-building negotiations. In most instances, though, unilateral action creates a false efficiency. Were the mayor of Middletown to act on the recommendations of his task force without consulting anyone else, he might achieve quick headlines and perhaps even preliminary results, but he would soon run into obstacles. Implementation problems would almost certainly arise. Based on our experience, we suggest that the public official who acts unilaterally in a public dispute "trades" several months of negotiation for roughly twice as many months or years in court. In public disputes, it is often necessary to "go slow to go fast."

There is, finally, an important tradeoff between the attributes of fairness and efficiency. It may well be possible for an informed observer to invent quickly a set of policies identical to those developed by a group of negotiators working over a long period of time. Such a brilliant individual effort would undoubtedly be more efficient than a group process. Our experience suggests, however, that perceived fairness depends on participation. Those who participate feel that they "own" the agreement, and are therefore more likely to support its implementation. The goal of efficiency, therefore, cannot be considered in isolation. Indeed, at times, it should be secondary.

At other times, efficiency must be considered paramount. When severe time constraints are imposed externally, negotiating parties must work within those limits. Some percentage of the homeless in Middletown, for example, might not survive another winter. If consensus is to be useful, it must be reached within a specific time frame.

WISDOM

What is a "wise" outcome? In one sense, wisdom is only obvious in hindsight. Most dispute resolution processes involve forecasts of some sort. It may take months, or even years, before the wisdom of such forecasts and the accuracy of the assumptions upon which they were based can be ascertained.

The key to wisdom is what has been called "prospective hindsight."[3] The participants in the Middletown dispute should have had enough experience with their own community and with similar problems of resource allocation to anticipate the impasse they were creating. They also should have known enough about their own city to imagine which policies would work and which would not. In some situations, of course, prospective hindsight is harder to develop.

This was the case in a Massachusetts dispute concerning the construction of a proposed shopping mall in a large wetland.[4] To satisfy state regulations, as well as the "dredge and fill" requirements of the federal government, the developer proposed to create replacement wetlands several miles away from the site he wanted to fill.

The state regulatory agency had to decide whether or not man-made wetlands would function enough like natural wetlands to meet the same ecological needs. If the developer's assertions proved wrong, it would be too late. By the time the artificial wetlands failed, the natural wetlands would have been destroyed to make way for the shopping mall. At the same time, it would be impractical to insist that the developer prove his man-made wetlands would work satisfactorily before granting him a permit to build the mall. He would have had to pay several hundred thousand additional dollars, and wait more than a decade, before he had any idea whether he would be allowed to build his mall. This would be financially infeasible and probably legally unacceptable.

If a credible research organization had been studying the functioning of artificial wetlands for a decade or more, the regulators might have had the information they needed to make a wise decision. On the other hand, they might not. Suppose such experiments had only been conducted in California. A skeptic would surely point out that tests done in California could not necessarily predict what would happen in Massachusetts, given that ecological conditions in the two states are so different. Moreover, the results of a decade-long study might be mixed. They might indicate, for example, that artificial wetlands only function like natural wetlands in certain respects. Moreover, someone in Massachusetts would almost certainly argue that natural wetlands should not be destroyed in favor of man-made wetlands on the basis of a single study.

In fact, scientists know very little about how natural wetlands are created.[5] Developers know even less. In the Massachusetts example, the developer secured the services of several environmental consulting firms who assured the state that wetlands could indeed be designed and created successfully. The state regulatory agency, relying on its own experts, disagreed.

Sometimes we have no relevant experience and prospective hindsight is hard to muster. In other situations, we have partially relevant experience that is interpreted differently by competing experts.

This often leads to the dismal process of "advocacy science," in which disputing parties use hired experts to undercut each other's claims. As a result, useful information is obscured. Instead of being examined and resolved, legitimate scientific and technical differences are exaggerated, as each side attempts to bolster its position by attacking the validity of the information provided by others. This is a particularly dangerous practice when lives are at stake. It is therefore worth considering how advocacy science can be avoided, and how scientific and technical advisors can be employed more productively in distributional disputes.

Under present circumstances, advocacy scientists tend to "cancel each other out." Decision makers (and the public) may well throw up their hands in frustration, and decide to ignore the scientific aspects of the debate altogether. "If *they* can't agree," the public asks, "how are *we* supposed to?"

A wise settlement is one that contains the most relevant information. Advocacy science, therefore, is undesirable because it impairs the development and incorporation of wisdom.[6] But how is wisdom to be achieved if the impact of a decision only becomes evident months, or years, later? The answer lies in cooperation: both sides must participate in an effort to minimize the risk of being wrong. They must develop a working approach that accommodates the best possible technical evidence—no matter which "side" that evidence supports.

The search for a wise resolution of differences requires a collaborative inquiry—one that breaks down a complex problem into a series of mutually agreed-upon pieces. These pieces are often defined by a series of questions. What small-scale experiment could we perform to test a critical assumption upon which we disagree? What information should we try to get that would settle a key disagreement? Can we identify which evidence, obtained by agreed-upon means, would cause us to abandon our own argument and accept someone else's? Can we be educated together in the complexities of this issue?

It is not enough for the parties to reach an accord with which they are willing to live. Rather than engaging in a test of will, contending interests must examine the merits of all the arguments and evidence being put forward, including their own. To achieve a wise agreement, advocacy science must be avoided.

STABILITY

Finally, stability is a key attribute of a good settlement. An agreement that is perceived as fair, is reached efficiently, and seems technically wise is nevertheless unsatisfactory if it does not endure.

Instability can result from several sources, including unrealistic expectations. Participants in a public dispute resolution effort should put an emphasis on *feasibility*. They should not strike a deal they will be unable to implement. If one party represents a coalition, for example, that party must take responsibility for cultivating support from the full spectrum of coalition members. Otherwise, members may split off and seek to block implementation of the agreement. Each negotiating party's representative must take responsibility for meeting all internal organizational restrictions on what he or she can offer, and for handling subsequent objections from coalition members.

Feasibility may also depend on setting realistic timetables. Being overly ambitious can cause trouble later, especially if implementation depends on a sequence of reciprocal actions.

Another way of thinking about feasibility is to focus on the commitments that the parties make to each other. It is not helpful to extract unrealistic commitments from other participants, even if such promises seem like victories at the time they are secured.[7] It is better to seek and offer modest commitments rather than all-encompassing and unrealistic promises. By appointing a task force, the mayor of Middletown implied that he would solve the problem. The city council promised decisive action several times, only to find that it did not have the capacity to act. In both instances, the mayor and the council overstated what they could do. Had they forced agreement, it would surely have been temporary at best.

At times, disputants are lured into making unrealistic promises by the unexpected spirit of harmony that develops as an agreement appears within reach; at other times, disputants close their eyes to the technical, legal, economic, or financial obstacles simply because they are exhausted, and want to reach closure. In either case, a "domino effect" can eventually ensue: first one commitment falls victim to reality, and then another, until finally the whole agreement collapses.

Negotiated agreements ought to include provisions for renegotiation. Just as the quest for wisdom means that negotiators must assimilate new information, the quest for stability requires adjusting negotiated agreements in light of changing circumstances. One useful model is the "severability clause" that appears at the end of most pieces of legislation. That clause says, in effect, that if any section of the preceding law is found to be in conflict with some existing law or with the Constitution, then only the offending clause—and not the whole law—will be invalidated. This gives legislators a chance to reconvene and correct the offending clause while the rest of the law remains intact.

When framing written agreements, negotiators should include a summary paragraph stating, "If we have based our agreement on a mistaken assumption, then we will reconvene and correct that mistake." In Middletown, for example, the parties might have agreed to meet every six months to monitor implementation of their negotiated settlement, as well as to review new information on the status of the homeless.

Participants in a public dispute resolution process must recognize that stability depends upon *relationships.* Conventional methods of settling disagreements, as we have already stressed, are win-lose, confrontational encounters that create hostility and ill will. As a result, the slightest flaw in an agreement imposed by such methods will be seized upon by a disgruntled disputant and used to scuttle the entire agreement. New information and unexpected turns of events pose grave threats to nonconsensual solutions. Any wedge that a loser can find will be used to topple the agreement.

If disputing parties build a good working relationship, the prospects for stability are greatly enhanced.[8] Even under the best of circumstances, something in an agreement can go awry. At that point, the success of a renegotiation may well depend on the quality of the relationships developed during the preceding round of talks. The parties are likely to come back to fix the agreement and make it work if they feel positively about how they were treated.

FROM WIN-LOSE
TO ALL-GAIN SOLUTIONS

It is not easy to transform win-lose disputes into all-gain agreements. Above all, it involves the efficient "packaging" of items that disputants value differently.[9] This concept may sound something like the "logrolling" that leads to unstable political compromises, but it differs in several crucial respects. In the first place, the most efficient trades are only possible if all parties exchange accurate information about their true priorities. The lack of trust that typifies political bargaining often prevents the exchange of such information. In addition, it is necessary for all stakeholding groups to designate ad hoc representatives—not general-purpose public officials—to speak for them in each negotiation. This precludes the trading away of votes on items of deep concern to a small segment of a constituency. Ad hoc representatives chosen to speak for small groups do not feel the same pressure to logroll.

All-gain agreements can only be achieved when the parties stress the cooperative, and not just the competitive, aspects of their relationship.[10] These dual concerns or mixed motives must be confronted simultaneously. Conflict should not be suppressed. Indeed, it is often the only available tool for achieving badly needed reforms. But incessant confrontation—especially when everyone agrees that some action is necessary—is destructive. All-gain solutions depend on each disputant's ability to invent a way of satisfying his or her own needs while meeting the opponent's needs. This requires cooperation, even in the face of competing self-interests.

In the next chapter we recount several distributional disputes in some detail. They represent actual experiences in large cities and small towns across the United States. These disputes were not chosen at random. Rather, they were included because they illustrate certain flaws in our representative democratic system which constitute both the source of recurring public disputes and obstacles to their resolution.

CHAPTER 3

Sources
of Difficulty

It is important to stress that some of our current difficulties in formulating and implementing public policies are the result of two generations of tinkering. We are living with a paradox: many well-intentioned efforts to enhance the legitimacy of our governmental process have in fact undermined its effectiveness.

There are numerous illustrations. For example, Congress and the courts have tried to enhance the legitimacy of the rule-making process—the procedure by which administrative agencies translate the general mandate of Congress into specific regulations. Congress has passed laws requiring that rule making be conducted "in the sunshine," that adequate notice of rule making be given in the *Federal Register,* and that agencies refrain from communicating with regulatees while proposed regulations are being reviewed (to avoid the possibility of "backroom deals"). The courts have broadened the number and range of parties eligible to challenge proposed rules; they have also insisted that a detailed record of each rule-making endeavor be kept, and have made clear their intention to take a "hard look" at any and all rules to ensure that agencies conform closely to the intent of Congress. Thus we now have a hybrid rule-making process that is quite time-consuming and requires a permanent "Washington presence" for groups that want to be guaranteed timely input.[1]

These and other changes were implemented to increase the effectiveness of government, but the result has been the opposite. In 1984, for example, more than 80 percent of the regulations proposed by the EPA were challenged in court.[2] Challenges were as likely to come from environmental advocacy groups (who claimed that the agency was too sympathetic to industry) as they were from trade associations and other industry lobbies (who asserted that the agency was being too hard on them).

Standard setting is another realm in which continued efforts to make the government system more accountable has hindered its efficiency. Once a legislature has indicated its desire to clean up a region's air or a body of water, for example, it becomes the responsibility of an administrative agency to determine what the hoped-for standard of purity should be. But that agency's problem, typically, is that any given standard will please some groups and offend others, and the available scientific data (or a review of "best practice") rarely offer a definitive basis by which to justify the choice of one standard over another.

The problem is compounded when the issue is taken to court. The courts, with no particular scientific expertise, have no good way of determining whether a given standard of so many parts per million for a specific water pollutant is adequate or appropriate. All the courts can do is determine whether or not the agency has followed required procedures, and whether or not the standard seems generally consistent with the intent of Congress. Because of the scientific complexity and technical uncertainty surrounding most standard setting, expert testimony can be produced to substantiate almost every side of every question.

Advocacy science only contributes to the emerging paradox. Challenges to standard setting, in most instances, involve substantive disputes rather than procedural deficiencies. But the myriad procedural safeguards added by Congress create obstacles to reaching consensus on the substantive issues.

The pressure for openness in government decision making, combined with the willingness of the courts to take a "hard look" at agency actions, has had two unfortunate results. Although efforts to enhance the legitimacy and accountability of government are commendable in their intent, their practical effects are less laudable. It now takes much longer for our administrative and legislative bodies to reach decisions, and subsequently to implement them. Those to whom delay is an advantage have learned how to use (or abuse) these new procedural safeguards for selfish purposes. In response, agency staff realize that they are better off "going by the book," given that almost any action they take has a good chance of being scrutinized by the courts. By bureaucratizing the actions of administrative agencies (and, to some extent, of our legislative bodies as well), we have bogged them down. Moreover, we have made it less likely that a given proposal will be considered on its merits, because case-by-case reviews and interpretations force agencies to exercise precisely the sort of discretion that they now seek to avoid.

Good intentions, it seems, have led to unexpected and paradoxical outcomes. None of the many reformers who tinkered with our governmental structure suspected that more openness and accountability in government might actually reduce the likelihood that policies would be applied more wisely, respecting the unique aspects of each application. Nevertheless, that has been the effect.

Intensive lobbying is another recent and problematic innovation. The founding fathers never anticipated a permanent cadre of lobbyists—although the lobbyists evidently arrived in force shortly after the government began to operate. But it is the explosion in the numbers and influence of lobbyists since the 1960s that has forced us to confront this issue. As a society, we are of two minds about lobbying. On the one hand, we encourage all citizens to lobby their congressional representatives—after all, we reason, they must do this if they expect to be heard. At the same time, we tend to regard the permanent highly organized legislative lobbyists of special interests with suspicion.

If anything, we are even more uncomfortable with evidence of lobbying applied to the administrative arm of government. We expect administrative decisions to be based on the facts of a given situation. We fear "agency capture"—the control of the regulators by the regulated.[3]

The judicial branch is arguably the least vulnerable to lobbying. This is small comfort, though, as it must bear the burden of our efforts to control lobbying elsewhere. When we suspect that legislative and administrative decisions are the result of effective lobbying, rather than judgments based on unvarnished facts, we challenge those decisions in court. Again, this expands the courts' burden.

In sum, we have sought in various ways to bolster the legitimacy and accountability of our political system. By so doing, we have added to the time and cost of carrying out the government's business, while not necessarily addressing the difficulties that moved us to action in the first place. Rather than adopting new mechanisms more appropriate to the nature of distributional disputes, we have tried to force existing institutions into new and uncomfortable roles.

We can identify five major flaws in our representative democracy—shortcomings that foster and prolong distributional disputes. Some were inherent in the system as designed; others are the result of efforts to correct the initial deficiencies. All have become more problematic as the number and intensity of distributional disputes have risen. The five flaws—the tyranny of the majority, short-term political commitment, the inadequacies of the voting process, today's technical complexities, and the emphasis on winner-takes-all solutions—are discussed, with examples, in the following sections.

THE TYRANNY OF THE MAJORITY

If a bare majority of the electorate determines the makeup of a legislative body, and a bare majority of that legislative body controls its direction, what happens to the only slightly smaller minorities? In theory, those minorities must wait their turn, hoping to reverse their fortunes in the next election (or, when coalitions exist, on the next vote). For the minority, lobbying the winning side holds little promise—first, because those representatives themselves hold the views of the majority, and second, because those representatives are not likely to abandon their proven supporters. The obvious question that the winners ask the losers is, "But what did you do for me on the last vote?"

Of course, we have safeguards built into our governmental processes to prevent outright oppression. Also, we have shifted a great many responsibilities to the executive branch—the administrative side of government—and invested administrators with significantly more authority to blunt the power of majorities.

But an ideological component has accompanied this trend. Our implicit sense has been that minorities should be able to seek the protection of administrative agencies on technical grounds. In other words, administrators—particularly administrators whose tenure is not affected by fluctuations in leadership—should be the repository of technical expertise, and should use this expertise in nonpolitical ways. Administrative stability substitutes for political stability, and makes possible policy implementation by "professionals." These professionals, we assume, make the "correct" (and not the politically advantageous) decisions.

This implied protection of the rights of minorities has been reinforced by an activist judiciary. The courts are responsible for monitoring the fairness of administrative action. This completes the constellation of administrative safeguards. Administrative stability, procedural openness, and the "hard look" doctrine collectively ensure that the interests of the "other 49 percent" are not brushed aside.

Practically speaking, however, there are no such assurances, in part because we have thoroughly politicized our administrative and judicial processes. This sort of systematic tampering has always been a temptation to those in power, but in recent years it has been thoroughgoing and relatively aboveboard. A number of presidents and senators have proposed a "litmus test" for the politics of judges; and no one objects when incoming administrations "sweep the stables" in the agencies, reaching all the way down to the lowest levels of the bureaucracy to replace existing administrators with political allies. It is a reversion to the politics of the early nineteenth century: "To the victors belong the spoils."

In the long run, though, the spoils system did not serve Andrew Jackson's Democrats well in the 1800s and it is no more effective today. Now, as then, the minority correctly understands that judicial and administrative decisions are not always made on the merits or the facts of a matter. Those decisions may therefore have very little legitimacy—at least in the eyes of the minority—and aggrieved groups feel entirely justified in taking every conceivable step to block or overturn such decisions.

This problem is exacerbated by the fact that in real life we rarely encounter pure "majorities" and "minorities." Often, both consist of smaller, fragmented groups, usually bound together in fragile coalitions. Members of the minority may take advantage of a split in the majority on a crucial issue, "stealing" a faction to create a new majority. The result is a great and growing emphasis on coalition building, which leads directly to the growing instability of public policy. In other words, the more we make it clear that policymaking and resource allocation are purely a function of the size of the majority—and not an outgrowth of legitimate policy debate—the more we encourage majority building and policy instability.

We can identify several factors now contributing to the overall instability of government policies. Once such instability is perceived by the population at large, it becomes self-reinforcing. The minority understands that it need not heed the policy choices of the majority; the minority simply has to block implementation of those policies until the necessary realignment of interest groups can be completed. The minority correctly assumes that when they (re)gain power, they will be justified in reversing the offending policies implemented by their opponents, since those policies were manifestly political in nature. Unfortunately, there is no incentive to change the basic system—to correct the flaws that have created instability—because all parties look forward to the day when they will hold the reins and then will be able to institute self-serving policies across the broad reach of government. Contentiousness and instability, in the context of our current system, feed on themselves.

The RiverEnd case which follows is one of five stories we will present in this chapter to further illustrate the problems of resolving distributional disputes. RiverEnd, a disguised recounting of an actual conflict between environmentalists and development interests, illustrates what can happen when a minority is unwilling to accept the will of the majority.

RIVEREND: ENVIRONMENT VERSUS DEVELOPMENT

One spring morning, Dr. Horst Seybolt opened the newspaper at breakfast and scanned the front page.[4] He was stunned by what he saw. At a press conference the previous day, Governor Stratton had revealed plans for a massive transportation project. According to the governor, the state would apply for $750 million in special federal funds to extend the West Line—one of the four rapid transit lines in Capital City—out to the circumferential highway bordering the metropolitan area.

The newspaper account summarized Stratton's arguments in favor of the project. The point, the governor had said, was to reduce the number of cars coming into Capital City. The city had failed to meet the state and federal government's increasingly stringent air pollution control standards, and was now under court order to reduce traffic coming into the city. Extending the subway out to the beltway would give commuters in the suburbs to the north and west of the city a new means of getting to work without having to rely on their cars. Furthermore, Stratton had asserted, the severe traffic congestion in downtown Capital City was discouraging investment in the city. This was a problem that could only be addressed through a regional approach, with large-scale expenditures.

Seybolt, an ardent environmentalist, was well aware of Capital City's troubles with the regulatory agencies. Furthermore, as a resident of Alford, a town on Capital City's western border, he was only too familiar with the problems faced by the commuters who lived northwest of the city. But as head of the Watershed Association—a group that sought to protect the environmentally sensitive wetlands separating Alford and Capital City—Seybolt was particularly well informed about local environmental issues. He found himself reading the newspaper story with a growing sense of disbelief. The state was planning to build a massive new transportation facility, including a subway station and a huge parking garage at RiverEnd, in the heart of the local watershed.

Seybolt had no illusions about the current state of the River-End area. Originally part of a "necklace" of parks surrounding Capital City, RiverEnd had been alternately abused and neglected for decades. Local and regional officials had ignored completely the area's long-standing designation as a habitat for migratory birds and other types of wildlife. Several freight and passenger rail lines, and later a highway, had sliced the park into oddly shaped and isolated pieces. The highway actually terminated in the middle of the RiverEnd marshes, channeling high-speed traffic onto a rotary already congested with local traffic. The result was both chaotic and dangerous. More fatal car accidents had occurred at that traffic circle than at any other location in the state.

Development along the fringes of the RiverEnd area had also been haphazard. Capital City had constructed huge public housing high-rises nearby, and had encouraged industrial development along the rail lines to generate tax revenue. Some of those industries now found themselves dangerously isolated from city services, since the bridges over those same railroad tracks had been condemned. Capital City's fire engines, for example, could only reach the RiverEnd area by going through neighboring Alford.

This history of mistakes and bad planning had aroused the ire of environmentalists, including Seybolt's Watershed Association, who were by now well prepared to defend the RiverEnd area from further injury. The governor's plan, in Seybolt's estimation, was another huge step in the wrong direction. "Don't they know," he wondered to himself, "that RiverEnd is a floodplain, and a key piece of the larger watershed? Any more construction in the area will simply push flood waters into residential areas of Alford."

It was also clear that the towns between RiverEnd and the beltway (and there were quite a few) would fight hard to keep the subway out. As far as town residents were concerned, subways meant increased crime and other big-city problems. If they succeeded in blocking the subway extension, the RiverEnd stop would become the permanent end of the line, and might well have to grow even larger than the governor anticipated.

Finally, and perhaps most important, a project on the scale

that Stratton was describing would end forever the dream shared by many local residents: restoration of the mistreated RiverEnd environment.

In the following weeks, however, other groups expressed their willingness to back the governor. The state's secretary of transportation, who personally had supervised the preparation of the proposal, argued that it reflected one of the most open planning processes in the state's history. After all, he pointed out, the residents of Capital City and many of the surrounding communities had made it clear that they favored mass transit over new highways, as highways tended to destroy existing neighborhoods. The new plan was, therefore, consistent with their wishes. Officials of both Alford and Capital City, anticipating new tax revenues from the industrial and commercial development following the transit project, expressed their qualified support. Potential developers of the newly created building sites, and especially the owners of key parcels of developable land in the area, were strongly in favor of the plan. From their perspective, RiverEnd could not possibly be restored to a "natural" state. Given that reality, they said, it made sense to develop the region to its full industrial and commercial potential.

Within a month of the governor's announcement, battle lines had been drawn between the environmentalists and the advocates of development. The first step before the subway extension could begin was an environmental impact statement from the regional transportation authority, a statement required under both federal and state law. It was on this ground that the two camps would first meet formally. The governor, recognizing the growing controversy, announced that he was creating an Advisory Committee, which would enable all interested parties to have a role in the impact assessment process. Elliott Lawrence, a local university professor and mediator, was appointed chairman of the committee.

Lawrence quickly encountered the strong feelings and extreme positions that the RiverEnd transit proposal was generating. At the first meeting of the Advisory Committee, proponents of the project made their case. There was no RiverEnd "environment," they said flatly. If the state and federal government really intended to spend $750 million on the subway project, they should get their money's worth in the process—which meant constructing the largest possible parking facility, and undertaking a complete overhaul of the existing roads, rotary, bridges, and traffic patterns. The point of such a huge public investment, they said, should be to encourage a correspondingly large private investment, thereby improving the whole area.

The environmentalists, led by Horst Seybolt, responded with equal conviction. Past sins and abuses were no excuse, they argued. The only acceptable plan was a "no-build" approach, which would not only prevent future development at RiverEnd, but would also force the removal of existing environmental offenses, and mandate the upgrading and protection of the stream, wetlands, and wildlife preserve in the floodplain. This, they pointed out, would only bring the state into compliance with existing wetland protection regulations.

After a few sessions, it was clear to Committee Chairman Lawrence that the two camps were becoming dangerously polarized. The fact that the proposed project was supported unequivocally by almost all the relevant elected officials at the state and federal level had little impact on the environmentalists. The coalition of environmentalists threatened to withdraw from the advisory process and pursue their cause in court. The project proponents responded that they were perfectly willing to do battle in another arena—suggesting that they would find ways to exercise their considerable political and financial clout.

At a climactic meeting several months after the formation of the Advisory Committee, both sides announced their willingness to break off the talks. "Get off this 'no-build' craziness and talk about something realistic," a representative of the development community shouted across the crowded room at his environmental counterparts, "or we'll settle this politically. We have the elected officials on our side."

The environmentalists countered with their own threats. "Either you acknowledge the need to improve and restore this environment," Seybolt responded, "or we'll go to court. And we'll not only block this project—we'll kill every other development project you ever propose for RiverEnd."

The environmental advocates were not prepared to accept the decisions made by the governor, the congressional delegation, the state public works department, or the federal and state transit authorities. It did not matter that these were not arbitrary decisions. In fact, the agencies involved had spent millions of dollars on consultant studies, evaluating not only alternative designs for a regional transit stop, but also the feasibility of mitigating any and all adverse environmental impacts.

Nor were the environmentalists prepared to accept the decisions of their own elected local officials, most of whom endorsed the project as proposed by the state and regional agencies. Why were they unanimously in opposition? In part, it was because they assumed that all the various studies were self-serving. Indeed, they presumed that the initial decision to build a regional mass transit stop was at root a political decision, not the result of a dispassionate analysis of the transportation needs of the metropolitan population.

Environmental coalition members in the RiverEnd dispute sought support from local residents who opposed the project. They sought help from national environmental organizations. They worked through a key state representative from Alford who controlled the state legislative committee on transportation and had concerns about the impacts of the project in Alford. They approached Governor Stratton directly. Then they threatened legal action. They also tried to make support for the River-

End project an issue in municipal elections in Capital City, Alford, and other nearby towns.

In the end, through face-to-face negotiations that we will describe in detail in chapter 5, a solution emerged.

LACK OF LONG-TERM COMMITMENT

Concealed within the overall stability of our representative democracy are, of course, major fluctuations in leadership and policy. These are natural and necessary, enabling the system to accommodate changing circumstances and prevailing moods.

Our elected and appointed officials know that their tenure is likely to be short. They are therefore obliged to identify and "solve" problems within a limited time span. They know that their successors, often from opposing political factions, will be under no obligation to carry a given program or policy forward (unless, of course, there is a political advantage in doing so). As a result, huge sums of money are appropriated and spent in relatively short periods. Recent national examples include the "synfuels" program (the commercialization of coal-to-gas and other experimental technologies to decrease America's dependence on foreign energy sources), and Superfund, a large-scale effort to clean up toxic waste sites.

The synfuels program was initiated in response to the oil crises of the 1970s.[5] By 1985, when it was terminated, the synfuels board had spent several billion dollars. As soon as oil prices returned to an acceptable level, the market for synfuels— and the political consensus necessary to support an effort to reduce our dependence on foreign oil—collapsed. But the collapse of markets and consensus had little to do with the original perceived problem. America's long-term need for alternative fuel sources is no less important today than it was when the oil crisis first garnered headlines. Two lessons emerge from that experience. First, the disappearance of the immediate problem that the synfuels corporation was meant to solve dealt the program a mortal blow. Second, the synfuels program simply could not produce striking results fast enough to retain its political backing.

Similarly, Congress allocated almost $2 billion in Superfund dollars in less than five years.[6] A great many supporters of the Superfund concept were unsympathetic to the EPA's entreaties for more time and money to clean up the more than 800 chemical waste sites that had been identified.

The politicians argued that an immediate solution was needed. They were unwilling to wait for the basic research needed to make the clean-up efforts proceed effectively. (In fact, they needed results by the next congressional election.) In almost five years, the EPA was able to clean up fewer than half a dozen sites. When the 1985 debates over the reauthorization of the Superfund program began in earnest, critics of the program evidently were more concerned about the costs of clean-ups (and where the money would come from) than the clean-up problem itself. The Washington political agenda, in other words, again ignored the realities of the task.

Such short-term perspectives contribute to the inefficiency of our governmental processes. Just as government begins to master one set of responsibilities, its agenda changes. In some cases, inefficiency may be an acceptable price to pay for the short-term accountability our system provides. Other problems, however, do not lend themselves to solution by crash programs and rapid expenditures of large sums of money. Energy and environmental issues, unfortunately, are among them; this explains in part why the synfuels program and Superfund have been notably unproductive. Such problems demand steady, patient attention over years or decades and consistent appropriations (rather than massive, one-time funding). Even given boundless resources, what legislator or administrator could ever hope to "solve" our mass transit or educational problems? These are moving targets; they change even before the solutions to earlier definitions of problems can be implemented.

In some societies, a consensus on solutions to long-term problems is relatively easy to achieve. Totalitarian regimes, for instance, can simply dictate long-term policies, although they, too, have trouble implementing their intentions. Japan has been successful at consensus building, and that success has contributed greatly to Japan's postwar economic triumphs.[7] But neither the from-the-top-down methods of totalitarianism nor the facilitating cultural homogeneity of Japan hold much promise as models for American policymakers. What we need is bipartisan consensus—both on the definition of problems, and on the need for long-term commitments to their solution.

Such a consensus need not result in the removal of politics from the processes of government. Rather, politics—in certain specified instances—would be relegated a secondary role. Once bipartisan consensus had defined a given problem as deserving of this sort of special, long-term consideration, the identified problem would remain in that realm. (This would be the domestic equivalent of a long-term treaty with another country which must be honored regardless of which party or faction is in power in the United States.) The advantages would be twofold. First, the commitment to a solution would correctly be perceived as unwavering. (Our administrators, by and large, would certainly welcome the chance to avoid controversy by pointing out that they were constrained by long-term bipartisan agreements.) Second, and partly as a result, new information could be assimilated and proposed solutions revised without jeopardizing the commitment itself. Long-term commitments would accommodate frequent and sophisticated adjustments.

A case that illustrates the problems associated with the unwillingness of elected officials to take a longer-term perspective concerns the allocation of social service funds. In the mid-1970s the federal government began shifting responsibility to the states for deciding how to allocate the substantial sums of federal money provided each year in block grants. The funds had to be used for social services, but this broad stipulation left each state with substantial discretion.

Year by year, various groups within each state learned how to compete more effectively for a share of these funds. Those with longevity dominated. While social service needs continued to change, past grantees insisted that they should not be frozen out. And, because they were well organized, they were able to lobby effectively against changes in the allocation guidelines. By the mid-1980s, most officials and observers in one particular state—which we describe in the following section—agreed that it made no sense to continue allocating funds that enabled upper-middle-class children to spend their summers at camp while centers for battered women were closing for lack of financial support. Nevertheless, every effort to change this and other outdated spending priorities was defeated.

SETTING SOCIAL SERVICE PRIORITIES

State Social Service Commissioner Mary Dorada was frustrated. It was now the spring of 1983.[8] She had been trying for almost a year to put together a new set of guidelines. Her assistant commissioners had spent the better part of eighteen months preparing a detailed needs assessment; that assessment, now completed, provided unassailable evidence of shifting social service needs, particularly in poor areas of the state. Yet the cycle of the past four years was already starting to repeat itself. The telephone calls had begun and the legislative Commission on Social Services had scheduled a special hearing. That hearing, she knew, would surely degenerate into a nasty shouting match unless she withdrew her proposed guidelines. As she picked up the phone to return a call from the Associated Press, she reviewed her limited options, wondering for the thousandth time if there might be a workable alternative she had not yet considered.

Social service block grants are special in several respects. First, they offer the only unrestricted support for social services. All other human service grant programs are restricted to specific service categories or narrowly defined client groups. Second, in at least the state we are discussing, the program involves private "matching" funds. For each dollar a local service provider can raise on its own, it is eligible for matching funds from the block grant pool. (Through this and similar devices, the program attempts to be responsive to locally determined priorities.) And, finally, the pool of block grant dollars continues to grow through the contribution of state funds, because of a quirk in the original funding agreement between the state and the federal government. When the program started in the early 1970s it provided a total of $1 million to the state. By 1985 it channeled more than $20 million in state and federal funds, as well as another $4 million in private matching money, to nonprofit social service providers.

In Mary Dorada's state, there were at least four large groups with an important stake in the block grant program. The first was local officials. Even though the state share of the pool had grown larger than the federal share, local officials and social service providers viewed the money as "theirs," not the state's, to allocate. Thus, regardless of the statewide needs assessments produced annually by the commissioner's office, the majority of elected and appointed officials in the state were primarily interested in maintaining local control of funds.

But from the commissioner's standpoint the local control issue was a red herring designed to mask ulterior motives. After all, regional offices of the state social services agency had always been responsible for reviewing and approving all grants; the state was not now attempting to assert new authority. In fact, it was the commissioner's office that had originally organized local citizen advisory boards to help set priorities. Without that initial assistance, they most likely would never have been formed. Finally, the block grant program was operating under an outdated set of guidelines prepared years earlier by the Department of Social Services. Those guidelines certainly emphasized the importance of local priority setting, but they also indicated general categories of services and providers eligible for block grant funding. The fact that these guidelines existed, and had always existed, greatly undermined the argument for local control.

The second group with an important stake in the program was the Association of Social Service Providers, which represented more than 5,000 not-for-profit groups throughout the state. The association was especially vocal on the issue of wage parity between the social service workers who were supported with state monies and those whose salaries came from other sources. The gap between these two groups, everyone agreed, was substantial. For example, the average day-care worker supported by block grant funds was earning less than $8,000 annually while employees of private providers were making almost 50 percent more. The association argued that wages paid under existing block grant contracts should be increased substantially until parity was reached before any new grants were given. Understandably, the association argued (along with local officials) that priorities should continue to be set locally. This, after all, was the level at which they had the most influence.

A third important group was the private donors of matching funds, including corporations, foundations, and local governments. The majority of these donors agreed on certain key points. First, they felt that they should have the option of counting "in kind" and other noncash contributions as part of their matching contributions. They further wanted the right to target money to specific organizations, regardless of state priorities while still meeting the matching funds guidelines. Although they were as a whole somewhat sympathetic to the commissioner's argument that priorities had changed, and that grant allocations should change accordingly, they did not like the idea of the state determining what the new priorities should be. They were also displeased that the commissioner had not acknowledged one of their oft-stated concerns: that too much block grant money was going to central city neighborhoods and not enough to suburban and outlying areas—where, they argued, equally needy "pockets of poverty" existed.

The final stakeholders were citizen advocate groups, particularly representatives of minorities and the disabled. These groups complained bitterly that the existing priorities were a sham. In particular, they argued, much more money needed to be set aside for programs oriented toward cultural and linguistic minorities. They were angry that programs for the developmentally disabled were not eligible for support under the block grant program. (This was true because there were already other state funds set aside for this purpose.) Though this loose coalition of citizens' groups uniformly supported the idea of new state-imposed priorities, their united front dissolved quickly in the face of a need to be specific. Each group had its own strong ideas about how new priorities should be defined.

The commissioner had the formal authority to issue new guidelines, but she knew she lacked the political power. This fact had been made painfully clear at the beginning of each fiscal year. Dorada's annual attempt to issue new guidelines had been blocked by the legislature, which simply held the overall social services budget (close to $1 billion) "hostage" until the commissioner backed down and withdrew the proposed revisions.

The legislature was under constant and intense pressure from the Association of Social Service Providers, local officials, corporate donors, and citizen advocacy groups—who wanted either no change in the regulations or who advocated conflicting changes.

In 1982, Commissioner Dorada had made a concerted effort to meet privately with the legislative leadership and the legislative Commission on Social Services, but to no avail. She found few supporters of new guidelines. In fact, it hardly mattered what guidelines the commissioner suggested; there was bitter opposition to any changes that threatened to eliminate the eligibility of current grantees, or to add groups and thereby increase the competition for funds. Each group was committed to looking after its own interests.

The Commissioner's latest needs assessment identified four groups that were seriously underserved. The first was families functioning too poorly to make use of traditional forms of assistance. The second was young parents (or parents-to-be). The language of the needs assessment suggested that this group ought to be targeted to prevent child abuse and neglect; however, the unstated focus was on pregnancy counseling and birth control. This was a highly controversial priority in a state with a large Catholic population. The third group was adolescents with severe behavioral problems, and those not living in family settings; the final group was the homeless. None of these groups had been the focus of special programs before, and as a result, no organizations were receiving block grant funds on their behalf and few groups were prepared to act as their advocates.

The block grant program involved too small a fraction of Commissioner Dorada's overall budget for her to risk alienating the legislature. The governor, for his part, did not want a fight with the legislature; he had other budgetary concerns and did not want to trade for legislative support to prevail on such a small budget item. The legislators, elected every two years, felt other pressures. They were well aware, for example, that the Association of Social Service Providers had electoral clout. Moreover, no legislator wanted to risk being challenged for jeopardizing funding for social service providers.

In all likelihood, based on previous experience with other programs, the new guidelines would shift funds from some parts of the state to others. The precise flow of funds, however, would remain unknown until the guidelines were put into effect. That fact in itself represented an unacceptable risk for most legislators whose time horizon extended only to the next election. Solving an important—perhaps even critical—social problem presented few, if any, political rewards.

Through face-to-face negotiations we describe in chapter 5, more than one hundred groups with a stake in the block grant allocations were finally able to reach agreement on new priority-setting procedures.

SHORTCOMINGS
OF THE VOTING PROCESS

Americans attribute great significance to the voting process—even though they do not always act on that conviction. Yet it has become increasingly clear that the electoral process cannot ensure that all competing interests will be taken into account when public policy decisions must be made.

For example, voting is not timely. A great many issues can emerge between the last and the next election. Candidates elected on a platform that was relevant a year ago may not be the representatives we need today. Perhaps we discover that we have changed our minds on a certain critical issue because new information has emerged. We are still represented, however, by a politician we elected when we held the opposite view.

When candidates run for office, they adopt an array of positions on a broad range of issues. We identify and vote for individuals who seem to share our views—even when they hold some positions we dislike on issues we consider minor. But what happens when no candidate attaches much importance to an issue that concerns us greatly? We are likely to vote for the least objectionable candidate, or choose one whose positions on other issues suggest he or she is at least somewhat sympathetic to our way of thinking. In the end, we are not really able to express the intensity of our feelings on a particular issue by voting for a certain candidate. In fact, citizens with whom we disagree utterly on a key issue may find reason to vote for the same candidate.

Voters, furthermore, are never offered contingent choices. Americans would most likely be shocked by a ballot (even a referendum) that allowed them to vote one way under one set of assumptions and another way if key events worked out differently. Yet without this opportunity, voters are forced to choose among overly generalized or simplified options.

Contingencies are often the crucial ingredient in all-gain solutions to distributional disputes, yet voting does not allow this flexibility.

Lobbying is a means for voters to supplement their electoral intentions and to express the intensity of their concerns in a manner not presented by a yes-or-no vote. As was noted earlier, though, Americans are ambivalent about the type of lobbying that should be encouraged.[9] We want limitations on the money that certain lobbyists can spend, we want all lobbyists registered, and we want to know which of our elected representatives are under obligation, and to whom.

Simply put, we are uncomfortable with lobbying because it is unfair. It is a patently inequitable supplement to the electoral process, all the more inequitable because it is so effective. In short, lobbying works—but only if you are in Washington, with ample resources and a good organization, and with friends in the right places. Lobbying is most often condemned for furthering the interests of business and industry to an inappropriate degree. (The arms lobby is the most obvious and most often cited example. But other, noncorporate lobbies are at least as effective. The recent repeal of gun control, for example, was in large part the result of efforts by the gun lobby.)

The converse is equally true. Groups that are disorganized or underfinanced are not likely to be effective advocates for their positions. In some cases, disorganization reflects a simple lack of concern. In others, though, it reflects the sudden emergence of a high-intensity issue for groups that have not yet had time to organize.

The state's plan to build a mass transit facility at RiverEnd (discussed earlier) illustrates the two perils of lobbyist intervention. It was clear to the participants in the negotiating process that the developers had excellent access to influential state politicians. Their lobbyists were already in place and could call upon well-cultivated relationships with state legislators and administrators. Through their political influence they were clearly able to dominate the decision-making process, and the "outsiders"—the environmentalists—were infuriated. The first peril of lobbying was already evident: the outcome of a dispute might well be determined by the relative political clout of each side, rather than by the merits of their arguments.

A second peril was also in the making. Because of the lobbyists' undue influence, the entire decision-making process was suspect. Early in the game, the potential losers became inclined to reject everything the state proposed. They would, they announced with understandable indignation, lie down in front of the bulldozers if necessary.

State officials ignored a crucial fact. Silence from an affected group may be deceptive. It may temporarily conceal a gathering storm of protest. If lobbying results in an action that is perceived as unfair, that action eventually will be jeopardized—even if initial reaction is muted.

Even when lobbying supplements the electoral process, therefore, problems of accommodating the concerns of all affected parties still persist. Public referendums, California-style, do not really solve this problem. Long lists of detailed referendum questions still present the issues in a yes-no, noncontingent format. The intensity of group concern cannot register. The rigidity of the voting process often locks people into positions they must abandon soon after they vote—or even as they cast their ballots.

The story of the Harmon Sewage Authority's failed effort to clean up that county's polluted rivers and harbor is a prime example of the ways voting can produce unwanted results.

HARMON COUNTY SEWAGE CLEAN-UP

Judge Rollenkamp looked down from the bench.[10] There were more than a hundred people seated in the courtroom, most of them lawyers. "This dispute has gone on twelve years," he said. "That's long enough. I'm going to impose a ban on all new sewer hook-ups and any further construction until this thing is settled."

Mike Aubrey, a lawyer hired to represent the city of Harmon, was not surprised, but he was unsure how the city's administrators would react when they heard the news. For almost eight years, Aubrey had taken every legal step he could think of to delay construction of the proposed Harmon County regional sewage system. As long as the system was not built, Harmon's fiscal health was ensured. This threatened ban, though, thought Aubrey—that was another story. The city was just about to announce an important downtown revitalization package involving significant amounts of new construction. That package was now in jeopardy.

When the state legislature first created the Harmon County Regional Sewage Authority in 1975, everyone had applauded, including officials in the city of Harmon. But when the Sewage Authority unveiled its plans in 1978 for a $100 million system, and indicated that the city of Harmon's annual share of capital and operating costs would exceed $10 million, the mayor and the city council initiated an all-out legal fight. The proposed facility was simply too expensive, they said.

Since that time, the problem had only gotten worse. Costs

had risen, interest rates had gone up, the county's bond rating had dropped, and federal subsidies for treatment facilities had all but been eliminated. In 1985, the Sewage Authority announced that the system would cost $300 million and the city's annual share would be $22 million. Stunned city officials dismissed the plan as absurd.

From Aubrey's point of view, the issue was simple—there was no way the city of Harmon could come up with that kind of money. The city's total revenue from property taxes in 1985 was only $20 million. Annual sewer bills of over $1,000 for each household would almost certainly drive out residents and discourage business investment. Under such a plan, the city could conceivably foreclose on more than half of its housing stock in the first year alone. How could the Sewage Authority's officials possibly expect Harmon—one of the poorest cities in America—to come up with that kind of money?

Aubrey listened as the judge went on. "I am appointing Ron Jones, an out-of-state mediator, to serve as a special master. He will be aided by a team of local experts and will work with you to see if a concerted effort to reach an agreement can work. You have eight weeks. On September 1, 1985, I will issue my decision. The hook-up ban is in effect until then."

John Renfrow, lawyer for the Sewage Authority, turned toward his employer Tom Glynn. "Well, now the communities will be forced to work with us," Renfrow asserted. "I have a hunch the judge is leaning in our direction."

Glynn, director of the Sewage Authority, was not so sure. "Why didn't he just rule?" he asked. "What's this business about a special master?"

Glynn tried to imagine the arguments the special master would hear when he began to meet privately with the parties to the dispute. The smaller towns in the county would argue—as they had for years—that they should not be forced to join a regional sewage system. In some ways, Glynn was sympathetic to this point of view. These little communities really could operate on septic systems, as they claimed; but once the Sewage Authority had crisscrossed the county with large pipes, it would make no sense not to tie in the small towns. Moreover, once future development necessitated it, these small towns would be clamoring to tie into the regional system. It therefore made sense to make them pay their fair share of the up-front costs, Glynn reasoned.

And then there was the case of Carlton and other well-to-do towns in the county. Glynn was less sympathetic toward those communities. They knew they needed the sewer system, but none of the local politicians wanted to take the political blame for increases in sewer charges. What was $700 or $800 a year to most of the residents of those towns? It was the spineless local politicians, Glynn thought resentfully, who were making the Sewage Authority out to be the bad guy.

Finally, there was the problem of the city of Harmon. Glynn knew how poor most of its residents were, but he bridled at the thought of the Randall Company, a major canned food producer, giving the city the money needed to hire Aubrey and his extensive staff. Randall's stake was clear: the company did not want to be charged for pretreatment of its waste water, which it pumped directly into the city sewer system. But when one counted the Randall Company's substantial effluent, Harmon generated 40 percent of the region's sewage—so why not have the city pay 40 percent of the building and operating cost of the system? Every other regional system that Glynn knew of calculated costs on the basis of flow. It should be the city's responsibility to decide how much to charge its residential customers and how much to charge the Randall Company. But there was the rub, Glynn knew: Randall was constantly threatening to leave the city. As far as Glynn was concerned, it was a hollow threat; but it was a risk the city could not afford to take.

The special master, Ron Jones, was soon at work; he found the views of the various groups to be roughly as Glynn had imagined. After talking to local officials, he met with the federal

Sources of Difficulty

EPA and the state Department of Environmental Protection. The federal EPA indicated that it had been trying to close more than half of the thirty local sewage treatment plants in Harmon County for over a decade. The plants did not meet federal standards, and could not be upgraded to meet the new 1988 Clean Water Act standards. In 1978, the EPA had offered the Sewage Authority almost $65 million to subsidize the cost of a new regional system, but regional officials had dragged their feet and the project had become bogged down in endless litigation. The $65 million was still set aside, but it would now (in 1985) cover only a fraction of the total cost. New subsidies were no longer available.

The state Department of Environmental Protection told a similar story. Its officials had been trying for years to do something about the deplorable levels of pollution in the rivers and streams in Harmon County. But all of their efforts to push the Sewage Authority toward building a new regional system had failed. Similarly, efforts to close down inadequate local treatment plants had been thwarted politically. Now, the city of Harmon was demanding more money from the state—and more money simply was not available. Back when the Harmon County system would have cost only $100 million, officials pointed out, the state had been prepared to cover 20 percent of the cost of a regional system. Now the state was in financial straits, and it could only offer the $20 million it had originally promised in 1978.

Special Master Jones continued to make his rounds, meeting separately with elected and appointed officials in all thirty-nine communities in the county; with the Sewage Authority, its lawyers, and staff; with the state's congressional delegation; with the County Homebuilders Association, which was up in arms because of the hook-up ban; with the governor's special assistant on local finance; and with numerous other experts and officials.

Jones came away from these meetings with three distinct

impressions. First, the municipalities had little faith in the Harmon County Regional Sewage Authority. It had run up a substantial debt in the ten years of its existence—in part because it had built itself an impressive headquarters known to local officials as the "Taj Mahal." Indeed, $75 million of the estimated $300 million the authority was seeking through bonds would be used to cover old debt. The authority had also handled its relations with the cities and towns poorly, often behaving in an autocratic manner. These tensions were exacerbated by an underlying political split between Republican local officials (and a Republican governor) and Democratic county officials. Second, there were real questions about whether the regional system proposed by the Sewage Authority was technically adequate and appropriately designed. The state thought there might well be less expensive options. Third, the city of Harmon was indeed in a bind. There was no way it could afford much beyond $8–$10 million a year in fees without going bankrupt, forcing out the Randall Company, its only major employer, or foreclosing on more than half of the residential buildings in town. The governor's special assistant and the state local financial assistance office had the numbers to back up the city's claims.

Jones met with Judge Rollenkamp. "I don't know that there is any way to generate a settlement in this case," said Jones. "I certainly don't think much can be done in the three weeks I have left."

The judge stared out the window impassively. "Keep trying, Jones," he responded. "I don't want to have to rule on this thing in September. What do I know about the design of regional sewage systems? I'll tell you what: If you're making any progress at all, I can give you a few more weeks. But don't tell anyone! I've already got armies of people knocking down my door with requests for special exceptions to the ban.

"Keep at it," he concluded.

Lost in thought, Jones left the judge's chambers. How could he get the parties to agree to something that would be acceptable to all of them, and also to the judge? What would they all regard as a fair allocation of costs?

Clearly, a majority of the local and county officials continued to vote against any proposed clean-up plan, because they did not want to be held responsible for imposing substantial new costs upon their constituents. The small towns believed they could avoid becoming part of the district. The well-to-do towns thought they were being asked to shoulder an unfair proportion of the costs. The poorest communities, including Harmon, did not have the resources to cover the share of the costs assigned to them. Faced with a yes-or-no question, local officials in each of these communities felt obliged to oppose the proposed clean-up plans. Moreover, as costs mounted, they were increasingly inclined toward opposition. County officials continued to block all plans that would raise county taxes—as every plan did. After years of expensive litigation, they were in a trap. A "yes" vote would be a tacit acknowledgment that they had already wasted millions of dollars through their past actions. Additional "no" votes merely increased the cost of the system that would have to be built eventually. In the most cynical interpretation, they were now waiting for a judge to impose a solution—which they all knew would be contested and appealed for years to come. As we describe in chapter 5, the mediator helped the parties find a way out of this bind.

TECHNICAL COMPLEXITY
OVERWHELMS SLOGANEERING

We have underscored the importance of consensus in resolving distributional disputes. There are many examples, however, of situations in which disparate groups of politicians and the constituents they represent have joined together in common cause but consensus has represented nothing more than a superficial commitment to a simple slogan. Many groups with fundamentally different values can identify with cries such as "Energy Independence," "Save Social Security," "Protect Our National Parks," "A Strong Defense," or "Clean Up Toxic Wastes."

In some cases slogans can be very effective. President John F. Kennedy's call to put a man on the moon by the end of the 1960s focused the nation's attention and resources on an unlikely goal, and thereby helped to achieve it. More often than not, though, technical complexity, or differences over which approach to implementation would be best, thwart such calls to action and dissipate the consensus that seems to exist.

Superfund is again a good example.[11] The initial call to clean up the nation's toxic waste dumps evoked a strong and favorable public response. Several recent public opinion surveys have suggested that the elimination of the health and safety threats posed by toxic wastes is still among the top objectives of a majority of Americans. Although appropriations always face inherent political challenges, Superfund was relatively nonpartisan. A national effort to reclaim despoiled environments, and to protect groundwater and the quality of the air, was embraced by both Democrats and Republicans when the initial $1.2 billion was allocated in 1981.

When the EPA began its work, however, a number of problems arose, mostly stemming from the technical complexity of the task at hand. It soon became obvious that the allotted funds would probably be inadequate. What would happen if the cleanup cost ten times as much? Would the consensus hold in the face of such a dramatic cost increase? Simultaneously the problems associated with restoring particular sites (and finding a permanent means of disposing of the wastes that were recovered) proved nearly intractable. Consensus was threatened by new questions: How do you "clean up" toxic wastes? Do you relocate them? Where?

The technical dilemmas and legal complexities of the toxic waste issue unfolded over several years. It was assumed, for example, the investigators could readily identify a given toxic substance, determine where it had come from, select a means of neutralizing or containing it, and assign responsibility for the mess to culpable parties. More often than not, this proved impossible.

Our scientific and engineering knowledge is simply inadequate. For example, basic disagreements exist among equally qualified experts about what a particular mix of substances contains, how such a mass of undistinguishable substances might have migrated underground, what the cumulative impact on the environment has been, and what the adverse effects of tampering with the area might be.

Legal issues have intruded in unexpected ways. In several instances, for example, companies suspected of illegal dumping agreed to clean up a given site, only to learn that under our system of tort liability (that is, civil wrongs, not including breach of contract, for which victims are entitled to compensation), the voluntary cleaning up of a site amounted to an admission of guilt, and therefore entailed substantial additional liability for the company involved.

Thus, companies responding to EPA pressure by volunteering the funds for a clean-up found themselves vulnerable to claims (from residents near the sites and others) amounting to far more than the value of the proposed remedy suggested by the EPA. Subsequently, companies near other toxic waste dumps have refused to participate voluntarily, even in minimal ways, fearing similar findings of liability.

Consider the case of a proposed resource recovery (that is, trash-to-energy) plant. Few in the city of Metropolis disputed the pressing reality of the 10,000 tons of solid waste generated by the city each day, or the threat posed by the limited life expectancy of the city's only functioning landfill. Resource recovery seemed an obvious response. When a site was identified for the first of a proposed series of plants, however, a host of scientific and technical issues immediately complicated the equation. The city's fragile consensus—in the form of broad support for an alternative means of disposing of city waste—evaporated in the face of technical complexity.

Even in the midst of actions that enjoy reasonably broad support, we encounter second-level disputes. Of course we should have a safe way of disposing of our solid waste, or of meeting the housing needs of the poor. Speaking generally, we can all agree on such basic principles, but when the next obvious questions are asked, consensus dissolves. Which technology should we use? Who should pay for it? Where should we put it? To what extent should we rely on government to solve the problem? We simply do not know the answers, and we have no good way of working jointly to determine them.

THE DIOXIN DISPUTE

By early 1982, the Federal Navy Yard's neighbors had grown concerned and anxious.[12] Since its decommissioning as an active military facility a few years earlier, the Federal Navy Yard, one of the largest developable sites in Metropolis, had been the focus of a number of public and private development schemes. In the eyes of the Brownstone neighborhood, the latest proposal was the worst yet. It seemed that the city was proposing to build a "resource recovery plant" at the Navy Yard. That innocent-sounding phrase, it turned out, contained the seeds of trouble. "Resource recovery," to the Metropolis Department of Sanitation's engineers, meant the burning of trash to produce energy.

The citizens of the Brownstone neighborhood expressed their hostility to the plan at an impromptu public meeting in March 1982. Although the city had taken great pains to distinguish between resource recovery and simple dumping, many owners adjoining the Navy Yard said they did not intend to live next to a "garbage dump." Indeed, residents from a number of adjacent neighborhoods objected to the prospect of huge garbage trucks rolling in from the far reaches of Metropolis, adding congestion to their already crowded streets. The citizens' groups arrived at a quick consensus: if "resource recovery" meant odors, rodents, insects, and traffic, they did not want any part of it.

There were still other, more difficult questions to address. Rumors which had been circulating through the community were given voice at the meeting. Several people had heard that health hazards were associated with trash incineration—perhaps even explosions. One local resident related the experience of a city in the next state that had built the region's first resource recovery plant, only to see it shut down by the federal government for excessive air pollution. At that site, even the experts had been unable to agree on "safe" smokestack emission standards; now that city was stuck with an extremely expensive white elephant. Would the Navy Yard be the site of a similar technological and financial fiasco? If that were possible, then Brownstone's residents were even more strongly opposed to the project.

The city of Metropolis, though, had a different perspective. Its residents and businesses (including those in the Brownstone area) were generating more than 10,000 tons of garbage per day. At that rate, the city's only operating landfill would be filled to capacity and shut down in less than eight years. There was little remaining open land in the city, and in any case, the high local water table disqualified most of the city as a potential dump site. The federal government had strictly forbidden garbage disposal at sea, and neighboring states faced with their own solid waste disposal problems were not likely to welcome Metropolis's daily mountains of garbage.

Given this mounting crisis and its inescapable deadline, the city's Department of Sanitation had launched an investigation to find alternatives to landfill. After careful study, the department had finally settled on resource recovery, a technique used in many European cities since the Second World War, and more recently in over fifty American cities. This technique involves the controlled burning of garbage to generate steam, which in turn drives a turbine to produce electricity. The energy produced in this fashion is sold to help offset the cost of trash collection and disposal, and to repay the initial expense of building the incinerator. In the case of Metropolis, garbage could be collected, compacted into cubes, and trucked to incineration sites around the city. A feasibility study commissioned by the department concluded that a network of eight such plants could meet Metropolis's needs. The city's environmental impact assessment concluded that the Federal Navy Yard was an appropriate location for a pilot plant, with only minor health and safety implications.

It was these studies, in fact, that first alerted the Brownstone residents to the plan, and which prompted their March 1982 meeting. But it was a further development in June that really galvanized the neighborhood, as well as public interest groups across the city. At that point, Dr. Harry Lassiter, a nationally known ecologist recently appointed to the faculty of Metropolis University, released a detailed study criticizing the environmental impact assessment prepared by the Department of Sanitation. Lassiter claimed that the resource recovery plant proposed for the Navy Yard posed a substantial health risk, because it would be burning large quantities of plastic. The burning of plastic mixed with paper, he asserted, created dioxin and other deadly cancer-causing chemicals, which might well escape into surrounding neighborhoods.

Because of the seriousness of these charges, and also because of a sympathetic *Metropolis Times* editorial, Lassiter's report attracted national attention. It also further alarmed the residents of Brownstone. The city, unwilling to give up on resource recovery, responded by hiring an environmental risk-assessment consultant who was engaged to study the risk of dioxin formation and contamination. The consultant's report directly contradicted Lassiter's findings. There was, the consultant said, no additional health risk; Lassiter was wrong.

By now, the debate was out of the Sanitation Department's hands, and in the hands of the city council. Angry calls were coming in from around the city, accusing the Sanitation Department of doctoring the dioxin report, and condemning the city for imposing a dangerous facility on an unwilling neighborhood. In fact, the council's members felt every bit as confused as the anxious Brownstone residents. By this time, a series of experts had studied the dioxin question and had reached diametrically opposed conclusions. Who was to be believed?

After much debate, the city council appealed in the spring of 1984 to the local Academy of Sciences, a private organization of scientists with a long record of service to the community, for help. The council asked the academy to resolve the conflict, and to determine the truth about the dioxin risk.

The academy would not accept the assignment as outlined. Instead, the academy staff offered to host a public "dialogue," which would review the available scientific and technical evidence concerning dioxin. The discussion would be conducted in layperson's terms, the academy stressed. This would not only reassure the neighborhood and environmental interest groups— who would be invited to the meeting—that no serious questions were being ignored, but it would also serve to inform the members of the city council, who would have to make the final decision.

On the morning of 18 December 1984, nearly sixty people crowded into the academy's small auditorium. Anticipation, and no small measure of apprehension, filled the air. The Academy of Sciences had conducted extensive background discussions with experts on the combustion process, with pollution control engineers, and with epidemiologists (that is, public health specialists), but this was the first time they had gathered in the same place at the same time. These experts, who had already damned each other's conclusions in scientific language, were now prepared to restate their own cases in laypeople's terms. Advocates and opponents of resource recovery eyed each other across the room—the Department of Sanitation's engineers on the one hand, obligated to dispose of 10,000 tons of garbage a day; and the residents of the Brownstone neighborhood on the other, determined to protect themselves and their families from a perceived threat.

At 9:30 A.M., Dr. Gene McGerny, who had been appointed "facilitator" for the dialogue, called the meeting to order. "Let's talk about dioxin risks and public health standards," he began.

The informal policy dialogue, mediated by the local Academy of Sciences, was an unusual step. It took an enormous amount of time to arrange the event. No one was quite sure how to conduct such a dialogue in a way that would resolve the underlying scientific and technical dispute regarding the dioxin risk. The outcomes are described in chapter 5.

THE WINNER-TAKES-ALL MIND-SET

When our administrative and legislative efforts fail to resolve disputes, we go to court. We often see this as our only recourse, given the flaws of representative democracy described thus far. If a crucial decision is logrolled, the aggrieved parties take it to court. If lobbyists seem to have been overly influential in a legislative or administrative action, we challenge that action in court, usually on procedural grounds. An issue of technical complexity is highly likely to wind up in court, because both sides can usually produce experts to substantiate their own scientific claims.

Our successful efforts to broaden access to the courts have greatly increased the number of suits filed.[13] But to what end?

Our appellate courts are limited in their mandate and ability. They are empowered only to rule on the legal questions put before them. Practically speaking, this means either that the lawyers for the disputing parties must work something out behind the scenes, or that the distributional disputes brought into court must be decided in a "winner-takes-all" fashion. The dispute is usually not "arbitrated." In other words, the judge rarely strikes a compromise, giving each side a portion of what it wants. Moreover, the court almost never works with disputing parties to invent all-gain outcomes by getting the parties to look at options they have not considered. Judicial interpretation, in fact, typically leads to a narrowing of the scope of a dispute.

Within the courtroom, the adversary system introduces unfortunate "gaming" aspects to the process which impede the search for all-gain solutions.[14] For example, adversarial tactics, in conjunction with technical rules for the admission of evidence and testimony at a trial, practically ensure that potentially useful information will be excluded from consideration. In most court proceedings, contending parties possess relevant information that they are not allowed (or not willing) to communicate.

By restricting the range of legally recognizable causes of action, segmenting complex and interrelated problems into discrete legal actions, and limiting allowable information, the courts make it hard to reach judgments that accommodate the real concerns of all interested parties.

Judicial review of agency actions is equally frustrated by problems arising from the amount and quality of information available. Courts are limited to examining agency decisions for legal error; they must defer to the agency's judgment on factual matters. Despite this limitation on a court's consideration of the actions taken by an agency, however, one legal issue—whether the agency used reliable or sufficient evidence to make its decision—does indeed allow the court to determine whether an agency's decision is justifiable. This may lead to an examination of factual issues by the reviewing court, but such examination is sorely restricted, because the court has no access to further information (additional research or expert testimony, for example) that might assist such an evaluation.

Congress and the Supreme Court have searched for a solution to the problem of regulatory delay caused by courts second-guessing agency decisions. Unfortunately, they are working at cross purposes. In the Vermont Yankee case (a dispute between the Vermont Yankee Nuclear Power Corporation and the Natural Resources Defense Council in 1978) the Court indicated its support for judicial deference to agency judgment. In a sharply worded opinion, Justice William Rehnquist criticized the lower court's actions (which included finding fault with Nuclear Regulatory Commission procedures in two power plant licensing cases) as "judicial intervention run riot." At the same time, Congress sought to push the courts further into substantive decision making. In 1979, for example, some members of Congress pressed for a law to force agencies to prove through a "preponderance of the evidence" the validity of their regulations, whenever those regulations are challenged.

The courts have been trying hard to escape from their growing involvement in the substance of scientific questions. We applaud that effort. The judicial process is not competent to resolve the scientific uncertainties inherent in distributional disputes.

Imagine a circumstance, for example, in which the court is forced to ignore important scientific evidence (because it was not part of an agency's decision) in favor of legal arguments for the opposite conclusion. In such a case, the court could use the correct legal process to arrive at a disastrous conclusion.

In the final illustrative case presented in this chapter, we describe a situation in which a court attempted to avoid involvement in a substantive review process. The judge perceived the complexity of the issues and relationships in the case, and appointed a special master to help the parties reach a satisfactory accord. A purely procedural decision might have been ill-informed, and almost certainly would have been vulnerable to reversal on appeal. What was needed, instead, was an informal, educational process—a joint fact-finding mechanism—through which the disputing parties could develop a shared understanding of the issues and options involved. Unlike the Harmon case, the question in this instance was how to allocate benefits, rather than costs.

NATIVE AMERICAN FISHING RIGHTS

The battle for the lake had been under way for more than twenty years before most state residents became aware of it.[15] The fact that it involved only a relatively small group of people—two Native American tribes, commercial and sports fishing organizations, and some state and federal officials—helped keep the story off the front pages. Furthermore, the controversy, which concerned fishing rights and overlapping governmental jurisdictions, proved too complex for a simple explanation on the evening news.

By 1984, however, the story could no longer be overlooked. It had evolved into a classic conflict between state and tribal authorities. Two dozen Native Americans were arrested in an angry sit-down protest at the offices of the state Natural Resources Authority. The state, for its part, had begun boarding and searching tribal boats in an apparent policy of harassment. Incidents of sabotage and gunfire were beginning to erupt. Belatedly, the conflict had caught the public's attention, and obvious questions were now being raised. What had started the dispute, and what could be done to resolve it?

The Native Americans—members of two Chippewa tribes located on the northern and eastern shores of the lake—claimed the right to fish anywhere in the lake, without restrictions on the size of their catch or the use of particular fishing gear. They based this claim on the Treaty of Wooster, signed by the Chippewa and the federal government in 1847, which gave the tribes "an unlimited right to fish the waters of the lake until the area is settled." They had been doing so for more than a century, they pointed out, and they intended to keep doing so.

The Chippewa competed for their catch with commercial fishers and sports fishers. By the 1960s, tensions among these groups had begun to mount. The tribes resented the ever-increasing number of competitors—especially those with sophisticated fishing gear, including the commercial fishers, who like the Chippewa were in search of whitefish. The sports fishers, for their part, claimed that the Chippewa's use of traditional gill nets indiscriminately destroyed the lake's blue trout population, which sports fishers particularly prized. Commercial and sports fishers squabbled over favorite fishing spots, and engaged in petty acts of vandalism against each other.

The stakes were raised significantly in 1969, when the state's Natural Resources Authority concluded that both the whitefish and the blue trout in the lake were threatened by overfishing. As a result, the authority established a strict licensing program which restricted all fishing on the lake. In response, the Chippewa and the federal government sued the state, claiming that the authorities had no right—given the Native Americans' sovereign status—to regulate them. Furthermore, said the Chippewa, the state was interfering with their right, guaranteed by the Treaty of Wooster, to exploit the lake's resources.

This, said the state, was nonsense. The lake was a resource to be shared by all residents, and state authorities had an obligation to protect it from abuses by any and all special-interest groups. The Treaty of Wooster, they pointed out, had only guaranteed the tribes rights until "settlement," and reasonable people would agree that the state was now "settled."

For the next fifteen years, while tensions mounted, the federal courts struggled with the complicated case. Memorial Day marked the opening of the fishing season in 1984; it also presented grim evidence that the conflict had escalated to a new level of violence. Two Chippewa fishermen were fatally shot on the lake's eastern shore by drunken sports fishermen, and another Indian was ambushed in a similar incident on the northern shore. Oliver Eastman, the state's presiding federal circuit court judge, had seen enough. He appointed an experienced mediator, Leslie Burmaster, to find a solution to the dispute. He also established the day before Memorial Day, 1985, as the absolute deadline for such an agreement. The court, he said flatly, would not permit a recurrence of the recent tragic events.

Over the course of the following year, Burmaster struggled to find terms that both the state and the tribes could accept. She was aware of the need to involve the commercial and sports fishers, who could undermine (both politically and through legal challenges) any agreement they found unacceptable. Burmaster commissioned independent technical studies of the lake's fish resources, thereby educating the disputing parties (and herself) about the complex issues of fish stocking, management, and harvesting. She felt that slow but significant progress was being made. Perhaps this was because all the parties involved had finally grasped one overriding fact. Under conditions of cooperation among the disputing parties, the court would permit a much larger annual fish harvest in the lake than in the past. But if a compromise could not be reached, the court would greatly reduce the total allowable catch. In that case, even the "winners" designated by the court might well lose.

Time ran out, however. On 29 May 1985 representatives of the various factions assembled in Eastman's courtroom. Burmaster had circulated the final draft of a proposed settlement two days earlier, with a pointed warning attached. Will you accept this agreement, she asked each faction, or would you rather risk a court-imposed settlement? Will you support this proposal—to which each of you has contributed in a manner that protects the interests you consider most vital—or will you "roll the dice" and hope that the court will take your side? Even

Burmaster was not sure how the Chippewa, the state, and the various fishing interests would answer her questions.

At noon, Justice Eastman held up a copy of Burmaster's draft. "I'm going to ask each of you the same question in turn," he announced to the lawyers assembled before the bench. "Will you accept this proposal, or won't you?"

The use of a mediator in the fishing rights case was quite unusual. In a sense, it represented judicial acknowledgment that a yes-or-no decision on the legal questions before the court would have been inappropriate. When constitutional questions are not really central, it makes more sense for the parties to work out an agreement that responds to their real concerns.

Even when the court picks a "winner," the issue may not be settled. The losing party, unwilling to lose everything, simply moves to another venue or adopts another tactic. The original suit is appealed to a higher court, or a new suit is filed on slightly different grounds. Legislation is sought which, if passed, effectively reverses the court's decision. The losers are spurred to continuing action by powerful incentives, including economic self-interest and the desire to save face.

Burmaster's approach to mediation is described further in chapter 5.

IMPROVED AD HOC APPROACHES

It should be clear from the preceding analysis that a new approach to resolving distributional disputes is needed to overcome the flaws of representative democracy. We can no longer expect our system—as flexible and stable as it has proven in the past—to accommodate endless tinkering. We have put effective tools, including our three branches of government, to inappropriate tasks. It is not surprising that we are dissatisfied with the results.

What is needed is an approach that is

- Ad hoc
- Informal
- Consensual (that is, consensus-seeking)
- Face-to-face (involving specially selected representatives of all stakeholding parties)
- Supplementary to our existing structures
- Restricted to distributional issues (not fundamental value questions, or issues of basic human rights)

By *ad hoc*, we mean there should be room in each situation for the participants to design the dispute resolution process they prefer. By *informal*, we mean the parties should deal with each other (and not through hired advocates) in a nonbureaucratized fashion. A *consensual* approach is achieved when everyone agrees to live with a particular formulation of a problem and its solution because everyone knows the settlement is the best available under the circumstances, and because it attends to each party's most important concerns. *Face-to-face* implies that the disputing parties should sit around a table and work together until they produce an agreement—or decide to give up. A *supplementary* approach suggests that if agreement is not reached, the parties will fall back upon conventional dispute resolution processes. And finally, to reiterate, we acknowledge that such an approach is *not* appropriate when the dispute is primarily about the definition of constitutional rights or legality.

Our goal is to encourage joint problem solving. Such an approach depends on establishing linkages among issues, packaging elements valued differently by the various participants, arranging compensatory actions or payments, and guaranteeing future behavior. In the end, all parties should gain. Consensual

T A B L E 3 . 1

Alternative Approaches to Resolving Distributional Disputes

Attributes	Conventional Approaches	Consensual Approaches
Outcomes	Win-lose; impaired relationships	All-gain; improved relationships
Participation	Mandatory	Voluntary
Style of interaction	Indirect (through lawyers or hired advocates)	Direct (parties deal face-to-face)
Procedures	Same ground rules and procedures apply in all cases	New ground rules and procedures designed for each case
Methods of reaching closure	Imposition of a final determination by a judge or an official	Voluntary acceptance of a final decision by the parties
Role of intermediaries	Unassisted; no role for intermediaries	Assisted or unassisted; various roles for intermediaries
Cost	Low to moderate in the short term; potentially very high in the long term	Moderate to high in the short term; low in the long term if successful
Representation	General-purpose elected or appointed officials	Ad hoc; specially selected for each negotiation

settlements should offer results for each party at least as attractive as those likely to be achieved through any other means. Moreover, the outcome of this type of problem solving ought to be viewed as fully legitimate, and participants consequently should be much less inclined to invent obstacles to implementation. Consensual agreements with these attributes typically incorporate mechanisms for review and alteration in the face of changing circumstances.

What does it take to produce fairer, more efficient, wiser, and more stable resolution of distributional disputes? Above all, it takes an understanding of the key steps in the process of consensus building. In table 3.1 we summarize the key differences between conventional and consensual approaches to resolving public disputes.

In some distributional disputes, the interested parties can handle all aspects of consensus building without special help. In a great many instances, however, the assistance of intermediaries is crucial. Thus, we distinguish between "unassisted negotiation" and "assisted negotiation." No matter which approach the parties use, they must understand and effectively carry out the same sequence of tasks. That sequence and those tasks are described in the following two chapters. We will also explain how the five disputes introduced in this chapter were resolved using the approaches we advocate. These five cases, as noted earlier, are typical of the distributional disputes that emerge because of the flaws in our system of representative democracy. What is atypical is the set of strategies used to resolve them.

CHAPTER 4

Unassisted
Negotiation

When we say that a fairer outcome is a "better" outcome, we mean that given a fairer outcome, the parties involved will be more satisfied. The same is true for "more efficient" outcomes, "wiser" outcomes, and "more stable" outcomes—they will all yield greater satisfaction for the stakeholding parties. This premise is restated here because it underscores the importance of *interests*.

The best way to gauge a group's satisfaction is to consider its short-term and long-term interests. If its interests are met, the group's satisfaction level will go up. Thus, for any group entering a public dispute, its first priority ought to be to clarify its interests. This involves more than just knowing what the members want; it also means estimating what they are likely to get through conventional channels (in other words, in the absence of consensus).

Public disputes can be resolved more effectively (that is, better outcomes are more likely) if the parties voluntarily negotiate an agreement that serves their interests. Consensus, defined and developed by the stakeholders, is more likely to resolve a dispute than a vote of a legislative body, a decision by an administrative agency, or a court decree because it is likely to meet more of their interests.

This brings us to a salient point. Consensual solutions are better—and will be accepted—only if all the stakeholding parties are confident they will get more from a negotiated agreement than they would from a unilateral action, or from conventional means for resolving distributional disputes. Put another way, when a party thinks that it can satisfy its minimum concerns by putting its case before an elected official, a legislative body, an administrator, or a judge—and a bare minimum is enough of a victory—that party is unlikely to go through a more elaborate and perhaps unpredictable process.

But if a group is not confident of victory, or wants to satisfy more than its minimum objectives, it has an incentive to negotiate. Negotiation researchers have invented the term "BATNA" to explain this point.[1] The acronym BATNA stands for "best alternative to a negotiated agreement." Negotiations hinge on this concept. No group should choose to be part of a negotiation if what it can obtain "away from the bargaining table" is better than what it is likely to get by negotiating. On the other hand, if a group sees an opportunity to get more than its BATNA through negotiation, it has ample reason to come to the table.

For example, imagine how this calculation would look from the standpoint of a group embroiled in a dispute concerning the allocation of a city's mythical "quark" supply. Our imaginary group's first step—after organizing itself because quarks are important to its members—is to determine how many quarks it is likely to end up with if the relevant legislative, administrative, and judicial authorities behave as expected.

Assume that their answer, according to their best "guesstimate," is thirty quarks. Thus, negotiations must offer a chance for them to secure more than thirty quarks (or something else that they value more than thirty quarks). Otherwise, they will have no incentive to come to the negotiating table. Thirty quarks, then, is their Best Alternative To a Negotiated Agreement (BATNA)—the minimum they expect to get if they do not negotiate.

The proposed negotiation, moreover, has to offer a better-than-BATNA guarantee to all the parties involved. That is, each party has to believe that it can exceed its BATNA, or else it will not come to and stay at the table. Unless all the parties are involved, a "better" agreement is not likely. A missing party could sabotage an agreement from which it was excluded.

A good outcome in our hypothetical quark case, therefore, is one in which all the stakeholders get more quarks (or something of equivalent value) than they would have gotten on their own. Their interests, in other words, must be served.

But BATNA calculations are tricky. The smart negotiator considers not only what he or she wants (or fears) most, but also what is most likely to happen. In effect, a smart negotiator calculates the "expected value" of each possible strategy and outcome.[2] Such calculations usually involve multiplying the probability of "winning it all" or "losing it all," times the value of the best or worst outcome. So—for example—the environmentalists in the RiverEnd case might have calculated the expected value of court action: first by figuring out what the overall "savings" would be if the project were blocked, as well as the overall loss if the court decision went against them; and then by multiplying this by the likelihood of winning or losing in court.

Depending on their attitudes toward risk taking, people treat BATNAs differently. A person who is a risk taker will probably figure his or her BATNA by calculating the expected value of a complete win. A person who is risk-averse will probably set a BATNA at a level equal to what he or she is willing to lose or pay. This sometimes makes it difficult to guess another group's BATNA because it is hard to know what risks they are willing to take.

Calculations of BATNA are also difficult when all considerations cannot be reduced to dollar values. Is a promise of future benefits of a completely different kind worth thirty quarks? As the RiverEnd case demonstrates, environmental values and other intangibles are extremely difficult to appraise.

Regardless of the difficulties involved, every group in a public dispute must try to calculate its BATNA so that it can compare the advantages and disadvantages of conventional versus consensual options. The expected value of a court settlement may well serve as a group's BATNA, and their awareness of that BATNA will help them establish a threshold against which to gauge possible negotiated settlements.

If a group could actually pursue its best unilateral course of action first, without foreclosing other options, it would then have an exact measure of its BATNA. Of course, this is rarely possible. Each option requires an expenditure of time, money, and perhaps political capital that cannot be recouped. Moreover, one course of action usually forecloses others. As a result, more practical techniques for estimating BATNAs are required. Negotiation researchers have developed a number of tools for making such calculations.[3]

In estimating a BATNA and the factors likely to alter the expected value of various courses of action, it is helpful to secure the assistance of an expert analyst. Such analysts look for pertinent precedents and prepare enlightened forecasts. Not all disputes call for such expertise, but the more dangerous or large-scale the possible consequences, the more important the help of such an analyst becomes.

One of the hardest parts of calculating a realistic BATNA is imagining what other parties are thinking. Each party's evaluation of its options (and therefore its motivation) affects every other party's estimate of its BATNA, because the cost of pursuing an option is partly a function of what other groups decide to do. It is difficult to guess what value others will attach to various alternatives, especially if there has been little or no communication among the parties. It is possible that the other parties' public statements may prove helpful, but such statements may have been deliberately designed to mislead.

It is especially hard to be objective when a great deal is at stake. We tend to underestimate the strength of others, and allow wishful thinking to color our estimates of our own options. This is another compelling reason to call in an outside analyst who may be more dispassionate in making the appropriate calculations.

No matter what information is available, it is not possible to remove all uncertainty in analyzing your own or another group's options. On the other hand, there is no better advice to groups involved in public disputes than "Know your BATNA and don't lose sight of it." This may seem painfully obvious, yet few groups involved in public disputes do nearly enough analysis before selecting a negotiation strategy. Many disputants, moreover, fail to reassess their BATNAs as events unfold.

Not only can BATNAs change as a result of the actions of others, but each individual can improve his or her BATNA through "self-help." For example, generating a genuine counteroffer can improve a BATNA (that is, our alternative to no agreement with Party A is the new offer from Party B). A second self-help approach involves coalition building. If we can piece together a coalition involving powerful allies, our new collective BATNA may well be higher than what we had originally calculated for ourselves. We can also improve our BATNA if we can discover a helpful precedent. If groups like ours in other places have received more, we might revise our estimate of what we can legitimately expect. Similarly, if we can find a powerful principle with which to justify our claim, we might revise our estimate, and thus our BATNA, upward.

Another form of self-help involves lowering expectations, or reducing the BATNAs of the other participants. This is usually done by raising doubts in their minds. If we can discover a weakness in their calculations, we may be able to shake their faith in their estimated BATNA. We might also be able to lower their expectations by wooing away a member of their coalition, shifting the venue of potential court proceedings, or moving an administrative proceeding to a different forum. Such changes can alter the assumptions upon which their BATNA is based.

Assuming a careful analysis has led all the stakeholders to try a consensual approach, their next step will be to select a specific negotiation strategy.

ZERO-SUM VERSUS
INTEGRATIVE NEGOTIATIONS

There are basically two approaches to negotiation. These have been observed by almost all negotiation experts.[4] The first, the "zero-sum" approach, assumes that there are only limited gains available. Whatever one group wins, the other groups lose. Thus, the pluses to one side are balanced out by the minuses to the other side, yielding a total of zero—a "zero sum."

If a dispute concerns the allocation of a limited supply of water, for example, the negotiation will undoubtedly be framed as a zero-sum exercise: additional gallons gained by one party must be given up by others. In such a situation, the opening positions taken by the parties are crucial. An opening bid, so to speak, can "anchor" the final outcome.

This is best illustrated by classic buyer-seller interactions, such as home buying. If the prospective buyer makes a low opening bid, the seller will not take the offer seriously, and the negotiations may end abruptly. If the prospective buyer opens with a bid above what the seller was going to hold out for (that is, the seller's BATNA), the seller will either accept the offer, or try for even more. Thus, the opening bid in a zero-sum situation provides a benchmark for the negotiations that follow.

The other type of negotiation—integrative bargaining—calls for different tactics. In this type of negotiation, the parties search for things to trade. If they can find enough items they value differently, they can make a deal that exploits those differences, and all will gain. The key factor, the element that makes integrative bargaining work, is the availability of items that the disputing parties value differently. These must be "integrated" into a package.

Parties in an integrative bargaining situation must work together to develop a list of things they can trade. This suggests that it is better to begin with questions rather than demands. The success of integrative bargaining depends on setting an appropriately cooperative tone. In the absence of cooperation, it is hard to discover what the others want most and assess what they might be willing to trade.

Imagine a situation, for example, in which a builder is attempting to win approval for a zoning change that would permit commercial development in a residential neighborhood. (Assume that the builder has organized an informal meeting with the neighbors before going to the municipal zoning board.) There will surely be numerous issues at stake; therefore, there ought to be items to trade. However, if the stakeholders treat the negotiation as zero-sum (that is, the project as proposed by the developer is either built or not built) they may never discover the opportunities for all sides to gain. If they approach the negotiation with the aim of integrative bargaining, then they will search for items to trade.

Some of the neighbors might begin by pointing out that they are most concerned about their property values. Others might indicate that they are worried about visual impacts, pollution potential, or increased traffic flows.

The developers might respond by offering to compensate

nearby residents for any real decline in property values once the commercial project is built. The developers could also offer to screen the project with appropriate landscaping, and to reroute traffic to minimize pollution and traffic noise.

Still another group of neighbors might be more concerned about the change in the character of the neighborhood—from strictly residential to commercial. The developers might respond by offering to blend new residential units into the proposed commercial space. The developers might even offer to design and build new residential units jointly with the neighbors so that they can provide housing for family or friends. Unfortunately, most development disputes are quickly framed in zero-sum terms. When this happens, the stakeholders never have a chance to explore the integrative possibilities.

The key to integrative bargaining is to avoid casting the dispute in "win-lose" or "yes-no" terms. The negotiators must try to invent alternatives that respond to the interests of all the parties involved. They must find items to trade. Note that this is not the same as searching for a compromise. If the parties can find and trade things they value differently, actual benefits—and not simply concessions—are possible. The developer, for example, might find it relatively inexpensive to have the project's security police patrol some of the neighboring streets, whereas the cost of a private security force might be prohibitive for the residents.

In public disputes, the search for all-gain packages can become quite complicated. Sometimes brand-new project designs, or intricate commitments to mitigate adverse impacts, are needed to achieve consensus. In other instances, cash compensation for losses or various "in-kind" trades may be necessary. Given a large number of groups and a broad array of issues, the number of possible combinations or packages is almost unlimited.

We do not intend to minimize the difficulties inherent in integrative bargaining. Some groups may feel compelled to try zero-sum bargaining before they agree to joint problem solving. If this is the case, integrative bargaining will have to wait. Before disputants can be sufficiently motivated to seek integrative solutions, they must first be convinced that they are not giving up a real chance of "winning big."

Some groups may be reluctant to reveal what they will and will not accept, especially at the outset of a negotiation, for fear of "anchoring" the final agreement below what they might otherwise get.[5] Thus, there is an inherent tension (especially at the outset) between treating the situation as a zero-sum negotiation (in which openness and cooperation could lead to exploitation by others) or as integrative bargaining (in which openness and cooperation are essential in the search for joint gains).

In many negotiating situations, it may seem that there is no choice but to assume a zero-sum posture. Certainly, if a buyer and a seller in a busy marketplace are haggling about a price, they have no choice but to treat the negotiation as a zero-sum interaction—especially if the two are not likely to have a continuing relationship. But the parties in public disputes too often assume that this is their only option.

By linking the outcome on one issue with the outcome on others of concern to the same parties, it is often possible to transform zero-sum situations into integrative bargaining opportunities. By thinking of the longer term, it is possible to exchange a small loss now for a large gain in the future. By reexamining the assumptions upon which positions were taken initially, it may be possible to recast "losses" as victories—especially when symbolic gestures cost one side very little, but mean a great deal to others.

Because of the structure of the conventional means of resolving public disputes, there is very little opportunity to search for joint gains. Indeed, under our present system, any group that even suggests a cooperative strategy might well be disadvantaged. Elected and appointed officials may assume that offers to cooperate are evidence of a weak bargaining position. A reluctance to file suit, honestly motivated by a desire to avoid escalating the conflict, may well be construed as a lack of commitment to one's position. Only by changing the context in which distributional disputes are addressed, and creating environments in which joint problem solving is rewarded, is it possible to move from zero-sum to integrative bargaining.

ESCALATION AND ENTRAPMENT

Much of the difficulty people have working collaboratively and in reaching good agreements is psychological. This is best illustrated by the dynamics of escalation and entrapment. Unless these psychological tendencies are understood and overcome, it is almost impossible to move from zero-sum to integrative bargaining.

It is important for disputants to recognize that emotions can overwhelm logic. In fact, people are sometimes trapped into acting against their own best interests, even when they recognize that they are doing so. The best illustration of this is the classic experiment in group psychology—the dollar bill auction.[6] In this experiment, the researcher announces to the test group that he intends to auction off a dollar bill to the highest bidder. He also establishes four seemingly innocuous ground rules. First, bidding must proceed in ten-cent increments. Second, the highest bidder will win the dollar, but the second-highest bidder must pay the "auctioneer" the amount of his or her losing bid. Third, bidders are not allowed to communicate with each other during the course of the auction. Fourth, the auction is over when a minute passes without a new bid being made.

The progress of these auctions is remarkably predictable. Most people are willing to participate in the early stages of the bidding, because it seems that they have a chance to get a dollar for ten or twenty cents. The bidding quickly proceeds to thirty or forty cents, and then begins to slow down. People are still willing to pay a half-dollar for a dollar, of course, but they are less willing to give up forty cents for nothing if they turn out to be the second-highest bidder. More important, they are beginning to see the direction this auction is taking.

At this point, the auctioneer can easily fuel the fires of escalation simply by asking the second-to-last bidder, "Are you really willing to let that person get this dollar for forty cents, and pay me thirty cents, to boot?" Most often, the answer is no. The bidding war resumes, and a subtle change comes over the proceedings. Now, there are bidders not only with an investment in winning, but also with a stake in not losing. Soon the dollar bill bargain is no longer a bargain. When the bids exceed a dollar—which they almost always do—there are no longer any prospective "winners." Now the point of the game is to minimize losses. Eventually, the dollar may sell for as much as six dollars, depending on how badly the bidders want to avoid losing.

In other words, the auctioneer has successfully turned the procedure into a psychological struggle between two bidders. (As soon as the bidding exceeds a dollar, of course, the auctioneer himself has nothing to lose, and his guaranteed profit on the dollar being auctioned only adds fuel to the fire.) In our field work, we have conducted this same exercise with groups of senior corporate executives—although in recognition of the relatively higher stakes to which that audience is accustomed, we used a twenty-dollar bill, which finally "sold" for over forty dollars. The participants, it should be noted, responded to the pressure by breaking one of our ground rules. "This is getting ridiculous!" one of the two final bidders yelled across the room. "Let's stop here and split our losses!"

How is this exercise relevant to public dispute resolution? The participants in the auction were "trapped by choice."[7] They let themselves be caught up in a pattern of escalation. The same is often true of the parties in distributional disputes. They enter a conflict with a selfish desire to advance their own interests. The dialogue is constrained—in part by the ground rules, but also by the increasingly competitive nature of the proceedings. No one wants to lose. When they finally realize they are trapped, they see no way out.

This same point is sometimes illustrated by the tragic story of Karl Wallenda, the famous aerialist. As part of the promotion for a new shopping center in Bermuda, Wallenda invited the public to a planned tightrope walk between two fifteen-story office buildings. On the morning of the scheduled stunt, a gusty wind came up, and Wallenda and other family members contemplated canceling the event. But a large crowd had turned out, and Wallenda felt compelled to go ahead—his reputation, he felt, was at stake. Even as he stepped out on the wire, according to eyewitnesses, he seemed to have second thoughts, but apparently felt obliged to demonstrate his courage. Wallenda refused to take the only sure route to safety—that is, to drop down to the wire and return hand-over-hand back to his starting point. Having rejected that option, and having passed the midpoint of the wire, it was then less difficult to go forward than to retreat. But as he reached the two-thirds point, an unusually strong gust of wind blew up, and he fell to his death.

Wallenda, like many negotiators, had too much invested to quit. At each critical decision point, he acted in what he thought were his best interests; nevertheless, that series of decisions led to a tragedy. Unfortunately, this is a psychological pattern that often occurs.

There are several other forms of escalation and entrapment.[8] One involves "self-fulfilling prophecies." In this trap, each disputant begins by sizing up the others. Person 1 says to himself, "Person 2 over there looks like trouble. In fact, I've heard about him. I'm determined not to let him get the better of me. I'm going to be just as nasty as he's going to be." Of course, when confronted by such hostility, Person 2 (whose initial intention was to be as accommodating as possible) responds in kind. He follows the behavioral clues that Person 1 gives him. In the process, he acts just as Person 1 expected—but only because Person 1's behavior was self-fulfilling.

Other traps involve "selective perception" and "attributional distortion." Once Person 1 has settled on a negative view of Person 2, he or she is unlikely to pay attention to evidence that contradicts that initial view. Both of these traps can take many forms. When someone else toward whom Person 1 is positively disposed acts in a supportive or responsible manner, for example, Person 1 says to herself, "I knew I could count on that person!" But when Person 2 (who Person 1 has decided in advance is untrustworthy) acts in exactly the same manner, Person 1 either does not see it—selective perception—or says to herself, "What is Person 2 up to now? She must have some trick up her sleeve. But [attributional distortion] she won't put anything over on me!" Thus, it is practically impossible for Person 2 ever to change Person 1's opinion of her. In this way, selective perception (that is, the attitude of only noticing things that confirm initial suppositions) and attributional distortion (if one person does it, it is judged positively; if another person does the same thing, it is viewed with suspicion) tend to lock negotiators into destructive patterns that are hard to escape. By only noticing things that confirm our worst impressions, by behaving in ways that trigger the worst possible response, and by asking only those questions likely to support our initial impressions, we make matters worse.

Distributional disputes can get very emotional, and for good reasons. A great deal may be at stake. Changes in public policy or resource allocation can threaten the quality of our lives. Reactions to proposed policy changes may reflect a rational response to a clear threat ("Property values are already plummeting"), or an emotional response ("Big business is trying to ram this monster down my throat!"), or both. The emotional dimension of public dispute resolution is shaped by our psychological makeup—in other words, that which makes us human.

One psychological and emotional pattern that emerges again and again is the dynamic of escalation. Once conflicts begin, the emotional levels of the participants tend to rise, and the situation becomes more and more difficult to defuse. It appears that we humans are good at escalating confrontations, but we are ill-equipped to promote de-escalation.

The stakeholders in public disputes tend to feel increasingly threatened as the dispute drags on; they are more and more likely to posture and "grandstand" as events get beyond their control. As the conflict intensifies, they are less likely to listen seriously and think clearly. Unfortunately, such behavior on the part of one party merely encourages similar behavior by the others. Like small boats on a rising river, it is easy for disputing parties to lose control of the circumstances. The suggestion that participants in distributional disputes should pay close attention to the dynamic of escalation may seem nothing more than common sense—and indeed it is. But in the heat of an emotional dispute, common sense is often the first victim.

THREE PHASES OF
CONSENSUS-BUILDING NEGOTIATION

Successful negotiations are difficult to manage, and when more than two parties are involved, they are especially complicated. Because distributional disputes typically involve quite a few groups (each made up of numerous members) who may have little or no experience working together, they are among the most difficult to resolve through face-to-face negotiation.

Based on our experience in the field of public dispute resolution, and given the daunting list of obstacles cited earlier, we have concluded that most distributional disputes—and certainly the most complex ones—can only be resolved with the aid of a professional intermediary, whose job it is to offer nonpartisan assistance at key steps in the negotiation process. The roles that such helpers play are described in detail in chapter 5. In some instances, though, the disputants can negotiate a successful resolution of their differences on their own—that is, without assistance. The steps they must go through are the same as those involved in assisted negotiations. Table 4.1 identifies three phases of the consensus-building process: prenegotiation, negotiation, and implementation (or postnegotiation).

PRENEGOTIATION

GETTING STARTED

Simply put, it is hard to start a negotiation. As in all human interactions, somebody has to make the first move. In a situation in which a dispute is not yet fully developed, but in which one or more groups are concerned about the possible consequences of a particular policy or resource allocation decision, it is possible for the parties to get together in an effort to avoid a conflict. It is much more likely, unfortunately, that the stakeholders will not enter into negotiations until after a conflict has erupted. Indeed, until a dispute has become full-blown, some groups may not even realize that they have a stake in a conflict.

Whether the parties convene early in an effort to head off a dispute, or only after the dispute has intensified or reached an impasse, the problem of getting started is the same. Someone has to contact the stakeholders and suggest that they come together to talk. In most distributional disputes, the parties involved are under considerable pressure not to make the first

T A B L E 4.1

The Consensus-Building Process

Prenegotiation Phase

Getting Started

Representation

Drafting Protocols and Setting the Agenda

Joint Fact Finding

Negotiation Phase

Inventing Options for Mutual Gain

Packaging Agreements

Producing a Written Agreement

Binding the Parties to Their Commitments

Ratification

Implementation or Postnegotiation Phase

Linking Informal Agreements to Formal Decision Making

Monitoring

Creating a Context for Renegotiation

move. Why? Because people fear that suggesting a meeting may be misconstrued as a sign of weakness or an expression of anxiety about the outcome.

If one party believes that it will prevail by following conventional decision-making procedures, that party has very little incentive to play a convening role. On the other hand, a party that feels it is likely to lose through the conventional procedures may have a hard time convincing other stakeholders that it is in their interest to consider a face-to-face negotiation.

Often, an outsider with absolutely no direct stake in the outcome of the dispute is in the best position to convene the parties. So, for instance, a mayor might invite the parties to a local development dispute to a city hall meeting to see if something can be worked out. In such a case, the mayor plays an intermediary role—a subject we will reserve for the next chapter.

One way to enhance the prospects of getting started is to reduce the risk associated with attending a first meeting. Whoever proposes the meeting should be sure that the possibility is kept confidential until after all sides have agreed to attend—or even until the meeting has been held. It should be made clear in the invitation to a first meeting that no commitments are implied by attendance. The voluntary nature of negotiations should be stressed. If the interactions do not proceed in a useful fashion, any and all parties have the right to walk away.

In one case, which we will present here as the "Jordan Lane" dispute, homeowners upset about a proposed halfway house faced precisely these issues. A church in the neighborhood decided to sponsor a halfway house for retarded citizens. Neighborhood residents quickly announced their willingness to go to court to block the church's plans. From the neighbors' standpoint, as well as that of the church leadership, it was worth exploring less expensive and time-consuming options. Nevertheless, it took some courage for the homeowners to make the first move. Similarly, it took a great deal of courage on the rector's part to agree to a meeting on "hostile turf." He agreed to come only if he could bring "reinforcements." For obvious reasons, he did not want to be outnumbered.

We will use the Jordan Lane case throughout this chapter to illustrate the steps involved in the process of unassisted negotiation. The Jordan Lane conflict typifies many of the distributional disputes that lend themselves to consensual resolution without outside assistance.

JORDAN LANE

The residents of Jordan Lane, on the north side of the city of Bexley, never expected to find themselves at the center of a public dispute.[9] Jordan Lane is a dead-end street of a dozen carefully maintained houses which appear to turn their backs on the busier Homer Street at the end of the block. There is a sense of community on the lane, and its residents generally watch out for each other. As a result, families find it a good place to raise their children, and elderly residents find it possible to stay on there, long after their own children have established households of their own.

Life on Jordan Lane was disrupted, however, in the summer of 1984, when St. Mark's Episcopal Church (on the corner of Jordan Lane and Homer Street) revealed plans for a new use of church facilities. The church had experienced a decline in membership for several decades. Income from the congregation could no longer support expenses; St. Mark's elders had decided to rent space in the church to Neighborhood Care, Inc., an organization serving mentally retarded teenagers and young adults. If the Bexley zoning board granted the necessary permit, Neighborhood Care would be open from 9:00 A.M. to 9:00 P.M., six days a week, providing guidance and recreational services to several dozen "clients" daily.

This, to the residents of Jordan Lane, was thoroughly unwelcome news. There already had been isolated incidents of break-ins on their street; now there would be an influx of strangers. Furthermore, this was no ordinary population of visitors that the church was planning to impose on the neighborhood. This was a group of mental patients, some of them recently released from state institutions and most of them under continuing care. Parents worried out loud about the safety of their children playing in the lane, and older residents wondered if they might soon find themselves unable to leave their homes. Without a doubt, the plan would generate unwanted noise, traffic, and garbage, since the church's kitchen facilities would be in constant use. Property values, most residents agreed, would plummet.

Some Jordan Lane residents objected to the specifics of the plan. The twelve-hour-a-day, six-day-a-week schedule seemed particularly inappropriate in a residential neighborhood. To make matters worse, it appeared that Neighborhood Care, Inc., would not have the necessary staff to supervise its clients, who might well wander off the church grounds unnoticed. Particularly troubling to the Jordan Lane neighborhood was the attitude demonstrated by St. Mark's. Rather than discussing these plans with the neighborhood, the church elders had simply applied to the zoning board for the required permit. This, said the neighbors, was unfortunately typical of the church. In the past, for example, the church had added day care and Sunday school programs without consulting them. Churchgoers often parked carelessly on lawns and sidewalks, and the church's trash was sometimes allowed to pile up alongside the lane. What could the neighborhood expect next from the church, the Jordan Lane community wondered? What else would the church do for money?

John Martin, rector of St. Mark's Church, found his neighbors' attitudes offensive. The church, faced with a financial crisis, had to do something, and the proposed relationship with Neighborhood Care seemed a reasonable response. It was more than that, too: the community and the region needed facilities for its mentally disadvantaged citizens, who legally were entitled to recreational services. Neighborhood Care was a not-for-profit organization that was generally well regarded, and was successfully operating similar facilities in three nearby towns. Unable to find suitable space elsewhere in Bexley, Neighborhood Care had approached the church and had proposed generous terms for renting space.

Martin suspected that the neighborhood's objections to the specifics of the plan were only a smokescreen. There were, he felt, two real issues at hand. First, most of his neighbors were Jewish, and had always resented the Episcopal church in their midst. They had found fault with every innovation, small or large, that the church had proposed over the years and they would probably continue to do so. The current tensions were clearly part of that larger context. Second, the neighborhood was demonstrating its basic ignorance and selfishness—traits displayed by most communities faced with the establishment of similar mental health facilities in their midst. Where did the church's responsibility lie, Martin asked? To a group of mean-spirited neighbors, or to a disadvantaged population that could not fend for itself?

Two weeks before the zoning board was to meet, Martin received a phone call from Joan Singer, the de facto leader and spokesperson for the Jordan Lane neighborhood. It was the first formal contact between the church and the neighborhood since the controversy had arisen. Would Martin be willing to talk to the neighborhood group about the church's plans, she asked?

Martin agreed to a meeting on the following evening, on condition that he could bring along two other church representatives and the director of Neighborhood Care, Inc. Singer suggested that the neighborhood's representative on the city council be invited. Again, Martin agreed. The neighbors already had expressed their willingness to go to court to block the church's plans, he reasoned; almost any outcome would be preferable to that. Perhaps it was not too late to have a reasonable discussion.

Entering Joan Singer's house the following evening, however, Martin had second thoughts. Almost the entire neighborhood had turned out for the meeting, and emotions seemed to be running high. No one mentioned the subject at hand while refreshments were being passed around, but that purposeful avoidance only contributed to the mounting tension.

Finally, a half-hour after the meeting was scheduled to begin, Martin cleared his throat nervously. In the small and crowded living room, that was enough to silence the gathering. "Well," he addressed his neighbors, "shall we begin?"

The Jordan Lane neighborhood, to its credit, had overcome its first major obstacle. In every such case, someone has to make the first move, or negotiations cannot begin. That first move—a call for discussions—depends on someone having both a clear vision of what a consensus-building process might involve as well as the ability to explain it to other potential participants. Inevitably, questions are asked at the initial meeting about what will happen. Unless someone can offer at least tentative answers to these questions, there probably will not be a first meeting. One of these questions is sure to be, "Where will the meeting be held?" Although neutral turf is usually the best choice, it is possible—as in the Jordan Lane case—that one side may agree to a location of the other side's choosing. At times, the side willing to make such a concession can trade it (or hopes it can) for subsequent commitments from the other side.

To summarize: getting started without an intermediary is extremely difficult. You need some measure of skill, persuasiveness, courage, flexibility, and luck. Members of the Jordan Lane neighborhood had all these attributes, which further served them in later stages of their unassisted negotiation.

REPRESENTATION

A second step in the prenegotiation phase involves the identification and selection of appropriate representatives of all stakeholding groups.[10] Productive negotiations cannot begin until two problems are solved: figuring out which groups should be represented, and choosing representatives empowered to speak for the groups they claim to represent.

On the first point, our experience suggests that it is always better to include too many people or groups than too few— especially at the outset. There is a logistical advantage, of course, in limiting the number of voices directly involved in consensus-building discussions. That advantage is far outweighed, however, by the problems that arise if someone decides they have been unfairly excluded.

It is possible to begin with a large number of potential stakeholders and reduce the size of the group through the election or designation of selected representatives. This can be achieved by shifting the focus from the number of parties to the categories of people who want (and ought) to participate.

For example, in the social services block grant negotiation described in chapter 3, each of the four listed categories of participants selected twenty-five representatives. The Association of Social Service Providers asked its members in each subregion of the state to choose a total of twenty-five representatives. The private-sector donors met in a well-advertised statewide session to choose twenty-five participants, being careful to include at least several corporate participants and a selection of foundation representatives, as well as representatives from the various United Ways in the state. The "citizen/consumer team" selected representatives from each of its several subcategories including cultural and linguistic minorities, geographically distributed advocacy organizations, and organizations involved with different types of client groups. And the state agency chose twenty-five representatives from its regional offices and headquarters.

By having each coalition caucus to choose its spokespeople (using whatever means of selection it preferred), credible representation was achieved. Each coalition also selected a "team leader." Although a face-to-face negotiation with one hundred people was difficult, it was certainly more feasible than a process involving ten times that number. The seeming unwieldiness of one hundred participants was in fact a necessary evil. Ad hoc processes must sometimes embrace elaborate selection procedures if they are to overcome the charge that they are less representative than conventional processes.

Several other representational issues, involving diffuse or inarticulate interests, must also be considered. What should be done about people who do not realize they have a stake in a decision that is about to be made? A proposal to locate an oil refinery in an exclusive shorefront neighborhood, for example, would certainly motivate residents to mount a strong campaign in opposition. But the gasoline and home heating oil consumers in the rest of the region might not realize that they, too, have a stake in this siting decision. They would certainly not have the same incentive to organize that the shorefront residents have. The fact that they might save a penny a gallon at the gas pump, were there a refinery in the region, would not generate financial support or bring out volunteers to stand in picket lines. Simply put, the potential gains to each gainer are just too small in such situations to call forth an active membership with adequate commitment.

In some such situations, it may prove impossible to put together an effective group in time. Some groups may need time to select representatives. Other groups (typically those representing the poor, people without political connections, or groups such as illegal aliens with dubious or no legal standing) may need financial assistance. Even when members of such groups perceive themselves to be a coherent interest group, they may be unable to present their views effectively. These unempowered groups often need organizational support to ensure fair representation.

There is no simple generalization to be made about the resolution of these problems. Nevertheless, the parties to a public dispute must agree that it is necessary to involve all legitimate stakeholding interests in whatever negotiations are planned. If they leave out a key group, even unintentionally, the credibility of ad hoc consensus building may be irretrievably damaged.

The groups that do ultimately convene ought to prepare a detailed "conflict assessment" as a means of ensuring that they have not left anyone out.[11] Ideally, such a conflict assessment lists affected individuals and groups in four categories: those with the necessary standing to claim legal protection; those with sufficient political clout to draw elected and appointed officials into the dispute; those with the power to block implementation of a negotiated agreement; and those with sufficient moral claim to generate public sympathy. If the initial participants—those willing to accept an invitation to a first meeting—carefully scrutinize the circumstances of their dispute, they can generally produce such a list. If those at the initial meeting then accept responsibility for contacting organizations and individuals associated with the identified interests—and in the process, ask those whom they contact who else should be included—the final numbers will snowball and credibility will be enhanced to the fullest degree.

In many instances, it is not obvious which individual or organization should represent a particular interest. All possible groups, therefore, should be contacted. Preliminary contacts can often serve as a bridge to others, who may well have a better idea about who best can represent a certain interest. The further and wider the initial group casts its net, the better the chance of identifying the appropriate range of stakeholders. This step is so important, in fact, that the first set of participants may want to employ an outside analyst to help with the conflict assessment. Such an analyst would not be influenced by past hostilities among or misapprehensions about potential participants. Tactically, the presence of an analyst can also make it easier to add groups at a later date if they were overlooked. The participants can honestly claim that an "outsider" made the omission.

In some instances it may be necessary to seek a stand-in, or surrogate, for a group that is not sufficiently organized. In other contexts, it may be desirable to stimulate the creation of a new group. This allows a particular subset of stakeholders to become an organization specifically to participate in the proposed negotiation. The responsibility to represent all stakeholders may seem daunting. (How can you be certain, after all, that one more unrepresented group does not exist, somewhere out there?) But in practice, with an appropriate commitment by all parties, the problem can be overcome. Similarly, the problem of group size often solves itself in practice. It does not take long before the same names keep turning up, no matter how many people are contacted. The size of the group, like its makeup, is finally self-limiting.

If the guidelines suggested so far have been observed by would-be negotiators, the representational issues that must precede negotiations will be adequately addressed. Negotiations can begin, although all participants should agree that any overlooked stakeholders will be invited to join the process as soon as their absence becomes obvious.

When the representatives arrive at the table, another challenge to effective negotiations presents itself. How can negotiators be sure that those at the table can actually commit the groups they purport to represent? This is a terribly important point. There is nothing more frustrating than discovering at the last minute that a designated spokesperson was not empowered to speak for his or her group.

One way of avoiding such letdowns is to clarify at the outset what representation means. Unlike elected officials with statutory authority, ad hoc representatives are rarely empowered to commit their members to anything. They should, however, be in a good position to shuttle back and forth between the negotiating group and the people they represent. Their task is not to speak for their constituents, but to speak with them. Representatives in ad hoc negotiations of the sort we advocate serve primarily to amplify the concerns of larger groups, to carry messages and information to them, and to return with a sense of the group's willingness to commit to whatever consensus emerges.

We have identified several useful strategies for enhancing the success of this form of representation. The first involves relying on networks of existing organizations to select spokespeople by special election. In the Jordan Lane case, for example, neighbors talked to friends, who talked to neighbors, and so on, until everyone involved was reasonably certain that a fair cross-section of residents had been contacted. That group then met to discuss its negotiating strategy and designate a spokeswoman.

If existing organizations have a structure that includes elected officers, these officers may be the most appropriate spokespeople. On the other hand, even some groups with officers may prefer to select ad hoc representatives, depending on the issues under discussion. If the full group is small enough, perhaps several leaders will decide to participate. In any case, these leaders need not be empowered to commit their members. They must, however, be willing to accept responsibility for the tasks of representation we have described.

In other circumstances, it may be desirable to rotate designated spokespeople. To the extent that an organization or a coalition has trouble identifying a single spokesperson, it may be preferable to create an executive committee to share responsibility. This may be the only way to ensure that splinter groups which feel inadequately represented do not break away from the larger group and later try to sabotage implementation of a negotiated agreement.

Openness and flexibility should be the watchwords in the process of selecting representatives for consensus building. It may be necessary, as noted, for one or more groups to change their representatives, or to alternate representatives. Different delegates may be assigned to represent a given group's interests during specific rounds of bargaining. (This is often the case, for example, when a dispute involves technical or scientific issues.) Such a "revolving membership" might seem unwieldy, but it is infinitely preferable to "figurehead" representatives—that is, representatives who are either not knowledgeable about or not interested in the subjects at hand. Each group should be afforded the latitude it needs to solve its internal representation problems.

Disputes may arise over who is entitled to participate, how many representatives are allotted to various blocs, or who should represent a specific group. Sometimes, representational issues may seem insurmountable—for example, when one group insists that it should be involved, but a second group demands that the first group be excluded. These sorts of disagreements can almost always be resolved through negotiation, but only if the organizers of the process are willing to invest the needed time and resources. All too often, such disputes are mistaken for obstacles, when in fact they are opportunities to explore how well the groups will be able to work together on the more difficult issues that lie ahead. Once missed, though, such opportunities do indeed become obstacles to the ultimate ratification of a proposed settlement. Early controversies over representation, in short, should not be papered over or brushed aside, no matter how frustrating they may be.

In the Jordan Lane dispute, the problem of representation was not especially hard to handle. As is usually the case, existing groups with a leadership structure were easiest to represent. Present at the first meeting, therefore, were the official representatives of the church, the director and senior staff of Neighborhood Care, Inc., and the city councilor representing the Jordan

Lane area of the city. (It is important to note that in the city of Bexley, the city council serves as the zoning board, and therefore is the body that would either grant or withhold the land use permit needed by Neighborhood Care.) The church had a formal leadership structure, so no one challenged the authority of the rector and the elders to represent the church. Neighborhood Care, Inc., as a registered not-for-profit organization, had a duly appointed director. There was no question, similarly, about the city council member's accountability to the Jordan Lane area—although some of the neighbors thought, in retrospect, that it might also have been a good idea to invite other city officials, such as the building inspector and a board of health representative.

The neighborhood, by contrast, was more difficult to represent as it had no formal organization. Through word of mouth, though, the date of the meeting was publicized, and the turnout was substantial. Almost 20 percent of the households in the several blocks surrounding the church were represented.

The one group that was not represented directly were the clients of the proposed center, although both the church and the director of Neighborhood Care, Inc., alluded at various times to the interests of this group. These clients typify a constituency that is underempowered and disorganized—in short, very difficult to represent.

A final word on representation: in most cases, not all participants involve themselves in the dispute resolution process equally, or for the same length of time. Those most directly affected participate sooner, more intensively, and longer than those less directly affected. As the process continues, moreover, the mix of participants may change. Groups whose concerns have been satisfied, or who find that their interests are not really at stake, may depart; new groups may become involved as their stakes becomes more evident. In any case, the ongoing participants must take responsibility for engaging these new representatives. One important aspect of this task is keeping minutes, or providing some other form of "group memory" that offers a clear picture of what has been accomplished.

In the Jordan Lane case, Joan Singer and four of her neighbors agreed, after the first meeting, to serve as a negotiating committee for the neighbors. Rector Martin, the director of Neighborhood Care, and a second church elder agreed to serve as a negotiating committee for the church.

DRAFTING PROTOCOLS AND SETTING AN AGENDA

After the appropriate parties are identified and spokespeople have been designated, but before the substantive negotiations begin, the disputing parties must agree on two key points. First, how will they work together? And second, what exactly will they discuss?

In general, protocols (or ground rules) need to be established before the items on a negotiation agenda can be addressed. Numerous questions must be resolved. Where will the meetings be held? How often? How will the participants be seated? Will minutes be kept? Who will keep them? How will individuals be recognized to speak? (Robert's Rules of Order and standard parliamentary procedures are not especially helpful in a negotiation context because they tend to overly formalize the proceedings.) What notice of meetings will be sent? Will the press be invited? Are observers welcome? Will they be allowed to speak? When will meetings end? How will new rules be adopted?

These and related questions must be worked out before the substantive agenda can be addressed. It is usually best to develop written ground rules. In some instances, when disputes are quite complex and numerous parties are involved, a subcommittee with at least one member from each of the primary interest groups can play a key role in drafting a proposed set of protocols, which the full body can then improve upon. The most important thing to remember is that there is no "correct" set of ground rules; protocols must be developed anew for each negotiation.

In the Jordan Lane case, the parties did not address the question of protocols before their initial meeting. Instead, everyone simply arrived. This large group was to meet only once; subsequent negotiations would be conducted through a negotiating committee and phone calls. Perhaps because of this two-stage process, protocols were never formally established. The large group met once and disbanded, and the smaller group dealt with procedural questions from meeting to meeting. Such inattention to protocols was in this case a survivable mistake, since the group managed to resolve procedural difficulties as they arose. Such an approach rarely works in more complicated settings.

In the social services block grant negotiations, by contrast, each of the four "teams" designated a member to serve on a drafting committee to prepare proposed protocols. The drafting committee produced a two-page document with brief paragraphs on each of eight subjects. One paragraph discussed the media:

DEALING WITH THE MEDIA

Participants agree not to negotiate through the media. No press releases concerning the ongoing negotiations will be distributed unless they are approved jointly. While the negotiations continue, no participant will speak directly to the media about the content of the negotiations except at joint press conferences. At these conferences, only team leaders will answer questions.

These documents were reviewed and revised at team meetings, and subsequently at a full negotiating session. Redrafting continued until all the participants could "live with" the revisions. Significantly, no votes were taken. (A formal "vote" can sometimes create undue pressure.)

Once the protocols are established, it is possible to draw up an agenda. This, again, is a key juncture. If the initial set of issues to be covered in the negotiations is too broad, the discussions of specific points may be superficial and therefore unproductive. A huge agenda, moreover, is disheartening and may demoralize even the most committed parties. On the other hand, if too narrow a range of issues is proposed, one or more participants may not find their particular burning issue on the agenda. Unless that issue is added, that group may decide that it is not worth continuing. And finally, if the agenda is too limited, there may not be enough items to "trade"—that is, those issues that the participants value differently may not emerge, and a creative, integrative settlement may not be possible.

It is helpful to remember that in some cases, the disputing parties may not be able to say clearly why they are for or against a given project or policy. Particularly at the outset, they may speak only in the most general terms about their positions or concerns. A proposal to build a dam, for example, almost always generates strong support and strong opposition, but the precise issues at stake are often hard to identify at the outset of discussion. What, exactly, are the opponents worried about—the flooding and loss of an endangered habitat, the loss of a heretofore "wild" river, or the prospect of water being siphoned off for other uses? Similarly, proponents of the dam may be motivated by a broad spectrum of perceived opportunities: power generation, real estate speculation, farming, sports fishing, and so on. With such a range of concerns, it is difficult to know initially which issues to put on the agenda for negotiation.

Even within a "pro" or "con" faction, there may be significant differences of opinion. If these are mistaken for trivial disagreements, that mistake may create serious problems later on. For example, a factory that flagrantly pollutes the air is likely to provoke the local community into forming an antipollution group. Within that ad hoc organization, however, there may be groups with very different attitudes. If one group feels strongly that air pollution kills people, while another thinks that it creates only minor health and esthetic problems, they will almost certainly disagree about what should be on a negotiation agenda.

It is important, therefore, to include all these concerns as potential agenda items before the actual negotiations begin. This must be done carefully, however: Simply listing everyone's concerns may produce such a lengthy agenda that the participants are discouraged from beginning. The key is to cluster potential agenda items under broader headings, and then to put those headings into a priority list. Note that although this is a prenegotiation task, it involves face-to-face negotiations. Like the issues of representation and protocol, it needs to be addressed collectively, before negotiations actually begin.

At a preliminary meeting of neighbors opposed to the Jordan Lane halfway house—to return to our example—a list of "demands" was drawn up by the residents. They provide important clues as to what the agenda in that case needed to include:

1. The church should not be allowed to rent its space for any use that will disturb the neighborhood. Many of us have lived here for more than 25 years. We've paid our taxes, and kept up our homes. We deserve peace and quiet.
2. If mentally retarded or disturbed people are attracted to this area in large numbers, there is bound to be trouble. Some of us are elderly and don't have the ability to defend ourselves. The facility will cause some of us to become shut-ins.
3. There have been burglaries in the area. This facility is likely to increase the crime rate. It will be impossible to walk in front of our own homes.
4. We are opposed to any new activity in the neighborhood that will increase parking and traffic hazards, raise noise levels, and diminish the value of our property.

5. In the past, the church has expanded its activities (Sunday school and day care) without consulting us. The results have been completely unacceptable—cars parking on our lawns, strangers coming and going at all hours. We demand that no additional activity be allowed.

6. We've heard that the group that the church proposes to rent to—Neighborhood Care, Inc.—will not be able to provide full-time supervision for the disturbed patients it hopes to serve. We are convinced this church is not an appropriate setting in which to provide health services. Moreover, we are concerned that neither the church nor Neighborhood Care, Inc., will be able to deal with the disturbed people who will wander in off the streets once they hear that shelter is available.

7. If the Zoning Board is not empowered to stop this intrusion into our community, we insist that very strict conditions be imposed: (a) hours of operation must be limited to 10 A.M. to 2 P.M. four days a week, with no activity on Fridays and weekends; (b) no more than ten people in the church at any time; (c) parking only in the church parking lot; (d) the church must accept responsibility for any and all damage caused by strangers in the neighborhood; and (e) no noise or trash.

8. Our group is prepared to go to court if necessary. We have contacted our council representative and demanded that the city council undertake an investigation to determine whether Neighborhood Care, Inc., is qualified to run such a facility. If this kind of facility is so important, why doesn't the city provide space for it in a public building?

Based on these eight points, the agenda from the neighbors' perspective could initially be summarized under four headings—operations (what is actually proposed, and how will it work?), impacts (what impacts will the proposed facility have on the neighborhood?), responsibilities (who will take responsibility for what and who will make the key decisions?), and options (what alternatives to the proposed facility are possible?). The church and Neighborhood Care, if they had prepared similar lists, would have added several more items: community and regional need (what is the demand for the kind of services that Neighborhood Care wants to provide?), property rights (can the church use its buildings as it wishes?), and regulation (which state and local rules apply to neighborhood mental health facilities?).

This is how the "clustering" process referred to earlier proceeds. A good agenda takes a complex task and breaks it into manageable pieces, which under ideal circumstances can be addressed sequentially. If such a sequencing proves impossible, items can often be worked on in parallel fashion, through the use of subcommittees. Above all, an agenda should always be renegotiable. If it takes longer than expected to handle an early agenda item, the remaining items may need to be reordered, or perhaps some can be eliminated. In the same vein, as new issues emerge in the course of the negotiations, the agenda should be flexible enough to accommodate additions or refinements.

JOINT FACT FINDING

We are now at the last step in what we define as the prenegotiation phase—although, of course, the first phone call between disputing parties might well be considered the start of negotiations. Having established an agenda, the parties must now engage in a process of joint fact finding. Together, they must ask and attempt to answer a major question: "What do we know, and what don't we know about the issues, contexts, and experiences relevant to this dispute?"

In the Jordan Lane case, the residents came to a great many conclusions before checking with the proponents of the halfway house. When Rector Martin addressed the full group he made the following statement:

We have, after careful consideration, decided to rent space in our building to Neighborhood Care, Inc. This is a highly regarded, not-for-profit mental health organization that provides recreational and counseling services to residents of Bexley and several neighboring towns. They are licensed by the state department of mental health. They operate three facilities in nearby cities. We have checked with officials in those communities and heard only good things about them.

Neighborhood Care proposes to operate its programs from 9 A.M. to 9 P.M., six days a week, although it may take them a year or two to reach that scale of operation. They expect to provide counseling for ten to twelve clients a day, whom they will pick up by van and drive home. They will also offer recreational activities for twenty to thirty clients each day from 3 P.M. to 9 P.M.

Our Church feels strongly that mentally retarded teenagers and adults who have been deinstitutionalized deserve a comfortable setting in which to meet and play. Furthermore, Neighborhood Care, Inc., will be serving clients from our own community.

Our Church has lost many of its members over the past ten to fifteen years. Our congregation has dispersed. To maintain our physical plant, we must generate new income. Neighborhood Care's request to us came at just the right time. From what we've heard, they have no other place available at the reasonable price we offered. In the future, they may be willing to pay to renovate the lower floor of the Church.

Neighborhood Care assures us that they will always have a trained counselor on hand and a trained nurse on call.

Residents of almost every community oppose halfway houses and other facilities designed to serve the mentally disadvantaged. We expect opposition, and we see no reason to abandon a good plan simply because of that expectation.

In short, we feel that this important service to the community must be provided.

Speaking more personally, it seems to me that the residents of this neighborhood have complained about almost everything innovative we have ever attempted. Perhaps I'm being unfair, but I suspect that this is in part a result of our being of different faiths.

The fact that the rector made these statements did not necessarily make them true, of course. But just as the neighbors' list of demands helped in agenda setting, these statements provided an outline of issues on which joint fact finding might be productive. The point is that assumptions, opinions, and even values can change in the face of believable information; in order to achieve this important end, such assumptions must be identified and scrutinized.

If a group's assumptions have been based on incorrect or misinterpreted data, for example, a member of that group may be persuaded to help correct the error. He or she can point out that the group's initial error may have been compounded by a tendency to accept only evidence which supported that original position (an approach that we have previously referred to as "selective perception"). People do change positions on issues. Therefore, it is essential to specify the information, and the sources of information, that a group will accept as a valid basis for rethinking.

Early in the negotiating process, each side should describe, even if only in general terms, the sorts of evidence that would persuade them to abandon their initial positions. Subsequent efforts should be aimed at gathering relevant data jointly, and avoiding what in technical or science-intensive disputes is often called "the battle of the print-out." Advocacy science— my expert versus your expert—here operates at its worst. As noted in chapter 2, advocacy science tends to undercut the credibility of all technical evidence, whereas the point of joint fact finding is to develop a shared base of knowledge. Of course, that knowledge will be interpreted differently and valued differently, reflecting the basic differences among the contending parties. But precisely these different interests must be addressed in a productive negotiating process. The basic guideline should be, "Let's make our fight concentrate on basic differences of interpretation, rather than on disputed facts or precedents," which all too often conceal or distract attention from conflicting interests.

In the case of the dam proposal cited earlier, for example, the proponents of hydroelectric power might admit that if building and operating the dam would mean much higher utility rates, then the project should be abandoned. Perhaps the "wild river" advocates could imagine a combination of compensatory measures (fish ladders, guaranteed flow rates, purchase of land along the river for permanent protection from development, and so on) that would persuade them to support the project. All parties, including the most vocal opponents of the dam, should want the design of the facility to "work." They all have a shared interest (although they are not likely to admit it) in getting the best possible technical advice on the design of the dam. Although they may prefer, for strategic reasons, not to talk about designs they could live with, they would undoubtedly prefer a well-built dam if one is eventually built.

Joint fact finding in the dam proposal case might consist of several separate processes. The participants might commission an independent forecast of the impacts the project is likely to have on future utility rates. They might also jointly select a consultant to prepare an environmental impact assessment, spelling out the potential adverse effects that the project could have on the environment. They could hire mutually agreed-upon experts to prepare brief case histories of similar situations in which mitigation efforts were attempted.

In addition to sorting out fact from fiction, a joint fact-finding effort can create a positive psychological context for the next and most creative step in the consensus-building process.

NEGOTIATION

INVENTING OPTIONS FOR MUTUAL GAIN

Assuming that successful fact finding has occurred, or is occurring, how does the process proceed from prenegotiation to negotiation? What is needed is a wide-ranging exercise in invention. Working together and separately, all participants begin to envision and articulate at least one solution, whole or partial, that they find satisfactory. Obviously, if either side restricts itself to its ideal-world option—"No dam of any sort, ever!" or "Build it now, and just the way we've designed it!"—the negotiations are in serious trouble. But such inflexibility usually reflects a preliminary tactic rather than a working posture. As the dispute continues and the stakes rise, most groups eventually get around to considering their BATNA, rather than holding out for an extreme outcome.

In the dam proposal example, it is unlikely that the opponents of the dam will insist on a complete victory, refusing indefinitely to discuss options. Once they realize that they cannot be entirely confident of stopping the project, they must consider (albeit grudgingly) the most likely outcome and what it would mean to them. If they remain entirely confident about stopping the project, it is up to their opponents to shake that confidence, either by raising doubts or by altering key circumstances (and thus forcing recalculation of BATNAs).

Most often, negotiators begin by stating inflated positions (on the presumption that compromise will eventually be necessary) and by presenting nonnegotiable demands.[12] Neither tactic fools very many people. More often than not, each side realizes the other's demands have been inflated, and if they wait long enough more reasonable demands will be forthcoming. This is a terribly inefficient way to negotiate because it wastes not only time, but also creative energy. The same creativity could be devoted instead to inventing ways of serving the interests of all the stakeholders.

The all-important point is to "focus on interests, not positions."[13] This means the parties should spend their time outlining their concerns as candidly as possible. Instead of opening with a nonnegotiable demand, such as "The project must be withdrawn," a concerned citizens group should enumerate the possible impacts that worry them: "We are concerned about increasing noise, traffic, and possible loss of property values." The project proponents, instead of asserting their claim that "each person has a right to use his land as he wants," should respond by listing their concerns: meeting obligations to investors and lenders, realizing a reasonable profit on their investment, building a project they can be proud of, achieving a positive reputation in the development community, and so forth. Until all the disputants have presented a clear picture of their concerns, it is impossible to collaborate on integrative solutions that will allow each group to do better than its BATNA.

A recitation of interests should be followed by a period of "inventing without committing."[14] If all sides can be convinced to participate in a brainstorming process, the chances of coming up with a mutually satisfactory proposal will improve. Unfortunately, most disputants are afraid to suggest options responsive to the concerns of others out of fear that such suggestions will be seen as concessions or signs of weakness. Instead, they keep repeating unrealistic and antagonistic demands which eventually lead to deadlock.

To overcome this, the participants can declare an official period of "inventing without committing." They then work hard to produce a list of good ideas for addressing the items on the agenda, while assuring each other that whatever is said will not be taken as a firm commitment. For this process of brainstorming to work, there must be a moratorium on commitment. "Trust" need not enter the picture: Such collaboration can proceed independently of trust as long as the moratorium is honored.

In the Jordan Lane case, the necessary brainstorming took place through the efforts of a negotiating subcommittee, rather than in a full bargaining session. Everyone on the subcommittee understood that no one present could make commitments without checking back, so there was no danger of being held to inadvertent promises. This simple fact "freed" the group, and allowed it to be creative. They could always advise their membership to disavow any proposal that, in retrospect, seemed not to be advantageous.

Several mechanical aspects of brainstorming are worth mentioning. It is important for some member of the group to keep a record of the suggestions that emerge. If the group finds it difficult to invent useful options, there are techniques—such as "Synectics," a copyrighted brainstorming technique that emphasizes "free association"—which have been proven successful in a wide variety of problem-solving situations.[15]

The more complex the dispute, the more likely it is that subcommittees (sometimes with the help of outside advisors) will need to study each agenda item, and work hard to develop alternatives to deal with the concerns of all the disputants. To the extent that such subcommittees include at least one person from each identifiable faction or coalition, the proposals that emerge will be more likely to find favor with the full group. Also, such subcommittees should spend as much time as possible generating a wealth of good ideas rather than elaborating a single proposal. In fact, the more work the subcommittee does on a particular idea, the greater the risk that some participants will conclude that they have made an implicit commitment to that idea. This, as suggested previously, is counterproductive, and defeats the purpose of brainstorming.

The Jordan Lane negotiating committee was fortunate, finding it fairly easy to come up with ideas on each agenda item. That work proved immensely helpful in the next step of the negotiations.

PACKAGING AGREEMENTS

When the inventing process is sufficiently creative and productive, the next step comes easily. The negotiating parties now have to figure out which responses to each agenda item should be included in the final agreement. Disagreements will surely arise at this stage; trading, or "packaging," provides a helpful way of handling them.

One way to think about using trades to deal with disagreements is to consider the example of two talent-laden professional sports franchises. Both clubs are concerned about making a profit. Because they will be competing head-to-head in coming years, neither wants to trade a player that will allow the other to gain a clear-cut advantage. Through careful questioning, each team determines which players on the other team are "untouchable," and which could be considered available for a package deal. In many such cases, the negotiations gather momentum as each club sees additional ways to improve its own roster at an acceptable cost. When the overall package is sufficiently attractive, both clubs willingly agree to it.

The key to such packaging is that the opposing teams *value the same things differently.* For instance, if a baseball team has three possible shortstops, it will value the third on its list somewhat less than the other two. If the other team lacks depth in that position because of injuries, it may value that same player very highly. Because each team comes to the table in different circumstances, it attaches different value to the same players. In short, if both sides can find players on whom they place a low value, but whom the other values highly, they can trade to their mutual advantage.

In the Jordan Lane case, the three negotiating parties found numerous issues to trade. The neighborhood group agreed to five things: (1) to accept the Neighborhood Care mental health center in a spirit of goodwill, and to cooperate in phasing in its operations; (2) to notify the center if problems or concerns arose; (3) to attend open houses at the center, both to better understand the facility's operations and to meet its clients; (4) to serve on a joint review committee, in order to ensure the safety of residents and build goodwill toward the facility; and (5) to support the center's request for zoning approval, with the understanding that the joint committee would meet prior to each phase in the expansion of the program. A vital element of this section of their agreement was that subsequent expansion would not occur until every effort had been made to resolve any problems that emerged. If problems could not be resolved, the services of an impartial mediator would be employed. This would not, however, delay implementation of scheduled phase-ins.

The church, for its part, promised three things: (1) to notify the residents of the neighborhood should the church plan any additional long-term or recurring rentals of its building or grounds; (2) to place all trash in appropriate containers and to put out these containers only on the morning of scheduled city pick-up; and (3) to appoint a representative to meet with the neighbors, when necessary, to discuss their concerns.

Neighborhood Care, Inc., which would operate the center, made fourteen specific promises: (1) to avoid parking on Jordan Lane; (2) to use only the Homer Street entrance to the church; (3) to form a joint review committee with the neighborhood; (4)

to phase in its hours of operations according to a jointly agreed-upon schedule (that is, three days a week for two months, four days a week for two months, five days a week for one month, and six days a week in the sixth month), and to convene the joint committee before each phase-in. If the neighbors reported problems, the center agreed, as a show of good faith, to work to resolve those problems before the next increase in hours; (5) to send a monthly calendar to local residents informing them of the scheduling of events and activities; (6) to provide adequate staffing (at ratio of 1:8), with professional trained staff members on hand at all times; (7) to limit the maximum number of clients at any given time to thirty-five, and the maximum number of people present (including staff) to fifty-five; (8) to monitor clients' arrivals and departures by keeping a sign-in sheet; (9) to operate a van for the pick-up and return of clients to day and evening programs; (10) to encourage phone calls from the neighborhood residents should clients become disoriented after leaving the church; (11) to carry insurance sufficient to cover potential property damage to neighbors, should the center or its clients be found liable; (12) to refrain from holding activities on Jordan Lane, or the church grounds on Jordan Lane; (13) to keep noise levels to a point where they did not disturb the neighbors; and (14) to keep a staff person on the premises after the end of each day's programming until all the clients had safely left the area.

These promises represented victory for all sides. The neighborhood group got all the guarantees it wanted, including promises from the church that no future surprises would occur, and from Neighborhood Care that every reasonable measure would be taken to reduce the level of risk presented by the facility. The church won the neighbors' support for the proposed zoning change, and put the residents on notice that other uses of the church might be necessary in the future. Neighborhood Care won a promise of goodwill from the neighbors that would allow positive long-term relationships to develop, and—as it turned out—had to promise nothing that it had not originally intended to.

PRODUCING A WRITTEN AGREEMENT

The next step in the consensus-building process is to produce a written agreement. This is important for two reasons. First, it ensures that the parties have heard and understood each other. In the absence of a written agreement, it is very common for participants to come away from negotiations with slightly different interpretations of what was promised. This, of course, can lead to problems of implementation later on. The second function of a written agreement is to be certain that the parties have something concrete to take back to their members for review and ratification. The negotiators must leave the table with identical documents to show their respective constituencies.

In a public negotiation, it is especially important to be explicit. (Unlike a sports trade, most public dispute settlements cannot allow for the proverbial "player to be named later.") Even though ad hoc negotiations such as we have described often produce informal agreements, written documents may be needed to transform such informal agreements to formally binding contracts. (We will discuss this point in detail in a subsequent section.) Given the large number of participants in most public disputes, as well as the complexity of the issues involved, no one should have to trust their memories or rely on word-of-mouth reports about a proposed settlement.

There are better and worse ways of translating oral understandings into written agreements. A not-so-helpful way is to ask each group to prepare its own written version of what has been agreed. This typically leads to each stakeholder presenting a version of the agreement that puts the very best light on things from his or her perspective. An exchange of such purposeful drafts could well force yet another round of negotiations—an unwelcome outcome, when the goal is simply to formalize what has already been decided.

A more helpful approach is the "single-text procedure."[16] One person (or a very small group of participants) is designated to produce a draft that captures his or her sense of the agreement. This draft is circulated back and forth among the participants until agreement, or "closure," is reached. It should be clearly understood by all that the text is a working draft and not a final document. Participants should be asked to "improve the draft"—as opposed to preparing written comments about its shortcomings—by adding language that is both more acceptable to them, and likely to be acceptable to everyone else as well.

One of the positive aspects of the ad hoc or informal dispute resolution process we are describing is that no one needs to worry about drafting agreements in "legalese." In fact, the entire process we have described thus far can be handled by the disputants themselves (although they may want their lawyers to look over the final draft before they sign).

One key to capturing in writing the inventive quality of a negotiated agreement is to emphasize "contingencies"—statements of what will happen under different sets of circumstances. An "if-then" format is often an excellent device for recording different assumptions about the future. So, for example, the Jordan Lane negotiators indicated in writing how they would proceed if the neighbors found themselves unhappy with further expansion of the center's operating hours.

Just as a great many people have difficulty with marriage contracts that spell out what happens in the event of a divorce, negotiators in distributional disputes often want to avoid discussing what will be done if the worst occurs. But explicit reference to such contingencies may be necessary to satisfy the most pessimistic partners in a negotiation. Moreover, only by covering all such possibilities in the written agreement will the negotiators be able to convince their constituents that the most important issues have been addressed.

BINDING PARTIES TO COMMITMENTS

It is extremely important to devise a means of holding the various parties to the terms of what is still an informal agreement. The participants must be confident that the bargain they have struck will be honored. For this to be true, the negotiating parties must devise appropriate mechanisms to hold each other to their commitments. Some agreements can be designed to be self-enforcing, while others can be made enforceable through legal means. In either case, some decision about enforcement must be made in time to include a description of the relevant mechanisms in the written agreement.

A basic element in binding the parties is the specification of "performance measures"—that is, objective measures of success. Some settlements, for example, require that certain outcomes be measured and assessed at prescribed intervals, and that funding be provided for this purpose. Previous joint fact-finding efforts can have a bearing on what happens at this point. If the disputants have already agreed upon acceptable sources of data and ways of measuring performance, this sharply reduces the likelihood of subsequent challenges to the agreement.

Self-enforcing agreements require a careful sequencing of reciprocal actions—in other words, no one is required to meet their next commitment until everyone else has completed their tasks on schedule. So, for example, the residents on Jordan Lane were not obliged to testify in favor of the proposed zoning change at the city council hearing until Neighborhood Care and

St. Mark's Church appointed members to the joint review committee.

Another approach to designing self-enforcing agreements is based on traditional betting procedures. The concept is simple. If two parties make a bet, they may ask a third person to hold the stakes. When the outcome of the bet is clear, the holder of the stakes pays the winner.

In one development dispute in the Washington, D.C., area, a variant of this procedure was put to very effective use.[17] The developer of a shopping center was seeking neighborhood support for a needed zoning change. The residents expressed concern about the impact the new development might have on their property values. In response, the developer offered to put up a bond of several hundred thousand dollars to be held by a mutually agreed-upon private party. According to the agreement, if any nearby resident sold a house within five years after construction of the shopping center, some of that bond money would be available to make up any difference between the actual sales price and what the price would have been had the shopping center not been built. (This hypothetical price reflected an initial appraisal and an allowance for inflation.)

Because the money was being held by someone trusted by all the parties, there was no question that the agreement would be honored. No legal sleight of hand was possible, and it was not necessary to go to court to claim the money. As it turned out, no one suffered a loss, no claims were filed, and the funds were returned with interest to the developer after the allotted time had passed.

In some instances, it may be necessary to write legally binding contracts to ensure that future members of certain groups or subsequent officeholders honor their commitments. If such a step is necessary, it is desirable to have one attorney acceptable to all the participants prepare a draft of such a contract. Again, each person covered by the contract may want to have his or her attorney review the draft.

RATIFICATION

Depending on how the original issues of representation were handled, many of the individuals involved in the negotiations may well speak for several people or organizations. These representatives must now return to their constituents and say, "This is the final draft of the agreement. Do you support it? Are you willing to have me sign it on your behalf?" Or, in some cases, "Are you each willing to sign it?"

This is a critical juncture in many negotiations. If the representation issue has not been addressed effectively, the affected groups may repudiate not only the agreement, but also their representative. Even if the representative began his or her work with adequate backing, the negotiations may have ranged far afield and produced a settlement very different from what the group expected. This, as we said earlier, implies a crucial responsibility for the negotiator, who must educate his or her constituency throughout the course of the negotiations. Early on, the negotiator must help the group assess its initial expectations in light of the information that emerges. Later, the negotiator must explain how the settlement is reasonably reflective of the group's interests, even if it does not meet all their expectations.

This is an appropriate point to note that the binding and ratification steps can be greatly complicated by the emergence of splinter groups. Imagine, for example, representatives of an environmental group involved in negotiations concerning a controversial development such as the RiverEnd mass transit facility. They have helped to draft a tentative settlement which they must take back to their membership for a vote. The vote is taken; the agreement is ratified, and the group is now bound to live by its terms. Then—unexpectedly—an individual member of the group announces that he or she is dissatisfied with the agreement and is suing to block its implementation.

Some organizations are sufficiently hierarchical that they can force their members to live with the terms of an agreement. Most are not. Painfully aware of this reality, public officials and business interests are sometimes reluctant to begin informal negotiations with citizen or consumer groups, environmental organizations, or similar adversaries. "Why negotiate with these people?" they ask. "It's a waste of time talking to groups that can't bind their members." Of course, from the standpoint of the consumer or citizen group, the problem looks the same: "Why negotiate with this administration when it's likely to be turned out of office in a year or two?" Or, "Why negotiate with the leadership of this company, when its directors may well appoint a new executive in the near future?" There are no easy answers to this problem. We will examine the issue further in chapter 6, which presents a series of practical approaches to taking action.

At this point, we mention the splinter group problem only in a cautionary way. Each party to a negotiation must take responsibility for assessing the legitimacy and authority of the other parties at the table. Some disaffected subgroups cannot be anticipated; others can. If Group A's representative suspects that a faction of Group B is unhappy with the progress of the negotiations, the representatives of Groups A and B should meet to discuss the problem. The earlier they do so, the less likelihood there is that a splinter group will emerge later.

In addition, the process by which each participant seeks ratification from his or her constituency should be spelled out in the protocols. Although flexibility should be the watchword in determining what is required of each group (because organizations are designed and function differently), all participants should be satisfied that realistic ratification procedures will be followed. In some instances, the officers or even one individual in a group can commit that organization. In other instances, a poll of the full membership is necessary. In still others, the best that can be achieved is a nonbinding personal pledge from the leadership of an organization that it will work to help implement the negotiated agreement.

In some public dispute resolution efforts, elected or appointed officials may designate staff to participate on their behalf. This may be a legal necessity when elected or appointed officials are bound by statute to avoid behind-the-scenes (or, in legal terms, "ex parte") communication with regulatees. The staff members in the negotiations may be limited to promising a personal "best effort" to live up to the commitments spelled out in the agreement. Presumably such designees remain in contact with their agency or supervisors, so that their promise of a best effort can be read as an unofficial agency commitment. This certainly is a great distance removed from open agency support, but it may be sufficient as a prelude to implementation.

Often, negotiators return to the full group to report that final ratification is only possible if some additional changes are made in the draft. The other representatives may well object. This may mean that every negotiator has to return to his or her constituents once again with a revised version of the final agreement. Why did no one raise these concerns earlier, they may ask?

Such occurrences, however, are common, and are not necessarily a sign that a negotiator has done a poor job. Many factors may come into play at such a juncture. Some groups, for example, may not pay serious attention to a proposed agreement until it comes time to vote on it.

Ratification sometimes takes the form of contingent commitments: "We agree to support the agreement if the following changes are made," or, "We support the agreement in principle, but something must be done about [one or another matter]." Agreements in principle are valuable because they make it possible to avoid another full round of review—assuming, of course, that minor changes can be agreed upon by the participants without further need to touch base.

IMPLEMENTATION OR POSTNEGOTIATION

LINKING THE INFORMAL AGREEMENT TO THE FORMAL PROCESSES OF GOVERNMENT DECISION MAKING

After the agreement is ratified, the negotiating parties must find a way to link the ad hoc, informal agreement they have fashioned to the formal decision-making processes of government. Up to this point, typically, the negotiating process has been kept "unofficial." (It may have been this very ad hoc quality, in fact, which persuaded some of the key players to participate.) An unofficial process has produced an informal result, which probably could not have been reached by other means; the challenge now is to formalize that result. It seems paradoxical: How can an informal agreement be formalized?

The answer to this question varies, of course, depending on individual circumstances. In some instances, the negotiated agreement can be converted into a statute or a bylaw by a legislative vote. In others, it may be converted into a legally enforceable contract with city, state, or federal agencies. In still others, an executive order or administrative action may put an agency of the government on record as the enforcer of the agreement. Each of these approaches presents its own advantages and perils. (A statute, for example, is only as permanent as the legislative and judicial branches allow it to be.) Nevertheless, the negotiating parties must seek and employ the most effective means for linking the formal and the informal processes of decision making.

In the Jordan Lane case, the participants were quite ingenious. They asked the member of the city council who had attended their initial session to add the terms of their written agreement as conditions of the zoning variance awarded by the council. The city council, of course, still had the power to decide whether or not to grant the variance. But when the member of the council who had followed the informal negotiations described, in detail, how that process had worked and what it had produced, the full council quickly agreed to add the requested conditions to the permit. Thus, implementation of the informally negotiated agreement was ensured through government regulation, although no new laws were written and no formal precedent regarding future halfway houses was set.

The question of the precedent-setting nature of informally negotiated agreements is often raised by elected and appointed officials. One of the best arguments for pursuing a negotiated approach to a distributional dispute is that both the procedures and the resolution can be matched with the particulars of the situation. Precedent does not apply the way it does when more conventional modes of dispute resolution are used. Of course, it must be recognized that when it comes time to transform an informally negotiated agreement into a formal statement of public policy, a precedent of sorts may well be set, unless all the parties take great care to ensure that it is not. The negotiated agreement should state that the terms reached by the disputants are not viewed as setting a precedent by which any of them will feel bound in other distributional disputes. The formal action of the government body implementing the agreement should underscore this. By explicitly denying the precedent-setting nature of decisions reached by consensus, public officials can create incentives for other groups to work out their differences in ways that satisfy those groups, while protecting themselves from implied commitments to future agreements.

MONITORING IMPLEMENTATION

The step of monitoring implementation of an agreement has already been mentioned in the context of binding the parties. In addition to checking compliance and measuring the success of the settlement in terms of certain objective standards, the monitoring process must take account of changing circumstances. As individuals who participated in the negotiations are replaced by newcomers, it is important for some designated body to inform them of the terms of the agreement. Monitoring is a means of achieving this.

In some public disputes, the design of a monitoring process is a difficult and elaborate task. The outcome of the resource recovery/dioxin dispute will be described in detail in chapter 5; we will note here that the final agreement in that case hinged on the design of a scientifically acceptable monitoring plan. The parties were able to agree on the emission standards that the trash-to-energy plant would have to meet. They also recognized that the technology for measuring emissions would be very expensive. (Indeed, it might cost as much as $500,000 to take a full set of measurements every few months.) Further, it might take several months for the results of the tests to be known, and crucial decisions might hinge on numbers that could vary depending on when, where, and how the samples were taken. Thus, the monitoring plan had to be extraordinarily detailed to forestall disputes over the reliability and meaning of the results.

In short, designing a monitoring process can be a formidable task. Certain cases do require such an effort—especially disputes involving complex scientific and technical issues.

CREATING A CONTEXT FOR RENEGOTIATION

By the time an agreement is reached, it often reflects an enormous investment of time and energy. It is important to protect that investment with a provision for reconvening the parties should something go wrong. Such a reconvening might be restricted to certain well-defined circumstances, such as an apparent violation of the terms of the agreement by one party or the failure of the settlement to produce agreed-upon results. The renegotiation provision could be invoked when one of the involved parties felt its interests were threatened. In all cases, however, the attitude of all concerned should be, "What can we do to hold this agreement together, in the event that something goes wrong?"

In the Jordan Lane case, the parties assumed that if anything went awry the joint monitoring committee would reconvene all the participants. They also felt that reasonably good relationships had developed as a result of the consensus-building process, and that opening a renegotiation, if necessary, would be much easier than starting the original negotiations.

Many negotiated agreements spell out the terms under which the parties will reconvene. They also indicate exactly what the reconvening procedure should be, so that precipitous action is not taken on the basis of untested claims or misinformation.

PRECONDITIONS FOR THE SUCCESS OF UNASSISTED NEGOTIATION

We have observed three preconditions for the success of unassisted negotiations: (1) the issues in dispute, as well as the array of stakeholding parties, should be relatively few in number and readily identifiable; (2) the stakeholders must be able to establish sufficient channels of communication to permit joint problem solving; and (3) the uncertainty surrounding the outcome of unilateral action must be moderately high for all stakeholders. When these conditions do not pertain, it may still be possible for the parties to deal with their differences on their own, but it will be much harder.

"Unassisted negotiation," we should emphasize, in summary, does not mean that the parties have no access to technical or scientific advice. (In fact, if specialists are available to assist the parties in joint fact finding, for example, they should be used.) Instead, "unassisted negotiation" means that no one has been asked to help manage the process of negotiating. The parties get together on their own—on mutually agreed-upon terms—and work things out.

Despite the success of the Jordan Lane negotiation, it is unusual for people caught up in distributional disputes to deal with their differences so effectively without assistance. One of the most common reasons why an unassisted negotiation fails to begin, or fails to produce a satisfactory outcome, is an imbalance of power among the stakeholders. (Such an imbalance violates the third precondition stated previously. Powerful groups are tempted to take unilateral actions.) In negotiations, each group must protect its own interests. Without assistance, less powerful parties often have trouble protecting their interests at every step in the consensus-building process.

Groups that are unorganized or fearful of speaking out, for example, may go unheeded in an unassisted negotiation. Groups that lack enough technical expertise (or the funds to purchase the advice they need) may not realize that a proposed package is not in their interests. Groups that are not sophisticated in the process of negotiation may miss opportunities to pursue their interests in a way that could lead to greater advantages. And finally, groups with unpopular views may find their concerns trivialized or ignored during the course of an unassisted negotiation.

Of course, less powerful groups can always drop out of negotiations in such cases; but we maintain that they would be better served by remaining in the negotiations and maximizing joint gains with the aid of a competent helper. Departing from a negotiation is, very occasionally, risky. Less powerful groups may be worse off for having participated in and then dropped out of a negotiation, because others may claim that the disaffected group had an adequate opportunity to represent its views.

Negotiation is not an antidote to inequality. Groups can be, and sometimes are, outnumbered or outmaneuvered. Politically powerless groups are appropriately skeptical about their potential for success in negotiations. As a result, they tend to conclude that lying down in front of the bulldozers or similar forms of direct action are more effective approaches for them. In rare cases, they may be right. On the other hand, we maintain that power in negotiations is dynamic, and that political power away from the bargaining table is not necessarily a good predictor of what will happen once negotiations begin. Coalitions can form, tipping the scales in unexpected ways. Creative thinking—in the form of packages that maximize joint gains—can give a less powerful group a surprising degree of leverage. Access to information through joint fact finding, and the improved relationships that often result from joint problem solving, can also serve to balance the scales.

Negotiation researchers have documented a host of ways in which less powerful groups can gain power by handling themselves effectively in negotiations.[18] Most often, though, the key is the presence of a facilitator or mediator. In the same way that the players in a sporting match are aided—regardless of their ability—by the presence of a referee or umpire who enforces the rules, so, too, do the participants in a negotiation benefit from the presence of a nonpartisan intervenor, who manages the process of negotiation fairly and efficiently.

In the next chapter, we describe the variety of roles that neutral intervenors can play to augment and reinforce the efforts of the negotiating parties.

CHAPTER 5

Mediation and Other Forms of Assisted Negotiation

In an ideal world distributional disputes would be settled by the parties themselves, as in the Jordan Lane case. But, because the participants in multiparty, many-issue disputes are usually unable to deal with their differences on their own, assisted negotiation is often necessary.

Assisted negotiation is the complement to unassisted negotiation. Many public disputes—in fact, the great majority of the distributional disputes to which we have alluded—do not meet the preconditions outlined in the last chapter for successful unassisted negotiation. Most public disputes are highly complex, for example, and the affected groups are hard to identify and difficult to represent. Disputing parties often have great difficulty initiating and pursuing discussions. Emotional, psychological, or financial stakes may be so high that the disputants are unable to sustain the collaborative aspects of unassisted negotiation. Finally, power imbalances may preclude direct and unassisted dealings among disputants.

Consider, for example, the problems posed by the relatively simple task of initiating a dialogue—or, as we have labeled the first step in the prenegotiation phase, "getting started." We have already discussed some of the psychological traps that come into play as disputing parties consider whether or not to pursue negotiations. Like some couples involved in marital squabbles, each partner refuses to make the first conciliatory gesture. "You started this," each says, "so you solve it." In other words, public postures alone may preclude unassisted negotiation. If that is the case, then the disputing parties have only two choices: they can resort to the conventional legislative, administrative, or judicial means of resolving distributional disputes, or they can seek the help of a nonpartisan intermediary—a facilitator, mediator, or arbitrator—and engage in assisted negotiation.

"Getting started" is relatively easy, when compared with some of the subsequent phases of negotiation. Suffice it to say that when complexities arise, a neutral intermediary is often the only solution.

ENTRY

There are numerous ways that intermediaries can arrive on the scene. As suggested earlier, an unassisted negotiation can easily get bogged down; and as the frustration level rises, one of the disputing parties may suggest the need for a "neutral." Alternatively, a neutral may present himself or herself to the various stakeholders and indicate a willingness to provide assistance. Finally, a disinterested observer may advise the disputing parties to seek outside assistance.

This last approach is particularly fruitful when the various parties are "frozen" into uncompromising public postures. In such cases, all parties may in fact want to initiate negotiations, but fear the consequences of appearing weak. ("If I seem eager to negotiate, the others will attempt to gain more by hardening their positions.") This may be partially true, but the overriding reality is that these parties are unlikely to resolve their dispute without help. Therefore, the neutral may have to be introduced into the dispute by a nonparticipant.

A second problem of entry has to do with perceptions of control. In many cases, one or more disputants is convinced that employing an intermediary will amount to surrendering control over the outcome. This is a common misperception, which arises out of the publicity that often accompanies binding arbitration, a process in which an arbitrator listens to each side's arguments and arrives at a judgment by which the parties have agreed to be bound. In contrast, there are several types of assisted negotiation which are not binding, and which proceed only with the continuing assent of the negotiating parties. In other words, all parties must be satisfied with the settlement reached through such a consensual process, or there is no settlement. Because the stakeholders retain veto power over the final outcome, they retain a vital measure of control.

Government agencies and officials are particularly sensitive to issues of control. "I have a legal mandate," such officials frequently tell us. "It would be inappropriate and perhaps illegal for me to accept terms dictated by someone else." The answer, of course, is that in the types of consensual negotiations described in this book, no one dictates terms, or has terms dictated to them. Government agencies are constantly entering into negotiations that produce legally binding agreements—for example, labor contracts. Given that fact, nothing prevents government officials from engaging in nonbinding negotiations, assuming, of course, that they are attentive to "sunshine" laws and other due process considerations.

Two other issues of entry—the neutrality and competence of the proposed helper—often present themselves early in the negotiating process. How can all sides be certain that the go-between is unbiased, and will be equally helpful to all the parties? Wouldn't it be easy for a seemingly disinterested helper to favor one side over the others while disguising his or her stance as neutral? Even if all sides can be sure that the intermediary is impartial, can they be sure of his or her competence? What if the neutral botches the job, causing everything to take far longer and cost far more than would otherwise have been the case?

The question of neutrality is actually not difficult to resolve. Once again, "veto power" is the key. Any party to a dispute can disqualify a proposed helper who seems biased. Obviously, the background and affiliation of the intermediary are fundamental considerations. It is much easier for a helper to be accepted by all the parties, for example, if he or she has had no direct affiliation with any of the stakeholders. Also, the record and reputation of the proposed helper should be reviewed and approved by all the participants. If the helper begins work before all anticipated participants have joined the negotiations, it should be with a clear understanding that the helper may still be disqualified by a late participant with a complaint about bias.

These same four criteria—background, affiliation, record, and reputation—are equally useful in assessing a potential intermediary's competence. For specific advice about finding and hiring a helper, please consult the next chapter, in which we discuss these and other practical issues (who is going to pay?) in greater detail.

Different helpers have distinct styles. Some define their role very narrowly; others are willing to take on a broader set of roles. Some expect the disputants to handle many of the details of the negotiation; others are willing to carry more of the burden.[1] It makes sense to ask a potential helper to submit a proposed contract enumerating his or her concerns and commitments. It is not uncommon for disputants to collect written information about and interview half a dozen potential helpers before settling on one. A written agreement spelling out the disputants' expectations regarding the helper's role and obligations can avoid misunderstandings later.

ROLES AND FUNCTIONS OF AN INTERMEDIARY

The easiest way to think about the functions that a helper plays in a public dispute is to refer again to the three phases of the consensus-building process described in chapter 4. There are several tasks that the helper can complete at each step (see table 5.1).

Getting started, as we have already emphasized, may well depend on the assistance of a nonpartisan convenor. The helper, however he or she entered the process, will probably have to spend a substantial amount of time meeting with potential stakeholders to convince them that a negotiated approach can work. Because the notion of joint problem solving is alien to most parties in public disputes, helpers often find it necessary to describe situations in which consensual approaches produced better outcomes than conventional approaches. This means that the intermediary needs to be well versed in the actual practice, and not just the theory, of dispute resolution.

The neutral can allow all parties to maintain the appearance of "toughness" while still supporting the search for integrative outcomes. This is accomplished by allowing the parties to communicate cooperative messages through the helper while maintaining a less cooperative "public" stance in meetings of the full group. To the extent that the helper can alert the parties ahead of time to the fact that an uncompromising statement is about to made, but that the statement does not really represent that stakeholder's "bottom line," the helper can head off confrontations. In addition, by suggesting neutral turf for the first meeting, handling all the logistical arrangements, and proposing a provisional set of protocols to guide the initial discussions, the helper can assist the parties in overcoming many of the initial obstacles to successful negotiation.

It may appear that we are describing a "chicken-and-egg" problem: The parties must meet in order to identify a helper who will help them arrange a meeting. This is rarely the case in practice. Typically, a potential helper is contacted by one side (without the concurrence of the others) or by a noninvolved observer. The helper then calls the other parties and (assuming conditions are right) proposes either an initial get-together, at which everyone can talk, or a round of private caucuses between the helper and each stakeholding group. The helper has no guarantee that he or she will be paid, or that negotiations are even likely to happen. This is an "up-front" investment of time that potential helpers must make, comparable to the investment builders make when they prepare a bid for a possible project.

Representation is another prenegotiation task that helpers are often called upon to handle. Before a professional mediator or facilitator will invest the time needed to complete a conflict assessment or to help with representation, however, he or she will probably require a contract. Such a contract might cover only the first few steps in the proposed negotiation process. It might be written initially with just the key stakeholders, and amended later as more groups are added, and as the stakeholders decide to commit to a full-fledged negotiation. The preliminary contract gives the helper an indication of the seriousness of the group's commitment to the process.

Intermediaries can advise potential stakeholders about strategies for selecting spokespersons. They can also assist all the participants in undertaking a preliminary analysis of their alternatives to negotiation. They can make it clear to groups anxious about perceived imbalances of power that everyone will have a

T A B L E 5 . 1

Tasks of the Mediator

Phases	Tasks
PRENEGOTIATION	
Getting started	Meeting with potential stakeholders to assess their interests and describe the consensus-building process; handling logistics and convening initial meetings; assist groups in initial calculation of BATNAs
Representation	Caucusing with stakeholders to help choose spokespeople or team leaders; working with initial stakeholders to identify missing groups or strategies for representing diffuse interests
Drafting protocols and agenda setting	Preparing draft protocols based on past experience and the concerns of the parties; managing the process of agenda setting
Joint fact finding	Helping to draft fact-finding protocols; identifying technical consultants or advisors to the group; raising and administering the funds in a resource pool; serving as a repository for confidential or proprietary information
NEGOTIATION	
Inventing options	Managing the brainstorming process; suggesting potential options for the group to consider; coordinating subcommittees to draft options
Packaging	Caucusing privately with each group to identify and test possible trades; suggesting possible packages for the group to consider

T A B L E 5 . 1 *(continued)*

Tasks of the Mediator

Phases	Tasks
NEGOTIATION (Continued)	
Written agreement	Working with a subcommitee to produce a draft agreement; managing a single-text procedure; preparing a preliminary draft of a single text
Binding the parties	Serving as the holder of the bond; approaching outsiders on behalf of the group; helping to invent new ways to bind the parties to their commitments
Ratification	Helping the participants "sell" the agreement to their constituents; ensuring that all representatives have been in touch with their constituents
IMPLEMENTATION OR POSTNEGOTIATION	
Linking informal agreements and formal decision making	Working with the parties to invent linkages; approaching elected or appointed officials on behalf of the group; identifying the legal constraints on implementation
Monitoring	Serving as the monitor of implementation; convening a monitoring group
Renegotiation	Reassembling the participants if subsequent disagreements emerge; helping to remind the group of its earlier intentions

chance to be heard, and that available information will be shared.

As a spokesperson for and manager of the process, the helper is the only one in a position to promise the parties that the rules of the game will be enforced. The helper can also serve as a link to the media. In fact, it is often advisable for the helper to be the only person who talks to the press during an ongoing negotiation. This minimizes the temptation some groups may feel to negotiate through the press.

The neutral can play a critical role in bringing recalcitrant parties to the bargaining table. For example, by offering assurances that the rules of the game will be strictly enforced, the helper may be able to sign on less powerful groups. Conversely, the neutral may bring subtle pressure to bear on more powerful parties, by convincing them that sitting on the sidelines could entail a high price. If used heavy-handedly, of course, such tactics usually backfire. But if used skillfully, they may overcome what would otherwise be insurmountable barriers to consensus building.

Development of protocols and agenda setting are tasks that are best managed by a neutral—first through private discussions with each party, and then in group discussion. The listing of potential agenda topics may seem a simple mechanical task, but in fact there is an art to compressing numerous items into a manageable set of priorities that all parties can accept.

Experienced intermediaries can also save disputants a great deal of time by drafting preliminary protocols. Blending elements from past dispute situations, the helper can provide a draft that the group can use as a starting point. At the very least, illustrations of the ways in which other groups have handled similar problems are reassuring. The helper can also include the draft agenda and the agreed-upon protocols as conditions of his or her contract. This not only commits the neutral to procedures the participants want, but it also reassures mistrustful parties that the protocols will not be ignored.

Joint fact finding may require various kinds of assistance from a neutral. For example, the group may rely on a helper to come up with names of potential expert advisors that all stakeholders can accept. The intermediary may serve as the "banker" for studies that are jointly commissioned—holding and allocating funds contributed by each of the stakeholders. In situations involving confidential or proprietary information, the helper may be asked to summarize data in ways that protect one party's legitimate need for privacy, without concealing useful data. A variation on this role arises when negotiators must share business information, but such sharing may constitute a violation of antitrust laws. The neutral, in such a circumstance, can serve as a repository for information, issuing summaries of findings without mentioning particular companies.

A neutral may also be asked to assist in raising money to establish a resource pool—that is, a "kitty" of money which the group as a whole can draw upon. At one point, for example, the EPA created a resource pool to ensure the availability of funds to the participants in that agency's "negotiated rule makings."[2] The participants were meeting, at EPA's request, to help draft regulations to implement a portion of the Clean Air Act. The funds in the resource pool were available to any of the twenty-five participating groups who needed reimbursement for travel or other expenses incurred during the negotiations. Resources were also available to the group as a whole to commission joint fact-finding studies. The convenor—not an EPA official—held the funds for the group and allocated them in accordance with decisions made by the group as a whole.

Sometimes a *team* of intermediaries is needed. This is particularly useful in complex disputes hinging on scientific questions. In such a case, an expert in process management may want to team up with a neutral who has relevant technical background. Again, the second member of the team would also have to be acceptable to all the stakeholders, even though he or she would advise the process manager rather than the participants.

Even more elaborate teams are sometimes appropriate. In the Harmon County sewage clean-up case described in chapter 3, the out-of-state mediator appointed by the court teamed up with a local mediator—who had a thorough knowledge of the state's political and legal systems—as well as with several engineering professionals, who developed a computer model the mediators could use to forecast the costs of various settlement proposals.

Inventing options, as we indicated in the previous chapter, requires a process of brainstorming and intensive subcommittee work. The neutral can be the one to declare a period of "inventing without committing." He or she can also be the compiler of good ideas. The helper may even put forward options that participants want considered but feel uneasy about suggesting themselves. So, for example, one or another group might approach the helper privately and ask that he or she mention an option without revealing its source.

Inventing options has its perils, though. Intermediaries have to be careful not to become too closely identified with particular options or proposals, for if a participant feels that the helper has become too supportive of a specific proposal, that stakeholder may feel that the helper can no longer be trusted to remain neutral. This does not mean, of course, that intermediaries cannot offer suggestions. Skilled neutrals should know how to present ideas in a dispassionate fashion, thereby reassuring the participants that the intermediary is nonpartisan.

Packaging is the step that generally involves the greatest skill and insight. It is here that helpers can play their most important role. By meeting privately with each participant, an intermediary should be able to discover which items are tradeable. Typically, the helper says to each party in a private caucus, "What's most important to you?" Or, "What can you most readily give up?" Through confidential questioning, an effective intermediary should be able to figure out a set of trades that will bring the participants as close to agreement as they can possibly get.

(Of course, this can only occur if the neutral has already demonstrated competence and earned the trust of the parties.)

An intermediary can offer the parties a chance to suggest possible trades without making commitments. In a private conversation, the helper might say, "I know what you've said in the full meetings, but tell me: Would you be willing to trade X if the others offered you Y and Z?" At this point, the disputant might say, "I won't say it out loud in the meeting, but if I were offered Y and Z, yes, I would trade X." This is crucial information which the helper must find a way of testing with the other parties—without violating a confidence, of course.

A skilled intermediary can, in private meetings with the other participants, explore whether they would be willing to give up Y and Z in exchange for X. This might be phrased, "What if I could get them to give up X? Would you trade Y and Z?" Of course, the neutral already knows that such a trade is possible. He or she must phrase the question, though, in a what-if format to protect the confidentiality of the information secured earlier. If the answer is "yes," the helper might call everyone together and offer the following observation: "I have a hunch that if the folks on this side of the room were willing to offer X the others would promise to give Y and Z. Am I correct?"

By proceeding in this fashion, the intermediary has made no promises, and has attributed no commitments to anyone. The end result, if all goes well, is a package that everyone can accept.

Written agreements need to be drafted by someone, and in most cases the neutral is the obvious person to play this role. To the extent that an intermediary can produce a single text and carry it from party to party, he or she can ensure that everyone agrees to the same thing. This is a great advantage in negotiations. Long-time international treaty negotiators use the "single-text" procedure described earlier, which is much more likely to produce agreement than a process in which each party drafts its own version of the final agreement and those versions are later integrated.

In the single-text procedure, the helper asks each party to suggest "improvements" in a draft attributed to the intermediary. Because the draft is not "extreme" and refrains from arguing only for what one side or the other wants most, progress is likely to ensue.

Binding the parties involves the invention of enforcement mechanisms. We have already described the device of setting aside funds. In some instances, the intermediary may be the person favored by all sides to "hold the bet." In other instances, the helper may be asked to approach someone who has not been involved in the negotiations, to see whether that individual might play a role in binding the parties. It is usually the case that skilled helpers can assist disputing parties in inventing new ways to bind each other to an agreement.

Ratification requires each participant to go back to his or her constituents and seek approval of the draft agreement. For some participants, this may present difficulties, particularly if their group began the negotiations with utterly unrealistic expectations. The helper may be able to aid such participants in "selling" the agreement to their members, perhaps by pointing out how far all the other stakeholders have come in accepting the draft agreement. The helper may also be able to emphasize truthfully how effective the group's negotiator was. ("You should have seen how far along your spokesperson was able to pull the rest of the group. She was an incredibly effective advocate of your interests.") The group's spokesperson, of course, could not make such claims without seeming to brag. If true, though, the fact of effectiveness is significant, and needs to be pointed out.

The process of *linking the informal agreement and formal decision making* requires interaction with elected or appointed officials, who may not have participated directly in the negotiations (although they should have been apprised of the progress of the negotiations by their staff or appointed observers). Because the neutral is an advocate of the process and not of any particular outcome, it is usually easier for officials to accept a helper's claims regarding the legitimacy of the process than the claims of a stakeholder.

The participants may want the helper to play a role in *monitoring* implementation of the agreement. Although this is not often the case (it is better to have monitoring performed by people on the scene), it is sometimes a possibility. The helper may be asked by the participants to approach outsiders who have not been involved in the negotiations to ask them to play a monitoring role. In many cases, it is easier for the helper to make these contacts, and to be convincing about the legitimacy of the process, than it is for any one of the disputants.

It is likely that the participants will want to specify in the agreement what the helper's role will be if *renegotiation* (or "remediation") is necessary. Who better to reassemble the parties, or to remind them of their previous commitments? Also, the parties are likely to feel that the helper will be a fair referee of what was originally intended, should subsequent disagreements arise. It should be noted, though, that very few helpers will accept a renegotiation role if they have assisted in drafting the original agreement; they prefer to move on to new disputes.

When we describe the roles and functions of intermediaries in distributional disputes, some people mistakenly conclude that helpers in public disputes do roughly what intermediaries in labor disputes or international disputes do. But those familiar with the roles of such intermediaries (or "third parties," as they are often called, as there are usually only two disputing sides in labor negotiations) will recognize immediately from the preceding descriptions that there are very substantial differences between assisted negotiation in distributional disputes and other kinds of assisted negotiation.

In short, neutrals in distributional disputes need to be more activist. They have a much broader array of responsibilities, because the context in which they work is much less structured. They need a different kind of background, different skills, and perhaps a different temperament from their counterparts in labor relations and international relations. Intermediaries in distributional disputes usually need to be quite conversant with the ways in which the public sector operates, because they may spend as much time creating the context in which negotiations take place as they do managing the consensus-building process. They also need more sharply honed communication skills, since they may have to spend significant amounts of time "selling the process" to potential participants and the community at large.

Given the scope of the intermediaries' involvement in most distributional disputes, it is important that they be willing to accept some responsibility for the fairness, efficiency, wisdom, and stability of the outcomes. This is not inconsistent with the concept of neutrality. While those who participate directly must "own" the agreement, the neutral must also assure himself or herself that everything possible has been done to meet the concerns of those who chose not to participate directly as well as the concerns of those who did. Long-term voluntary compliance requires that this test be met. Unless it is, the credibility of the consensus-building effort is likely to erode. In addition, to the extent that consensual dispute resolution processes are likely to be judged against the conventional judicial, administrative, and legislative mechanisms, assisted negotiation must meet the same tests of performance they do.

THREE FORMS OF ASSISTED NEGOTIATION

Within the realm of assisted negotiation, various approaches can be taken. We will consider three: *facilitation, mediation,* and *nonbinding arbitration.* These techniques, though distinguishable, are not mutually exclusive. In fact, a helper may find it advantageous to move back and forth among them as a negotiation progresses. These approaches are presented separately in the following pages primarily to make clear what each entails.

In general, the stakeholders must make a preliminary decision about the form of assistance they want—if only to help them choose an appropriately skilled neutral. The question they must first answer is, "How much help will we need in order to work together effectively?" Conceived differently, the same question might be phrased, "How much assistance in managing the negotiating process are we likely to require in order to reach a satisfactory conclusion?" Process is the key word here. Facilitation, mediation, and nonbinding arbitration assign different degrees of procedural responsibility to the helper. In all negotiations, the issue of managerial responsibility is paramount. Ideally, the disputing parties should retain as much control as possible over the dispute resolution process. If they do, they are much more likely to produce an agreement they will support.

Indeed, this was our rationale for focusing first on unassisted negotiation. We maintain that it is best when disputing parties retain full control over both the process and substance of a dispute resolution effort. But when unassisted negotiations fail, or when the problem is obviously too complex for resolution without help, the disputing parties must consider the various forms of assistance available.

As noted, we have chosen to limit our discussion and recommendations to facilitation, mediation, and nonbinding arbitration. We have not included a fourth technique: binding arbitration. One compelling argument against employing binding arbitration in distributional disputes is a legal one. In most cases, public officials are not permitted to delegate their authority to an arbitrator. Therefore, the application of binding arbitration is severely limited. More important, in the context of this book, is our conviction that disputing parties can and should deal with their differences themselves. They are more likely to confront the sources of difficulty and improve long-term relationships if they do. Turning over responsibility for decision making to an outsider rarely resolves underlying conflicts.

FACILITATION

Facilitation is the simplest form of assisted negotiation. The facilitator focuses almost entirely on process, makes sure meeting places and times are agreed upon, sees that meeting space is arranged appropriately, and ensures that notes and minutes of the meetings are kept. He or she sometimes acts as a moderator, usually when many parties are involved.

Even in the moderator's role, however, facilitators rarely volunteer their own ideas. Instead, they monitor the quality of the dialogue, and intervene with questions designed to enhance understanding. "Are you really listening to each other?" the facilitator might ask. "I've jotted down what each person has said. Are you sure you've identified what's most important to you? Why don't you say again what you are really concerned about, so that the others can focus on that?"

Comments of this type certainly touch on the substance of the issues being discussed, but the facilitator's emphasis is on communication. He or she uses whatever tools are available to create and foster an environment conducive to joint problem solving. Without pretending to be a therapist, the facilitator also tries to make it easier for the participants to express their emotions.

A facilitator must improvise from meeting to meeting, taking cues from the negotiations themselves. Perhaps the best way to illustrate this improvisational activity—as well as the more general and constant activities of the facilitator—is to return to two of our original cases: RiverEnd and the dioxin dispute.

FACILITATING THE RIVEREND DISPUTE
RESOLUTION EFFORT

The RiverEnd negotiations took place over fourteen months, with the participants meeting one evening every two weeks. Meetings were held in a state agency field office in the RiverEnd area. Attendance rarely dropped below twenty-five, and there were almost always observers and reporters present, in part because all meetings were listed in the local newspapers. Participants agreed at the outset that no formal votes would be taken, and that informal procedures would be used in preference to Robert's *Rules of Order*. Facilitator Elliott Lawrence was asked to chair all the meetings, to regulate the pace and topics of conversation, and to assume whatever other responsibilities for managing the process he deemed necessary.

Included in the group of active participants were engineers, landscape architects, and environmental scientists. All had backgrounds and professional credentials equal to or greater than those of the agency personnel or the consultants selected by the state government to assist the group. Neighborhood representatives had extensive firsthand information about such significant factors as flooding patterns, water flow, noise levels, and wildlife habitats. The citizen participants, to their credit, were not intimidated by claims that certain evidence or analytical techniques might be too complex for them to understand. They plowed through the reports, references, and documents produced by the consultants, and spent hours debating the merits of baseline estimates, forecasts, and impact assessments.

The negotiations generally confirmed the adage that the best ideas occur to prepared minds. A consensus could not have emerged before the individual stakeholders understood the details of the proposed project, and were familiar with each interest group's priorities. Preparation, therefore, was essential, and the facilitator Lawrence used five techniques to enhance the group's understanding: (1) "charettes," (2) opinion surveys and straw polls, (3) brainstorming sessions, (4) role playing, and (5) collective image building.

Charettes, or intensive problem-solving workshops, were used to explore specifics such as possible alignments of the transit tracks through residential areas. Participants sketched the most desirable alignments and station locations on a large map. Each participant or coalition presented its map and argued for its proposals. The rest of the participants then indicated their concerns and raised questions about possible engineering constraints.

Between meetings, participants were asked by Lawrence to mail back questionnaires designed to clarify underlying conflicts. For instance, a poll with multiple-choice answers detailing the probable advantages and disadvantages of different parking garage sizes narrowed the scope of the debate, and suggested that a broader basis of agreement existed than was indicated by the participants' public positions. Presentation of these survey results eliminated the need for extended debate, and sharpened the agenda to everyone's satisfaction.

Brainstorming sessions were used to generate additional design options, and also to identify issues about which the participants were confused. For instance, early attempts to generate new roadway and ramp designs indicated that many of the participants were unclear about the constraints posed by grade, slope, and soil characteristics, even though they had already heard general presentations on these subjects. As a result, the facilitator scheduled additional presentations by outside experts acceptable to the entire group.

Role-playing exercises, which encouraged disputants to switch positions, helped to build respect and understanding for opposing points of view. The most ardent developers, for example, were teamed up with the environmentalists to examine the probable environmental impacts of suggested roadway designs. Similarly, environmentalists were asked to look at the same roadway proposals with an eye toward maximizing the return on private investment and increasing tax revenues for Capital City.

Finally, in an effort to focus the participants' thinking about possible open-space improvements, the group examined color slides of parks and parklike elements—such as landscaping along highways, lighting, and pedestrian walkways—from other places in the country. These explorations helped the group crystallize its concerns about esthetics. One of the most interesting outcomes of the collective imaging process was that after viewing slides of other garages (including some superimposed on the proposed RiverEnd site), almost everyone agreed that a 10,000-car garage, the size proposed initially by the state, was utterly inappropriate.

As meeting after meeting clarified concerns and sharpened differences, facilitator Lawrence searched for ways to help the parties put together a package that would be acceptable to everyone. He encouraged the formation of a subcommittee to think about the opportunities created by the regional mass transit facility, rather than just the problems or adverse impacts it was likely to cause. At his suggestion, the group was headed by the most ardent environmentalist, Horst Seybolt, and dubbed itself the "Linear Park group." It envisioned parklike landscaping along the transportation corridor that would connect open space areas, soften the impact of the automobile, and create a pleasant atmosphere for pedestrians. Other environmentalists supported this idea because they thought it would reinforce the hoped-for "human scale" of the new transit facilities, and enhance the visual appearance of the area. It also had some potential to channel federal and state transportation money into a "kitty" that could be used to add recreational and open spaces, improve pedestrian and bicycle paths, and restore the long-vanished parklike atmosphere along the roadway.

The Linear Park group, with consulting assistance arranged by Lawrence, prepared and presented detailed proposals to the full group. The development-oriented members of the group agreed that the linear park concept would provide a competitive edge in attracting commercial investment and new customers. Landscaping and land acquisition would complement, rather than impede, construction of the new subway station and garage.

The linear park concept emerged in large part because the environmentalists were unhappy with most of the options put forward by the state and regional agencies. The proposals generated by the state presumed that the primary objective of the project was to create a regional transit stop that would spur economic development; it was clear that effecting environmental improvements was not an important agency objective.

The environmentalists originally felt they had no choice but to argue for the no-build option, which they did. They were immediately accused of impeding progress, of sabotaging the planning effort, and of frustrating the legitimate economic interests of the neighborhoods. This was an uncomfortable position. Moreover, they soon realized that a constructive alternative would give them additional bargaining leverage. Although they threatened more than once to block the entire project in the courts, they ultimately decided instead to use the proposed subway extension to seek environmental improvements. Why? Because they had reached a crucial realization: No outcome resulting from a lengthy court battle was likely to reverse River-End's decline, which after all had resulted from decades of neglect and unplanned development.

RiverEnd, then, can serve as a useful model of facilitation. Through the activities designed and managed by the facilitator, the stakeholders began to see items that could be traded. The emergence of the linear park proposal, through which almost every group could gain at least partially, helped to persuade skeptics that a consensual approach was both possible and promising. By managing meetings to ensure effective communication and by assisting the participants in programming their time, Lawrence created a climate in which joint problem solving was possible. Significantly, he did not offer proposals. He did not meet privately with the parties between meetings. He did not carry confidential messages back and forth among the factions at the bargaining table. He did not help the parties produce a written agreement, or design mechanisms for bind ding each other to their commitments. Lawrence basically "managed" the group discussions—and, by the time those discussions concluded, all parties felt they had achieved a fairer, more stable, more efficient, and wiser agreement than would otherwise have emerged.

FACILITATING THE DIOXIN NEGOTIATION

You will recall that Dr. Gene McGerny, the facilitator in the dioxin case, was asked by the Academy of Sciences to bring together the scientists and engineers who disagreed about the risks associated with the proposed resource recovery plant at the Federal Navy Yard. Most of the members of the city council (or representatives from their staff) were in the audience; they faced the assembled experts seated at the front of the room. Approximately thirty neighborhood and environmental groups, including many residents of the Brownstone neighborhood, were also in attendance.

Dr. McGerny had worked hard before the meeting to get the city council members to list in writing the issues that most concerned them. The questions he received in response were easily grouped under three headings: the nature of the dioxin risk, the possibility of reducing or eliminating the risk, and the health impacts of dioxin emissions. The first set of questions was most usefully put to environmental scientists; the second to engineers; and the third to medical or public health specialists. Dr. McGerny had taken special care to assemble balanced panels: None of the participants had as yet taken a public stand on the questions posed by the city council.

As Dr. McGerny put the first set of questions, one at a time, to the panel of scientists, he tried to avoid any indication that he was taking sides. Each panelist was given all the time he or she needed to answer each question. Panelists had the chance to pose questions to each other, as well as to comment on what the others had said. City council members had the opportunity to ask follow-up questions through Dr. McGerny. Whenever the interaction among the scientists drifted into highly technical exchanges, McGerny interrupted, seeking clarification in "plain English."

By the end of the first panel on the nature and sources of dioxin, it had become clear that there were two very different schools of thought. One side believed strongly that dioxin was the natural and inevitable by-product of incinerating plastic and paper at the same time (a theory popularized by the ubiquitous ecologist, Professor Lassiter, who attended the session). The other side disputed this view, arguing that dioxin and its dangers could be eliminated entirely by proper burning.

By the end of the second panel—which examined the prospects of controlling the dioxin risk, if it indeed arose—conflicting views had again emerged. One group of engineers believed that by burning municipal trash at a high enough temperature, and by simultaneously controlling the amount of oxygen present, dioxin emissions could be all but eliminated. Whatever tiny amounts remained could be captured in flue filters or removed by precipitators. But another group of engineers argued that based on the data they had obtained from resource recovery plants operating elsewhere, high temperatures, controlled oxygen flow, and filters and precipitators would still permit the escape of a significant amount of dioxin.

A split also developed among the health experts regarding the nature of the risk to humans posed by dioxin in the air. They disagreed on whether it was reasonable to infer from tests on laboratory rats what the effects of dioxin would be on people. Each side posited different models of events that might lead to unsafe dioxin emissions from the resource recovery plant. One model, for example, depicted a chain of the events in which the plant broke down during the summer. Emissions then drifted into homes through open windows, dust settled on the floors and windowsills, and dioxin was ultimately ingested through hand contact.

As the panelists talked, the facilitator highlighted their arguments on large pads of paper displayed at the front of the room. As each page was filled, the facilitator taped it to the wall. Soon paper covered practically every available inch of wall space. Dr. McGerny repeatedly checked with the panelists to be certain that he had recorded the points they thought were most important. This somewhat exhausting process lasted almost eight hours, but as certain patterns began to emerge, it proved to be time well spent.

For example, some of the conflicts arose from reliance on different sets of data, with one side claiming that precedents cited by the other were irrelevant. The engineers could not even agree on whether existing resource recovery plants were similar enough in design to the plant proposed for the Navy Yard to permit comparisons.

A second source of conflict could be traced to the different ways in which the experts framed their questions. For instance, one health-effects expert attempted to answer the question, "Is there any chance that a dangerous amount of dioxin could escape into the environment?" His answer was yes. His scientific adversary, however, was trying to answer a different question, "Is it likely that a dangerous amount of dioxin will escape?" His answer was no. When pressed by the facilitator, the first expert agreed that the chances of getting cancer from a dioxin leak were less than a nonsmoker's chances of getting cancer from living with a smoker. Both experts agreed, on the other hand, that if a large amount of dioxin did manage to escape into the air, the cancer rate in Metropolis might well increase significantly.

The most important source of controversy, however, did not result from these sorts of scientific, engineering, and epidemiological differences. The disagreement hinged, it turned out, on one side's use of a "worst case" scenario and the other's reliance on a "most likely case." It soon became clear that what had been thought of as a fundamental disagreement regarding the facts—in other words, the basic science of the dispute—was in reality a disagreement over the choice of a method of analysis. (Everyone had agreed, we should note, that the state's proposed dioxin emission standard was reasonable.)

Although the sessions were somewhat heated, the debate proceeded in an orderly fashion. After hearing the presentations, the council had to consider its options. First, however, after some prodding from Dr. McGerny, project foe Professor Lassiter made what appeared to be a significant concession. He agreed to support construction of a pilot resource recovery plant if the city would promise that (1) a careful and regular dioxin monitoring procedure would be adopted; (2) the commercial builder of the plant would sign a contract indicating a willingness to have the plant closed down permanently if it emitted more dioxin than permitted under the state standard; and (3) all liability for accidents or injuries caused by the plant would be covered by either the city or the commercial builder of the plant.

Professor Lassiter, it seems, was assuming that no commercial vendor would agree to build the plant under such unattractive conditions. He was evidently surprised when the Department of Sanitation immediately indicated its readiness to accept these terms. Perhaps that readiness should not have come as such a surprise. After all, from the city's standpoint, a plant ought not to be licensed unless it could meet the agreed-upon state standard. On this point, then, agreement was possible because the contending interests continued to operate with totally different assessments of probable risks. Lassiter, for his part, thought the risk of significant dioxin emissions was high and that no vendor would be willing to live with a double-edged sword of shut-down and liability dangling over its head. The city, on the other hand, was convinced that the technology had been proven effective, and that finding a vendor willing to build a plant that would meet the state standards would be no problem. Therefore, the financial risk was, in their view, small. Although the disputing parties continued to disagree on the nature of the risk, they were—by exploiting their differences— able to agree on how to proceed.

In this case, the facilitator spent little or no time meeting privately with the parties. Instead, McGerny devoted most of his energies to making the meeting work. He was able to clarify the sources and nature of the disagreements, and to make sure everyone understood what was being said. Finally, the facilitator played almost no role in devising the actual terms of an agreement. Instead, Dr. McGerny focused on achieving an agreement in principle.

FACILITATION: A SUMMARY

Because facilitation is the simplest form of assisted negotiation, and because the facilitator restricts himself or herself to procedural questions, it might seem that the facilitator's role is insignificant. This is not the case. The facilitator makes possible a negotiating process that would otherwise be impossible. Consider a situation in which each of the disputing parties is unwilling to make the first phone call. ("We don't want to look too anxious; let's wait for them to call us.") Clearly, unassisted negotiation is unlikely to begin in such a situation, let alone succeed. In other cases, one or more of the parties may make it clear that they will not even consider coming to the table, if by so doing they must give up any control over the substance of the negotiation. Again, the facilitator makes otherwise impossible negotiations possible.

Even after negotiations have begun and seem to be proceeding well, the facilitator can play a vital role. What happens, for example, if one of the disputing parties stalks out of the proceedings as a result of a real or imagined slight? Without a facilitator, the negotiations simply stop. With a facilitator, there is a chance that they can resume, perhaps on an improved footing. "Let me talk with the others privately," the facilitator can say to the aggrieved party. "Let me see if I can get them to recognize that from your standpoint they are being unreasonable."

In summary, facilitation is called for when the disputing parties need some assistance, but want that help limited to focusing or moderating their discussions. The facilitator serves at the pleasure of all the negotiating parties. All parties must jointly choose the facilitator, but each group has the right to "fire" that person if they conclude that he or she is biased, incompetent, or otherwise unsatisfactory. The facilitator, a skilled process manager, takes whatever procedural steps are necessary to keep the discussion on a useful course.

MEDIATION

Mediation intensifies the substantive involvement of the neutral without removing control over the outcome from the parties. It also involves the helper in a great deal more confidential interaction with the parties. Just as some disputes are too complex for unassisted negotiation, others are too formidable for facilitation. In such cases, the disputing parties should decide ahead of time that they need more help from an outside neutral.

The parties may begin with facilitation and discover that they are not making much progress, or that the progress they are making is too slow. Or—simply put—the parties may not be good at sitting in a room together. The "hardness" of their public postures may preclude real give and take. If this is the case, they may need someone to relieve them of responsibility for devising and presenting options. "We know we need help," they may conclude, "and that means more than someone to facilitate communication and arrange meetings. We need some-one who can meet with each side privately and give us a sense of how far apart we really are."

For those private meetings to succeed, the neutral must be knowledgeable about the issues of concern to the parties. This is one important function of the mediator: carrying private messages among the parties. In essence, the mediator plays a transforming role—helping the parties out of a zero-sum mind-set into an integrative bargaining framework. Early in the nego-tiating process, private caucuses are crucial to understanding the real interests of the parties and the ways they have cal-culated their BATNAs. To ensure candid exchanges, the medi-ator must be able to promise confidentiality.

With the inside knowledge that comes from these meetings, the mediator is in a position to understand what is tradeable and what is not. Moving back and forth among the parties, the mediator is in a position to launch trial balloons. As we men-tioned earlier, the mediator may begin meetings with statements like this: "I have a hunch that if Group A offers this and Group B offers that, you will find yourselves much closer together than you imagined."

While taking a large measure of responsibility for the sub-stance of the agreement that emerges, the mediator must remain neutral. In other words, the mediator must submerge his or her sense of what is "best," and focus instead on the disputing parties' own measures of success. For many professional media-tors, this is a very difficult role to play. Many of them have extensive knowledge about the substance of the dispute; this means they are likely to have personal feelings about what will work and what will not. Their previous mediation experience, furthermore, may tempt them to "steer" the negotiations to-ward solutions that have proven successful in the past.

Both of these temptations must be resisted. As for the media-tor's own conclusions regarding the substance of the negotiated agreement, they can be destructive if expressed in a way that implies partiality. A mediator with a commitment to a particular outcome is akin to a real estate agent—who seems to act as a neutral intermediary, but is in fact an advocate for one side, with a direct financial interest in the sales price. At the same time, the mediator must generate enthusiasm and support for a proposed settlement. If the mediator steers a negotiation in a direction that the parties only halfheartedly support, subsequent implementation of the agreement will be difficult.

There are qualities of a negotiated agreement for which a mediator must be willing to be held accountable. The perceived fairness of the outcome, for example, is as much the mediator's responsibility as it is the parties'. If the mediator permits a process that is viewed as unfair at its conclusion, and does not urge the parties to consider other, more appropriate ways of proceeding, he or she will not have done a creditable job. This is very much an interventionist posture, because raising such concerns does not necessarily guarantee that the parties will make adjustments. (If they fail to do so, of course, the mediator must ultimately decide whether or not to remain a part of the negotiations.) The long-term credibility of a mediator depends on ensuring that every possible effort was made to meet the interests of all the parties involved. If a proposed settlement appears exploitative or unworkable, the mediator is obligated to question the validity of such a settlement. He or she should seek to "raise doubts," either by invoking concerns about subsequent implementability or fairness.

Sharing responsibility means that the mediator will raise these concerns. It is not the mediator's role, however, to dictate terms, or to represent specific interests who may be having trouble representing themselves effectively. When conflicts arise—whether between the disputing parties or between the parties and "outside-world" interests—the mediator rarely says, "I'll tell you what you ought to do." Instead, the mediator tends to ask, "Can't we review the procedures we have followed, and come up with something that will get everyone closer to their individual objectives? I'll tell you how I think the outside world will respond to what we have come up with so far; but my job is to help you reach an agreement that is yours."

Three of the cases introduced in chapter 3—the fishing rights dispute, the Harmon County sewage dispute, and the conflict over social service block grant priorities—were resolved with the help of mediators. The circumstances were different and therefore different approaches to mediation were required. Nevertheless, they illustrate clearly the advantages of mediation.

MEDIATING THE FISHING RIGHTS DISPUTE

Judge Eastman encouraged the disputants to select a mediator from the list of twelve candidates he had identified. (His assumption was that the parties would be more inclined to work with someone they had selected.) The disputants settled upon mediator Leslie Burmaster, who was hired with funds provided by the federal and state governments. Each level of government put $100,000 into a "kitty," from which the mediator could be paid by the court (at a specified hourly rate), and through which technical studies could be purchased.

Burmaster spent three months getting to know the parties. The key participants included the director of the state's Department of Natural Resources, a lawyer for the state, the deputy undersecretary of the U.S. Department of the Interior, and the negotiators for the tribes. Burmaster also spent the first few months assembling a team of technical consultants, whose responsibility it would be to advise the parties about the impact of alternative management policies on the total fish catch. The consultants, including specialists from a range of disciplines, put together detailed models of the lake's ecology.

Before beginning the full negotiations, Burmaster decided to bring the tribes together to negotiate an intertribal allocation plan. She encouraged them to negotiate an agreement that would go into effect whether or not the tribes and the state reached a broader agreement. From Burmaster's perspective, whether the tribes collectively ended up with 20 percent or 80 percent of the overall catch, they would still have to agree on how to divide their share. Burmaster saw a successful intertribal negotiation as an inducement to the state to bargain seriously. Finally, she knew that the intertribal negotiations could only help the relatively inexperienced tribal negotiators sharpen their bargaining skills.

The tribes met for five days under Burmaster's watchful eye. Burmaster spent most of the time helping the parties understand each other's positions. She talked to them in a way that they could not, or would not, talk to each other. Burmaster made no effort to develop specific proposals; these, she felt, should come from them. In a relatively short period, the tribes were able to reach agreement, allocating certain sections of the lake to each tribe, and indicating specific times of the year when each tribe would be allowed to fish in given areas.

Having settled their internal differences, the tribes then collectively demanded 70 percent of the whitefish catch, leaving the remainder of the whitefish and the blue trout to commercial and sports fishermen. State officials resisted this demand for an overall allocation of the catch; they preferred instead to allocate the right to fish in certain zones of the lake. This might have been a difficult point, except for the fact that the federal government offered substantially more money than expected to cover the costs of managing the fisheries. The state, by prior agreement, was forced to match this increased federal allocation. The combined sums available for fish management assured the tribes that the total catch would increase, and that a rigid allocation of the catch was unnecessary.

In brief, the agreement divided the lake into zones for tribal fishing, nontribal commercial fishing, and game fishing. Several blue trout refuges were established, and made off limits to all parties. Federal and state funds were assigned to a biological monitoring system, as well as the new fisheries management program. Mechanisms for implementing the agreement (which was to remain operative for fifteen years, until 2000) were also negotiated. Three joint committees were established: one to monitor the fish, one to decide how to manage the resources, and one to resolve disputes.

Although the drafting of a written agreement took a great deal of time, the final version was completed in a two-day session. Working through the night, the parties had nearly completed a final draft when the process stalled in the predawn hours. Everyone at the table was exhausted and short-tempered. Nevertheless, Burmaster feared that if she allowed the parties to break for even a few hours, the fragile understandings arrived at to that point might well unravel. She took a calculated risk: leading the key parties into a private room, she closed the door and staged a mock tantrum. Burmaster told them curtly that the agreement would almost certainly fall apart if they did not finish quickly. In fact, she said, they had to decide then and there whether they really wanted an agreement; then she stalked out of the room. The ploy worked: The parties quickly agreed on a final draft of the document.

Burmaster made several strategic choices that paid off. She decided to play a less intrusive role in shaping the agenda and formulating specific proposals than she might have. She encouraged the parties to think in terms of a fifteen-year agreement, rather than one that would last "in perpetuity." This took some of the pressure off the parties: If they made a mistake, there would be an opportunity to renegotiate. She also realized that "zoning" the lake was the key to transforming a win-lose situation into an all-gain opportunity.

As noted, she worked first with the tribes to produce an intertribal agreement, which in turn could be used to bring the state to the table. Burmaster decided to work directly with the parties, rather than their lawyers. (The lawyers were later assigned the task of drafting a document consistent with the commitments the parties had made to each other.) In short, she concentrated on enhancing the parties' ability to understand each other. Through her active interventions, the parties were able to reframe issues, share and generate new information, and develop procedures that allowed them to work together in spite of a lack of trust.

Above all, Burmaster focused on getting agreement in principle, assuming that the design of an implementation strategy could be handled afterward. This assumption turned out to be correct—largely because Burmaster was functioning as a special master under the aegis of the court. When one of the tribes unexpectedly reneged at the last minute on the terms of the final agreement, Judge Eastman ruled that the negotiated agreement was the agreement that the court would enforce. All the parties eventually concurred.

MEDIATING THE REGIONAL SEWAGE DISPUTE

Ron Jones and his local assistants, the mediation team, did as Judge Rollenkamp suggested: They searched for a cost allocation formula that all sides could accept. For the first few months, Jones did nothing but meet privately with the stakeholders—thirty-nine municipalities, the Harmon County Regional Sewage Authority, the Randall Company, the state agencies, and various other interests such as the County Homebuilders Association. At each meeting, he asked the same two questions, "What do you think a fair formula would be, and why?"

Jones also consulted with a variety of experts in the area of utility cost allocation. He needed a computer program that the parties could use to forecast the cost implications of alternative formulas.

As the private meetings progressed, the mediation team clarified and added to the list of concerns previously expressed by the parties. From the standpoint of the city of Harmon, the dominant issue was affordability, while the suburban communities and smaller towns were much more concerned about fair cost allocation. The communities in the northern part of the county wanted the sewage system in their district to be designed differently and to operate independently of the main plant in Harmon. This, they argued, would save everyone money. Finally, many of the communities expressed strong distrust of the regional Sewage Authority.

The mediators called in experts to review the detailed design of the sewage system proposed by the Sewage Authority. They sought advice on alternative strategies for financing the system. The more they explored the technical complexity of the dispute, however, the more mired in details they became. Small but worrisome questions arose by the hundreds. Who, for example, would do quarterly billing? Who would be responsible for unpaid sewer bills?

The development community, for its part, was worried that the overall capacity of the new regional system might not be sufficient to sustain future growth. Local officials were determined to receive compensation for past investments in local collection systems and treatment plants. Moreover, almost all the local officials wanted some additional role in the management of the new regional system, arguing that the Sewage Authority was not adequately accountable to local concerns.

At a large meeting to which all interested parties were invited, Jones asked for responses to a preliminary "package" of ideas the mediation team had drafted. The proposal had been sent to more than one hundred stakeholders before the meeting. The all-day session produced a number of suggested refinements that were blended into a revised proposal, which Jones submitted to Judge Rollenkamp for review. The judge distributed it for formal comment.

Jones was surprised when negative reactions began pouring into the judge's office. He thought the proposed agreement had responded to all the issues raised by the parties. As it turned out, though, the city of Harmon had decided to press for an even more favorable cost allocation. From Jones's point of view, the adverse reaction arose at least in part because the judge had asked the wrong question. Judge Rollenkamp had asked, "Are you completely happy with this agreement?" Jones would have preferred the judge to ask, "Can you live with this agreement?

While agreeing that the mediators' package was reasonable, some of the smaller communities argued that they still preferred not to be included in the regional system at all. Indeed, almost every stakeholding group indicated some change it wanted in the proposed agreement.

The judge thanked Jones, and indicated his satisfaction that the issues in dispute had been narrowed. He also found all the background material and forecasts Jones and his staff had assembled to be quite useful. Jones was not satisfied, however; he asked for a six-week extension, and one more chance to develop an agreement that all the parties would accept. Judge Rollenkamp agreed.

The mediators began another round of private meetings, hoping to find out what it would take to bring the dissenters on board. They soon realized that there were three possible ways to reach closure: first, reduce the overall cost of the system through redesign; second, reduce the cost to the dissenters by bringing in new state or federal funds; or third, redefine the scope of the sewage clean-up problem so that the funds already in hand would be sufficient. Not wanting to limit his options prematurely, Jones decided to push on all three fronts. First, he pressed the regional authority to consider the merits of smaller treatment plants, instead of one large one. He and his staff met with federal and state officials to see if they would increase their financial contributions, in exchange for the parties dropping all pending litigation, and taking prompt action to clean up the rivers and streams. Finally, he pressed the EPA and the state Department of Environmental Protection to consider reducing the scope of the effort—or at least dividing the project into phases, which would have the effect of spreading the project's cost over a much longer time.

After five weeks of intensive negotiations, Jones proposed another package. This time, the city and the Randall Company promised in advance to support the package. The reason for their switch lay in a revised basis for calculating annual sewage charges. Previously, those charges were to be municipally defined "shares" based on each community's percentage of the total flow into the regional system. Under the new plan, there would be a consistent average household charge for everyone in the entire region. (This reduced Harmon's overall charge.) Other towns found tempting amendments in the new package as well. For example, the revised package included a promise of a long-term, no-interest loan from the state, a shift in responsibility for billing and collection from the local to the regional level, compensation to municipalities for abandoned treatment facilities, an option for smaller decentralized treatment plants (if they could be built at lower cost to the region), and the creation of a local advisory board that would ensure greater regional accountability to local concerns.

This time the package won practically unanimous approval. In response to his second "poll" of disputing groups, Judge Rollenkamp heard again from several municipalities that they would still prefer to stay out of the system altogether. This time, though, they indicated a new willingness to live with the proposal if the judge decided to impose it. All the other participants agreed to drop their lawsuits and work together to implement the plan.

Jones and his staff, obviously, played a very active role at every stage of the negotiations, generating proposals and working hard to "sell" those proposals to the parties. The mediators assembled a team of consultants across a broad range of disciplines to back up their efforts. They also worked out a sequence of hoped-for agreements. For example, although they focused first on generating an agreement on the basic components of a cost allocation formula, they also knew that each local official would require a precise forecast of what that formula would mean to his or her constituents before any commitments could be made.

Jones spent a great deal of time meeting behind the scenes with senior state officials. The state's promise of a no-interest, long-term loan to assist in the financing of the second stage of the regional sewage system proved to be the key to lowering each community's total cost. Indeed, when some municipal officials heard that the average annual sewerage charge for the new system would be less than $300 per household per year, they simply lost interest in the entire issue. They had been led to believe that such charges might exceed $1,000 a year. The mediators' success resulted in part from their ability to put together a package that was less onerous financially than what the parties had come to expect and dread.

SOCIAL SERVICE BLOCK GRANT ALLOCATIONS

When over one hundred participants met to discuss priorities for the allocation of the "public/private partnership" social services funds, they filled a large hall in one of the universities located in the central part of the state. The mediator, Denise Donovan, had met privately with each of the teams and with the team leaders prior to the first full negotiating session.

Donovan had been chosen by a mediator-selection committee that included five of the initial organizers from each of the four teams. She had been one of three finalists the committee interviewed. Her contract was officially with the state government (for a total of $35,000), but the terms of the contract had been approved by each of the teams.

It took six hours to reach agreement on the major agenda

items and on the protocols that would structure the negotiations. Throughout these initial steps, a great deal of skepticism was expressed by some team members, who felt that there was no chance of reaching a consensus.

The state agency team, headed by the assistant commissioner of the Department of Social Services, included staff from the department's various regional offices. This group pressed for new state guidelines that would give funding priority to underserved groups. The private donors team was headed by one of the directors of the United Way; this group made it clear that they wanted more flexible matching requirements for donors. The citizen/consumer team was headed by a professor of public administration who had been active on behalf of minority groups in the state, and whose particular interests she intended to serve. The Association of Social Service Providers team was headed by the elected chair of that statewide organization; on behalf of his constituents, he planned to press hard on the issue of wage parity between privately supported and publicly supported social service workers.

Donovan assembled a staff of assistant mediators, who began to meet regularly with each of the teams. They also served as support staff for subcommittees (consisting of two people from each team) assigned to generate possible responses to each of the agenda items: matching provisions, needs assessment, minority and underserved client groups, monitoring and evaluation of contracts, timing and duration of requests for proposals from new grantees, and overall service priorities.

The teams met monthly for almost a year. There were two points at which the process almost fell apart. First, the social service providers team refused to discuss any changes in priority setting procedures until the other three teams endorsed their position on wage parity. The others were put off by this "take-it-or-leave-it" attitude. At a team leader's meeting organized by Donovan, the four groups managed to work out an understanding. Formally, it was agreed that no one would be asked to commit to anything until the full draft of a package was complete. Informally, everyone agreed that the wages for providers in nonprofit agencies were much too low.

The second stumbling block arose when the state team presented its proposed changes in overall spending priorities—that is, naming specific client populations that ought to be the focus for further spending. The providers team insisted that no change in priorities should be permitted if it eliminated grantees who had been eligible in the past. The solution, suggested by Donovan, was to find the best way of spending any *increment* in block grant money that the group as a whole could get from the governor and the legislature. By concentrating on the allocation of an increment, the group was able to avoid a zero-sum situation. Indeed, by presenting a united front on the need for more money they were able to advance their individual as well as their common interests.

Eventually a draft agreement was worked out. Copies were distributed to more than 2,500 groups and individuals throughout the state prior to the final signing. The mediator prepared and distributed more than 10,000 copies of a quarterly newsletter describing the progress of the negotiations.

Almost eighteen months from the time they began, a consensus was reached. In their agreement, the groups spelled out monitoring and implementation procedures designed to ensure appropriate follow-up evaluation. A number of the procedural suggestions that emerged during the course of the negotiations were implemented immediately by Commissioner Dorada. Other reforms, everyone agreed, would take more time. Some real shifts in spending priorities were approved when it became clear that the public/private partnership program would receive a substantial overall increase in state funding. In the commissioner's view, these shifts were important; but more important, she had the consensus she wanted. She considered the negotiations extremely useful.

Mediator Donovan's success illustrates two facts that we feel are significant in an era of diminishing governmental resources. First, despite the apparent zero-sum aspect of fund allocations, it is possible to establish spending priorities through a consensus-building process. Second, such consensus building can take place even among a very large group of participants, none of whom have negotiated before.

NONBINDING ARBITRATION

As we have already explained, binding arbitration has only limited application in public disputes because most public officials cannot legally delegate their authority to an arbitrator. Public officials appear to be equally wary of nonbinding arbitration—a process whereby a private judge or panel listens to the arguments of all sides, and then suggests an appropriate solution that the parties can either accept or reject.

Because nonbinding arbitration is a relatively new and untried approach in distributional disputes, we will introduce it in hypothetical terms. The approach has been tested in complex private disputes, but these are only partially relevant. Based on these applications, it seems clear to us that nonbinding arbitration may well be an acceptable and desirable means of resolving the types of distributional disputes that do not give way to facilitation or mediation.

Imagine that the parties in a public dispute have reached an impasse even after working with a mediator. Perhaps their estimations of their BATNAs, constantly undergoing revision, have led them to question, once again, whether they could do better away from the table. They can agree on only one thing: They need a solution. A great deal of time, money, and energy has been invested in the negotiations to date, and deadlines of one sort or another are looming. What are their alternatives? One alternative, of course, is to admit failure and go to court. Let us assume, however, that the outcome of adjudication is unclear, that the case is likely to be resolved on a winner-takes-all basis, and that neither side wants to risk losing everything.

Instead, the disputants decide to submit to nonbinding arbitration. In so doing, they may adopt any one of a number of strategies. For example, they may jointly choose a private "judge"—perhaps a retired jurist, or someone else with a background the disputants think appropriate—to whom they present their respective arguments, and from whom they seek a judgment. "After you have heard our arguments, tell us how you think the case will come out if we go to court," the disputing parties might say. "We are not necessarily bound by your judgment, but we want to hear it." Alternatively, the disputing parties might assemble a jointly chosen panel of private arbitrators and ask for a majority ruling (again, not binding). Finally, with appropriate assistance, the parties might stage a mock trial, and invite the heads of all the participating groups or organizations (not just their negotiators) to watch. This last technique may be helpful when one or more of the constituent groups insists on demands that its own negotiators know to be unrealistic.

In many cases, stalled negotiations reflect the simple fact that the expectations of one or more parties are unrealistic. Learning what would probably happen in court, and why, can change those expectations. (In other words, nonbinding arbitration can make a BATNA seem less attractive.) Lowered expectations, in turn, allow the disputing parties to go back to the bargaining table—either unassisted, or with facilitation or mediation—and reach a mutually satisfactory accord.

As noted earlier, few distributional disputes have been resolved though nonbinding arbitration thus far. There have been a significant number of nonbinding arbitrations in the private sector, however, and it seems likely that some version of the technique will cross over into the public sector. We will therefore summarize the ways in which the private sector currently employs nonbinding arbitration, particularly through "minitrials."[3]

Since about 1980, minitrials have proven to be a quick, low-cost mechanism for settling disputes between corporations. Because minitrials are voluntary, confidential, and nonbinding, many corporations embrace them with enthusiasm. In general, corporate minitrials have had four objectives:

- Narrowing the dispute to each party's summary of the critical issues
- Promoting a face-to-face dialogue between the heads of the companies involved
- Encouraging more realistic BATNA calculations
- Preventing business disputes from turning into lawyers' disputes by avoiding many of the legalistic distractions of courtroom procedure

The elements of a minitrial generally include (1) a short period of pretrial preparation; (2) a meeting or meetings in which top management representatives—who are authorized to settle on behalf of their companies—meet to hear informal summaries of each party's "best case"; (3) a meeting or meetings for questioning and rebutting the best-case summaries; and (4) an opportunity to negotiate a settlement. In most cases, if the parties fail at this last stage to reach such a settlement, the judge or panel will present an analysis of the strengths and weaknesses of the positions they have heard.

All procedural aspects of a minitrial are negotiable, as the parties must feel comfortable with the process if settlement is to be reached. In general, there are only two essential aspects of a minitrial process: first, an opportunity for each side to state its case with an assurance of confidentiality; and second, the participation of leaders with the authority to enter into an agreement. (A neutral advisor, expert either in the subject matter of the dispute or in the processes of dispute resolution, is also typically involved.) Negotiation by top corporate officials—preferably without their lawyers—can be a chief ingredient for success.

Corporate minitrials held so far have proven relevant in cases involving product liability, patent infringement, and employee grievances. They also have been successful in antitrust cases, in instances when competitive practices were in question, and in circumstances requiring an expert analysis of highly technical issues. These private sector applications suggest a number of potential public sector applications especially in disputes over standards (that is, cases in which scientific authorities disagree on such subjects as acceptable health risks). Scientific and technical portions of distributional disputes could be presented before expert panels, which could then offer their views in an effort to encourage the disputants to settle.

To summarize: In nonbinding arbitration, the disputing parties still control the design of the process, and must still approve the ultimate outcome, but the intermediaries take more responsibility for devising possible solutions. The disputing parties are no longer saying, "Help us help ourselves." Instead, they are saying, "Give us an answer." Obviously, then, the intermediaries in nonbinding arbitration must be substantively knowledgeable—even more so than mediators. Ideally, they understand not only the complexities of the issues in dispute, but also the legal processes that may come to bear if all else fails.

FROM ZERO-SUM
TO INTEGRATIVE BARGAINING

Neutrals in any kind of dispute should seek to assist the parties in reaching satisfactory, as opposed to ideal, agreements. This process usually begins with an effort to ascertain that the parties understand their own interests, as well as what the others want and need. Once all the parties understand each other's interests, and they still find themselves in conflict, the neutral's next step is to assist the parties in exploring ways of reframing the dispute so that hidden common interests can be uncovered.

If it becomes clear that basic interests really are in conflict (and more than just communication or personality problems are involved) and that there is little common ground, the neutral switches gears. That is, when it becomes clear that disputants are in a zero-sum situation (in which it appears that the only way for one to gain is for the others to lose), the intermediary seeks to "change the game" by introducing the possibility of trading things, especially things that the parties value differently.

There are obviously limits on what can be traded, including constraints on what the parties in their real-life situations can offer. Finally, if a package of trades that would satisfy all sides cannot be found, the helper must work privately with the disputants to be sure that they have calculated their BATNAs realistically. If they have, and their away-from-the-table options are indeed more likely to produce "better outcomes" for some or all of them, the neutral should probably exit.

The search for satisfactory agreements, then, involves clarification of interests; the search for common ground; the creation of a setting in which the parties can work together to discover differences, which can then be exploited to produce joint gains; and the constant reassessment of alternatives to negotiation. If the parties have overlapping interests, a clarification of those interests and the search for common ground should produce a satisfactory agreement. If the parties have conflicting interests, the task of the neutral is to transform the dispute from a zero-sum situation to an integrative problem-solving activity. There is, of course, no magic wand that the helper can wave, and neutrals are not in the business of cajoling disputants into making concessions in the name of harmony or peaceful coexistence.

The transformation involves exploiting the multidimensionality of most conflict situations.

When there are lots of issues on the agenda and the parties rank them differently, this creates the possibility of trades. If the parties place a different value on certainty (or respond differently to risk), a small-but-certain victory sometimes can be traded for a larger-but-uncertain victory. If the parties calculate the time-value of money differently, this can open up trading possibilities. For example, one side may, for tax reasons, suggest a settlement that involves small payments, from the other side to them, each year for a number of years rather than a larger lump-sum payment. The other side may agree, finding this solution less of a strain in terms of cash flow. Even individual issues can be fragmented into smaller parts, permitting trades across elements of an issue. Symbolic commitments are a good example: They cost one side very little, and can often be exchanged for money or other tangible returns.

The transformation from zero-sum to integrative bargaining requires the invention and packaging of items to trade. A clear danger is that such trading may encourage extortionate behavior. If one side says to itself, "I get the idea; I'll gain by making my list of demands longer and longer," the game is then akin to blackmail. In such a case, the problem for the neutral is how to pursue the search for joint gains without encouraging excessive claiming.

Negotiation researchers have documented the inevitable tension between "creating and claiming value" in any dispute resolution situation.[4] This follows earlier studies of "mixed-motive bargaining." Every negotiation, whether zero-sum or integrative, recreates this tension.

In a zero-sum situation, the tension is obvious. Every proposal that one offers in an effort to discover possible joint gains—that is, to create value—will not be accepted by the others without promises in return. This is to be expected if the disputants are thinking solely in zero-sum terms. But even in an integrative bargaining situation, in which the parties have indicated a desire to find an all-gain outcome, the possibility exists that an honest statement of what one side might give up in exchange for something will be exploited by one of the other participants.

Even assuming that disputing parties have been successful in creating joint gains by exploiting differences, this fact alone is no guarantee that the gains they have created can or will be divided equally. So, for example, the parties may find things to trade that they value differently. One side may come out a little bit ahead and the other may come out way ahead. Nobody is worse off, but they are not equally better off.

Intermediaries in public disputes must be honest about this problem. When they say to the parties that they can help find all-gain outcomes, they should clarify that they are not promising that everyone will "beat their BATNA" (or satisfy their interests) to the same extent. We might imagine that everyone would be happy as long as assisted negotiation allowed them to satisfy their underlying interests; nevertheless, we are all aware of situations in which one side would rather not accept a gain if it means that another side gains even more. Thus, neutrals have to keep an eye on the overall "score card" as the parties search for joint gains. They should remind the parties that real costs are associated with not finding mutually beneficial trades. In addition, they should indicate that excessive or extortionate claiming will undermine the very process of inventing joint gains which leads to satisfactory agreements.

The transformation from a zero-sum perception of a conflict to a willingness to search for joint gains does not depend on the parties adopting "soft" (as opposed to "hard") negotiating styles. Based on extensive studies, negotiation researchers have established that cooperative negotiators are not necessarily more successful than competitive negotiators in reaching satisfactory agreement. Negotiators of either style can be effective or ineffective, and this is true regardless of the style of the negotiators they are matched against.[5] Thus, the search for joint gains does not require everyone to be "nice" or to make concessions; nor does it require one side to mimic the attitudes of the other. Effective but tough negotiators know their own interests, and they know that by participating in a collaborative process of creating joint gains they may be more likely to serve their own interests. They also know that there will be very little to claim if differences cannot be exploited through packaging and trading.

Creating and claiming, as noted earlier, are distinct activities. "Competitive-style" negotiators are likely to stress the claiming part of the process, and may require tangible "victories" at each step along the way. By contrast, "cooperative-style" negotiators are less inhibited about throwing themselves into the creating part of the creating and claiming process. They are also more willing to wait until the end to tote up the score.

But claiming can preempt creating, and it is important for the participants to realize this. Some negotiators attempt to solve this problem by constantly switching their negotiating posture: from claiming to creating and back again. It may be impossible to move back and forth between the two attitudes, however, if claiming creates tension or hostility. It may in fact be necessary in some disputes to go through a period of claiming, or zero-sum bargaining, so that the parties see what they might be able to achieve this way. Once the process of creating begins, though, and an integrative problem-solving mode is established, it is best to stay on this track.

Facilitators and mediators rarely try to convince the disputants to change their styles of negotiation. They do, however, take advantage of the emergence of the "group mentality" that develops as negotiations proceed.

As the parties "go at it" over an extended period of time,

relationships develop, just as they do when a jury is sequestered. The group may begin as total strangers, but constant interaction at close quarters can lead to accommodation, if not friendship. Though the negotiators are there to advance the interests of the groups they represent, they cannot help but get caught up in the new "group" of which they are a part.

This new group may pressure an individual who has not been very forthcoming into changing his or her attitude. As it approaches closure, the group may also bring pressure to bear on a party that is holding out. Momentum in such situations is almost tangible. While the intermediary may encourage all the parties to check back with their constituents before concluding a draft agreement, the group may prefer to push toward a conclusion. There is almost a "team spirit" that emerges as the disputants reach the end of their joint task.[6]

An effective intermediary may use the emergence of group pressure to move the transformation along, saying to one party, for example, "I don't know how much longer the rest of the group will stick with this, if you don't give some sign of your willingness to accept the trades that have been proposed." This is not to say that the neutral will encourage a party to ignore or sell short its own interests; rather, the neutral may use the pressure of the group to encourage a party to change its behavior, make a more realistic calculation of its BATNA, or offer a counterproposal that the others are likely to be able to accept.

We generally hold the view that any distributional dispute in the public sector that appears to be a zero-sum conflict can be transformed into an occasion for integrative bargaining, assuming the parties have adequate assistance. These sorts of conflicts are uniformly complex, but creative negotiators in any dispute usually will be able to find some possible trades—whether they be across issues, over time, relative to risk, or whatever.

This is not to say, though, that every distributional dispute will yield to resolution through assisted negotiation. The parties may have utterly unrealistic BATNAs, and they may refuse to reassess them regardless of what happens in the negotiations. Even though legitimate interests could be met through the creation of joint gains, the parties may hold out for more gains than can possibly be created.

Even with the assistance of a skilled intermediary, the parties may not be willing to move from inflated demands to ways of satisfying their true interests—either because they do not want to be seen as having backed down from their stated positions, because they are caught in psychological traps that work against their own best interests, or because internal pressures within their organizations lead them to attach a higher value to sustaining the conflict than to resolving it.

ASSISTED NEGOTIATION: CONCLUDING COMMENTS

At present, three techniques are available for assisted negotiation in the resolution of public disputes: facilitation, mediation, and nonbinding arbitration. By any rational accounting, these tools are underutilized. These techniques are not mutually exclusive. They can be used sequentially in the same dispute; in some situations, the line between facilitation and mediation may be blurred as the neutral moves into a more active behind-the-scenes role. They are highly mutable and can be applied in different ways by individual dispute resolution practitioners. In all cases, though, they involve the search for all-gain outcomes through a move from zero-sum to integrative bargaining.

We have already alluded to the biggest obstacle to their acceptance: fear on the part of public officials that facilitation, mediation, and nonbinding arbitration will infringe on their authority. We contend that this fear is misplaced, given that the outcomes of all three processes remain entirely under the control of the parties, including these same public officials.

In the next chapter we will describe in practical terms the ways in which public officials, citizens, and business interests can use consensual approaches to resolve distributional disputes.

CHAPTER 6

Taking Action

The two previous chapters focused on how to do better: that is, how to negotiate productively to settle distributional disputes in the public sector. We discussed the objectives of an effective negotiating process—particularly the transformation of apparently zero-sum bargaining situations into integrative bargaining situations, the psychological factors that may help or hinder the process, the three phases of consensus building, and the roles and functions of intermediaries.

In this chapter, we will carry these ideas one step further, giving specific recommendations about who should implement these better approaches to dispute resolution and the circumstances under which they should do so.

For the sake of convenience, we will group the key players in public disputes under three headings: public officials, citizens (the neighbors who are affected in their personal capacity or as representatives of voluntary associations), and business interests. By public officials, we mean both the elected and appointed individuals whose duties (such as standard setting, resource allocation, and formulating public policy) tend to involve them in distributional disputes. "Citizen" subsumes the wide spectrum of stakeholders affected by public decisions, including consumers, public interest groups, and advocacy organizations which can be either place-defined or issue-defined. (The Jordan Lane neighborhood group is an example of a place-defined citizen group on a small scale; the Sierra Club is, despite its name, issue-defined.) "Business interests" include all profit-motivated groups, including corporations, developers, entrepreneurs, trade associations, as well as nonprofit institutions (such as hospitals and universities) when they seek to maximize their return on investments.

Obviously, these labels have some shortcomings. Most people involved in public sector disputes are citizens. Business interests (particularly nonprofit institutions) have objectives other than profit maximization. But because we will use this framework to present three distinctive viewpoints, readers are encouraged to identify themselves as public officials, citizens, or business interests. In the category they select, they will find the material that is most relevant to their needs.

For these three groups, we will describe the opportunities and responsibilities present in the three phases of consensus building. We will instruct readers in the analysis of disputes, to help them determine when to participate in consensus-building efforts. We will suggest the most appropriate negotiation strategies. And, finally, we will describe some of the concerns, real or imagined, that may require attention.

Some aspects of dispute analysis are common to all three groups. These will be presented separately, before the more specific concerns of public officials, citizens, and business interests. But readers should also become familiar with the material that is specific to groups other than their own. As we explained in earlier chapters, a key part of negotiating successfully is understanding as much as possible about the interests and concerns of others. Each disputant must make not only a realistic assessment of its own BATNA, but an assessment of the others' BATNAs as well.

Much of what we are advocating can happen on a totally ad hoc basis. This is likely to be the case for some time to come. On the other hand, some attempts at institutionalization have been made, such as the adoption of enabling legislation to encourage the use of consensual approaches on a regular basis. We review these at the end of this chapter.

PREREQUISITES FOR NEGOTIATION

Imagine that you are a public official, citizen, or business interest faced with a distributional dispute. Having determined your BATNA (that is, the probable results of acting unilaterally, or going to court), you decide that it might be worth trying a consensual approach to dispute resolution. How can you determine whether such an approach is likely to prove fruitful? What prerequisites must be met?

Let us begin by identifying a prerequisite that does not need to be met. Many disputants assume that because relations between the parties are hostile, productive negotiations cannot take place. Negotiation researchers have shown that this is not true. Negotiations can proceed even when the parties have no trust in each other at all. Parties to a dispute ought to negotiate in ways that build trust (or they will never be able to conclude), but they need not begin with confidence in the other parties' reliability. Obviously, if trust were a prerequisite to public dispute resolution, very few negotiations would ever begin.

It is unrealistic to demand trust. Trust has to be earned. And the most important consideration for any stakeholder in deciding whether or not to trust another party is reciprocity: "Why should I act in a trustworthy manner if you won't?" Or, to put the same idea more positively, "If I don't act in a trustworthy manner, can I expect such behavior from others?"

Assuming that the parties begin in the absence of trust, it is only by acting in a trustworthy manner that each side can win the trust of the others.[1] No one wants their trust to be exploited, but all sides have a stake in the process of building trust; without it, agreements are hard to implement.

Although trust is not a prerequisite to consensus building, several other factors are. In the worst case, the absence of one or more of these prerequisites could thwart agreement. We will present them as questions. As you contemplate participating in a consensus-building process, you should ask and be able to answer these questions in the affirmative:

Can you identify the key players, and if so, can you persuade them that it is in their interest to sit down and talk? It may not be possible to identify every group or individual with an interest in a dispute, but it is usually quite easy to single out the key players. In the RiverEnd dispute, for example, it was obvious that the municipalities, regional agency, state agencies, area landowners, and existing environmental organizations had to agree to participate in the negotiations if those talks were to be worthwhile. In the Harmon sewage clean-up dispute, the regional Sewage Authority and each of the member municipalities had to be involved.

After identifying the significant groups, you should decide as realistically as possible whether you can imagine some way of getting them to come to the table. One possible method of convincing them that their alternative to negotiation is unattractive is to indicate that you may otherwise be forced to initiate a lawsuit, if only to protect your legal rights. You might even have to take the next step and begin legal proceedings, although we see this as an undesirable way of establishing a relationship conducive to joint problem solving.

What can the key players accomplish on their own? If

negotiations are not currently in their interests (that is, if their BATNA is better than what they are likely to get by coming to the table), can you alter circumstances enough to make it in their interest to participate? Can you alter their perception of their BATNA in a way that makes negotiation more attractive to them? If not, give up on a consensual solution, at least as long as these circumstances pertain. Consensus building can proceed without some of the secondary players, but not without all the key players.

Are the power relationships sufficiently balanced? This prerequisite is related to the first. The potential parties to a consensus-building effort cannot participate in a relationship in which one party holds all the power. Can one group get what it wants unilaterally? If so, there is no point in trying to get that group to come to the table when they will soon realize their power and attempt to act unilaterally.

Parties to a consensus-building effort need to have an interdependent relationship. This does not mean that they need to possess equal power. Rather, it means that each side has to have at least some leverage it can use, if necessary, to the other's disadvantage. This may be nothing more than the power to delay, but even this limited leverage can create interdependence.

Consider the following example of an utterly unbalanced power relationship. A development company owns a parcel of land on which it wants to build a residential development. Their plan conforms to all the existing municipal zoning requirements; they have the necessary building permits; the firm has made it clear that they intend to follow the letter of the law; and they are in no great rush to finish. Your counterproposal—which consists of another version of the project that you would prefer—would cost the developers considerably more and cut deeply into their profits. From the firm's public and private statements, it is clear that the developer has no compelling interest in doing further work in the community. In this situation, you are not likely to have sufficient leverage to succeed in achieving your objectives through negotiation.

Can you find a legitimate spokesperson for each group? Unfortunately, it is not enough to identify the key players. You must also ensure that someone can speak with authority on behalf of each group. If you find a key group without an empowered spokesperson, your negotiations will soon be in trouble. Spokespeople need to be able to speak for (but not necessarily bind) their members.

This is sometimes more difficult than it appears. For example, the elected leaders of some public interest organizations cannot take positions on specific proposals without a poll of their membership. This is a constraint imposed by their organizational bylaws. Often Native American negotiators must negotiate under similar constraints. By tribal custom, everything must be decided consensually. Many Native American negotiators are only empowered to carry messages back and forth between the tribe and the other parties. They cannot commit, even tentatively, to specific proposals.

Most negotiators cannot bind their members without checking back and going through a formal ratification process. But if a negotiator cannot even participate in a brainstorming process or give a preliminary indication of what his or her membership is likely to do, the negotiation process will drag on and on. This will almost assuredly thwart the building of consensus.

Do you have deadlines, and are they realistic? If there is an unrealistic deadline—whether imposed by one of the parties or by some external circumstance—you may find it impossible to assemble the disputing parties quickly enough to go through the necessary consensus-building steps. If, for example, a court is expected to impose a decision in a week or two, consensus may be impossible. On the other hand, if no deadline exists, it may be difficult to generate the momentum needed to bring the parties to the table.

Most deadlines in the public sector turn out to be flexible, and final decisions (especially those concerning difficult distributional questions) are postponed again and again. If you are facing a deadline, try to determine how "real" it is. As in the fishing rights dispute, a judge may prefer a consensual agreement to a court-imposed resolution; but he or she may also feel that the circumstances require action by a specific date.

Can you reframe the dispute so it does not focus primarily on sacrosanct values? It is risky for negotiators to trade commitments on issues in which basic values are involved. In such cases, constituents may disavow the commitments made on their behalf or move to appoint new spokespeople. This can create great instability. If public officials seek to settle policy disputes involving fundamental values (should public funds be used to pay for abortion? should additional nuclear power plants be built? should neo-Nazis have the right to march in public?), dissatisfied disputants will almost certainly pursue the matter in other forums until they are satisfied. If your dispute involves constitutional questions or revolves around definitions of basic rights, consensus may be unattainable. Unless there is room for inventing, packaging, trading, and redefining issues, it may not be possible to reach agreement.

Suppose a city decides to establish a municipal policy on handgun control. As has been amply demonstrated in recent years, this is an issue over which fundamental values come into conflict. It is primarily a question of constitutional rights. No proposal for compensation or mitigation, no linkage of issues or promises about the future will produce a consensus. The question is simply not amenable to consensus building. Until the constitutional or legal issue is settled, it would be fruitless to take up any distributional aspects of the dispute.

THE PUBLIC OFFICIAL:
ANALYSIS, STRATEGY, AND CONCERNS

The prerequisites mentioned thus far apply equally to public officials, citizens, and business interests. Public servants, however, must consider several more prerequisites. These can be summarized in one broad question: Can you participate in a consensus-building process without violating the terms of your office?

ANALYSIS

Imagine that you are a member of the commission responsible for adjudicating requests for public utility rate increases. In that capacity, you may be forbidden by law from having contact with the parties involved in a specific rate request. (This is referred to in the law as an ex parte communication prohibition.) On the other hand, rate increase requests are annual headaches, and do lend themselves to negotiated settlement. The stakeholders are obvious and usually well organized. Forecasts and other technical information can be shared, and allocation decisions typically hinge on the packaging of an array of trades including the way services are provided, long-term financing, and other costs and benefits.

In such a situation, you would have to proceed very carefully because strict rules govern the behavior of rate-setting commission members.[2] Perhaps your staff could help initiate an assisted negotiation, even though you cannot personally be involved in drafting a package that would eventually come before the commission for approval.

As a public official, you may be subject to prohibitions against private meetings of the commission, or meetings without adequate public notice. Such prohibitions, however, do not limit the use of a nonpartisan mediator who can meet privately with all the parties, including you. A number of states have "open meeting" laws which stipulate that if more than two members of a board intend to meet, the meeting must be announced and open to the public. As a public official, you are obviously aware of the regulations governing such private sessions. Because it is not usually clear whether a proposed negotiation will require the sorts of informal sessions or caucuses that are forbidden, you cannot make a blanket commitment to a process that might later put pressure on you to violate a statute.

One self-evident fact should also be noted in passing. If you have a personal stake in the outcome of a given public dispute, your actions will be constrained by conflict of interest laws. Citizens and business interests are permitted to reap private gain from a settlement, but you are not. Even discussing certain options might expose you to charges of corruption. Thus, you have to worry about both procedural due process and the appearance of fairness and propriety.

We have already mentioned the delegation of responsibility issues faced by public officials. It would be an abdication of responsibility, as well as a violation of law, for a city official to agree ahead of time to be bound by whatever came out of a consensus-building process. To avoid this trap, the public official who agrees to participate in an informal negotiation (or sends staff to participate) must be certain that all the participants understand that the only acceptable outcome is one that *all* parties find agreeable. Even then, the draft agreement must be ratified formally, and the informal settlement must be converted to a legally enforceable form. Thus, a city council member may promise to participate in an informal negotiation, but he or she should also point out that ratification by the full council is not guaranteed, and that the agreement may have to be converted to a bylaw before it can be considered by the council.

In summary, as a public official you are subject to numerous restrictions. Some are legal in nature (you cannot violate statutes), and others derive from the politics of appearances (you cannot seem to be profiting from your office or to have prejudged any matter). To the extent that these restrictions come into play during a negotiation, they may undercut your effectiveness. Consider them ahead of time and decide whether you can resolve them satisfactorily. If not, you must either delegate the negotiating effort to someone else or abandon it altogether. None of these constraints, we should emphasize again, negate the advantages of mediation. Indeed, the use of nonpartisan intermediaries who have no personal stake in any decision may be the key to overcoming many of the constraints we have described.

STRATEGY

Assume that you have met the prerequisites for fruitful negotiation, including the general prerequisites and those specific to the public official. Based on your analysis, you want to try to resolve a dispute through assisted negotiation. What specific steps should you take?

Obviously, there must be a first meeting of the key players. Those parties have to be introduced to the consensus-building idea. They need to meet each other in a relatively receptive frame of mind. In an unassisted negotiation—such as occurred in the Jordan Lane case—you might simply call together the disputing parties and begin discussions. In the more complicated assisted negotiation process, some important preliminaries need to be observed.

It is probably best if you, as an interested party, do not present the idea of consensus building yourself. Instead, seek the help of someone who is skilled in making such presentations. We refer to this sort of helper as a "convenor"—an experienced professional who can bring together disputing parties in a reasonably positive and productive frame of mind.

The first act of the convenor is to undertake a "conflict assessment." You have already identified the key players and are reasonably certain that they can be persuaded to participate. The convenor meets with all these parties, soliciting their views and trying to help them assess their interests. He or she may also locate and meet with additional players identified through the conflict assessment. Simultaneously, the convenor attempts to persuade all of the important players to come to a first meeting. In most cases, the idea of assisted negotiation will be foreign to at least some of the participants, and it may engender suspicion or hostility. ("What's this all about?" "Who's organizing it?" "Why should I come to his meeting?") The convenor, though, should have the ability to depict the process vividly and to make it seem both feasible and promising to the people who ought to participate.

There is no reason for you, as the public official initiating the process, not to share your own views with the convenor. Keep in mind, however, that you remain a party to the dispute even though you may be the one attempting to resolve it. The convenor will be ineffective if he or she is perceived as partisan; therefore, the convenor must consider your perspective to be only one of several pertinent points of view.

The convenor's role continues through at least the first meeting. At that meeting, the convenor helps the group begin the transition to the negotiation phase of the process. He or she informs the assembled representatives of their procedural options—facilitation, mediation, and so on. The convenor then describes the kinds of neutral assistance available and what it might cost. Some communities and states already provide convening and other process assistance free of charge. At the first meeting, or over a series of meetings, the convenor works with the group to develop a list of possible neutrals the group can subsequently interview.

The group then selects and hires the most appropriate intermediary. During this period, they may continue to call upon the convenor for help. The convenor may even prove to be the right person to continue in a facilitating or mediating role.

In most cases, the selection of a mediator is not a particularly contentious process. The disputing parties usually want the same characteristics in a neutral: a substantive understanding of the issues in dispute; a contextual understanding, or a familiarity with the legal constraints in the particular situation, the relevant regulations, and so on; and—above all else—a reputation for fairness. The group and the neutral then draw up a contract, perhaps based upon a standard contract supplied by the intermediary, modified as necessary to suit the specific circumstances.

Once the mediator is chosen, the convenor's work is done; and your role, as a public official involved in a dispute resolution process, is greatly clarified. Like the other parties, you can now concentrate on your own interests, without assuming further overall responsibility for whether or not consensus emerges. At this point, you should follow the three-phase negotiating process described in detail in the preceding chapter.

Keep in mind that when the issue of representation arises, you as a public official have a special responsibility. You will eventually be asked to commit to the agreed-upon solution, and your commitment—the commitment of the government—will be symbolically important. It is doubly important, therefore, that the people in your own organization respect and abide by that commitment. You should ask yourself, What are you able to do, during the negotiation process, that will generate support within your agency or elected body for the process and its outcome?

This responsibility continues through the postnegotiation phase. The key challenge for the public official—before, during, and after negotiations—is to be an effective spokesperson for your agency or constituency. You need to develop an internal mandate before negotiations are very far along; you need to sustain that mandate in order to sustain the negotiations; and you need to build consensus within your organization in support of the agreement that is eventually reached. Even if you are the head of your organization, or the elected head of the city or the state, you will not be able to "impose" a settlement on others. Subordinates and constituents must understand and support that settlement, which means that they need similarly to understand and support the process that produced it.

As a public official, you have an additional special responsibility in the postnegotiation phase: helping to transform the agreement from an informal understanding to a formally binding arrangement. Because the informal agreement that you have helped to reach cannot bind an agency or an elected body, you need to devise mechanisms that take account of the legal, administrative, and cultural restraints within which you operate. To the extent that you have functioned as a representative of an agency's or council's thinking, you should have mirrored (rather than spoken for) the others involved. This should make the next step relatively easy.

We can suggest four general approaches to converting informal to formal agreements:

1. Make the agreement into a legally enforceable contract. As noted previously, there are legal restrictions on the kinds of contracts that public bodies can make. There are also problems inherent in attempting to hold ad hoc citizens' groups to contractual commitments. If these limitations can be overcome (and they often can), a contract is a good solution. This is one realm in which creative legal advice can be very helpful.[3]

2. Convert the agreement into a statute, ordinance, or administrative regulation. Arrange to have a formal body adopt the agreement. City councils, for example, often adopt special ordinances embodying concepts that originated in informal

agreements. In these instances, make sure that everyone who has a vote participates in drafting or reviewing the informal agreement.

3. Attach conditions to permits, licenses, or other kinds of legal authorizations. This is often the simplest solution. If the informal agreement concerns a proposed development, for example, make sure that the agreed-upon conditions are stipulated in building permits, zoning variances, and so forth. Even though the local citizens' group will have no official standing in the formal agreement—which will exist in the form of an authorization to proceed—they can understand and accept this type of documented obligation.

4. Invent a creative solution. Sometimes a legal or cultural restraint requires an unorthodox approach. If restrictions on permits or licenses prove inadequate in the situation just mentioned, for example, the developer can post a bond to demonstrate good faith. A neutral party can hold the bond until the developer has delivered on his or her promises. If the developer fails to deliver, the bond will be turned over to the citizens' group. Such an approach remains "informal"—that is, not officially sanctioned—but it is self-enforcing, and there are always circumstances in which informality remains the most attractive option for one or more participants.

CONCERNS

We have described some of the issues that public officials ought to consider before entering into a consensus-building negotiation. But once negotiations have begun, certain additional concerns may arise or recur that are also of special importance to public officials. Some of these are "real" concerns, which can be anticipated and countered; others are often exaggerated or even imaginary.

We have already addressed the issue of the public official's authority to make binding commitments. "As a public official," this line of reasoning goes, "I can't bind a future legislature or administration." But this is simply untrue. Public officials make contracts all the time. Commitments that bind future legislatures are also contained in statutes. Everyone is bound by the law as it evolves. More accurately, the argument should be, "As a public official, I can't make informal agreements that bind others in the future."

Avoid short-circuiting a potentially productive process by worrying about your ability to bind your constituents to an informal agreement. What you should try to do is reach the best possible informal agreement you can. Then, worry about converting that agreement into one that can bind your constituents, using one of the techniques described earlier.

As a public official, you want to be sure that the people you are negotiating with can really commit (and subsequently bind) the stakeholders they ostensibly represent. What if they cannot? What if you spend six months negotiating an informal agreement and then a splinter group emerges and announces that they do not feel bound by the agreement?

This is a legitimate concern. The emergence of a splinter group cannot be fully guarded against. Your best insurance is to pay a great deal of attention to the representation issues throughout the negotiating process. Be sure to confirm, as often as you can, that the representatives are in close contact with their respective groups. When agreement is reached, be sure each representative takes it back to his or her constituents for ratification. Expect, furthermore, to be scrutinized by the other parties in the same way. Can you deliver your constituency?

What happens when a splinter group does emerge? This question can be broken into two parts. First, how do you interact with such a group? And second, what happens if that group resorts to litigation—the very outcome you have worked long and hard to avoid?

The first question is relatively easy to answer. You should

adopt the following stance: "Look—here is what we did. Here's how the process worked; it was open and thorough. Here's the agreement we reached; it attends to the interests of all those who chose to participate. I'm sorry, but this issue is not currently open to further discussion. I'm now committed to this outcome. Of course, if you can come up with an amendment to the agreement that everyone involved will accept, that's another story." In other words, use your commitment to the process to deflect the splinter group. And you need not hesitate to let your negotiating partners insulate you. Which of the other participants is ideologically closest to the splinter group? Ask that partner to put pressure on the dissidents, since you and that partner now share an interest in making the negotiated agreement work.

The second question is somewhat more troublesome. Perhaps if we phrase it differently—"Does litigation invalidate all that has gone before?"—the answer comes more easily: No. If you have kept an adequate record of your process (such as minutes of meetings), and if you have produced a public document that the interested parties have all signed, these facts may well be considered favorably by the courts. You certainly cannot prevent a group from litigating, but given a sound process and an outcome that all the participants support, you may be able to blunt a court's willingness to hear the complaint, or at least minimize the court's sympathy for the complainant.

Another concern of special interest to the public official is the sheer number of potential stakeholders. "I can't identify just a few key spokespeople," the beleaguered official complains. "There must be fifty people to deal with. How can I have a productive conversation with fifty people?" Our response is that we have seen such conversations work, mainly through the technique of "clustering" interest groups. For example, most of the antidevelopment groups in the RiverEnd case were persuaded to accept a relatively small number of designated spokespeople to represent them in the negotiations. All the groups still had the option of attending meetings (as observers), but only the designated spokespersons were empowered to participate.

This technique—also referred to as "pyramiding interests" or "snowballing"—requires skilled facilitation but offers many advantages. First, the number of voices at the table can be limited without reducing the legitimacy of the proceedings. It is crucial, though, that the groups involved choose their own designees. Second, a spirit of cooperation can be fostered among the groups within a cluster, thereby reducing the risk of subsequent splintering. And third, it increases the flexibility of the proceedings. Few effective negotiations begin and end with the same list of concerns. Spokespeople who represent several constituencies are likely to be especially sensitive to the evolution of interests during the course of negotiations.

In short, try not to fall victim to the old maxim that "a good meeting requires only seven-plus-or-minus-two people." Structured properly and with appropriate assistance, groups of up to fifty or sixty can function effectively.

The final concern of the public official is expense. By some reckonings, negotiations are expensive. They demand time and money. Moreover, current fiscal pressures often encourage public officials to think in the short term: "I could get a fire engine for that amount of money!" The temptation, therefore, is to act unilaterally. "Why don't I see if I can get away with it?" the public official asks himself or herself. "If that fails, I'll consider negotiation."

The answer, of course, is that when the "decide-announce-defend" approach fails, it does not leave the parties back where they were.[4] Consensus building is particularly hard to organize in the wake of a failed unilateral action. Trust is harder than ever to build. Equally important, the parties may be locked into hard postures. For example, you may be stuck with your opening position (because accepting less, even though you might be willing to, will make you look weak). Or, your initial attempt to act unilaterally will convince the other stakeholders that there is no use negotiating with you, since you have utterly unrealistic expectations.

We argue that public officials should take a slightly longer view. Instead of comparing the cost of consensus building with the cost of acting unilaterally, ask yourself what the real costs will be if your proposed action is blocked indefinitely. Compare that figure with the estimated cost of generating consensus. In some cases, you may decide that the costs of negotiation exceed the benefits. But in most cases, the cost of negotiating is minimal when considered as a percentage of the value of the project or proposal. Is a $10 billion facility worth an investment of, say, $50,000 to cover the cost of consensus building? If that facility were delayed for just six months (by court proceedings resulting from your unilateral action), would the $50,000 look paltry in retrospect?

One case in point is the Harmon County sewage clean-up example. By the time serious negotiations began, the Sewage Authority owed more in interest than the original facility would have cost.

There is, furthermore, some reasonable chance that most or even all of the hypothetical $50,000 will not come from the municipal purse. Several states have set up funding mechanisms to support negotiations of precisely this magnitude. Alternatively, some percentage of that $50,000 may be contributed by the other interested parties. Finally, you may be able to help reduce the overall cost of the process by offering "in-kind" support, such as public meeting places, secretarial assistance, copying services, or mailing.

To summarize, when it comes to assessing the costs of consensus building, you should know your BATNA. (What is your best estimate of the legal fees you may incur, if you opt for a decide-announce-defend strategy?) Keep in mind the scale of your proposal: the bigger the project, the less significant the proportional cost of consensus building, and the more "profitable" the results of a successful negotiation.

THE CITIZEN:
ANALYSIS, STRATEGY, AND CONCERNS

In this section, we present the perspective of a representative citizen—usually a member of an ad hoc group or a more permanent association. Again using the structure of analysis, strategy, and concerns, we will consider the sequence of issues that a party to a public dispute is likely to encounter. Please note that information of general usefulness precedes the public official section, and that the material defined as being of specific interest to one of our three groups (public officials, citizens, and business interests) should also be of use to members of the other two groups.

ANALYSIS

As a citizen, you must first determine whether your dispute meets the five general prerequisites to successful consensus building. Described at length earlier, they are simply listed here:

- Can you identify the key stakeholders and will they come to the bargaining table?
- Are the power relationships sufficiently balanced?
- Can you find a legitimate spokesperson for each group?
- Do you have deadlines, and are they reasonable?
- Can you free the dispute from a debate over sacrosanct values?

From the citizen's point of view, three additional prerequisites must be met. These, too, can be phrased as questions. If these and the preceding questions can be answered affirmatively, a consensual approach to dispute resolution will probably serve you well.

Do you have the resources to participate effectively? This is a question of particular concern in the prenegotiation phase of a consensus-building effort. Can your group find enough money to cover the basic costs of participation? (These would include, for example, travel to and from meetings, release time of a senior member of your group, back-up technical advice, secretarial time, and postage, phone, and related office expenses.) If not, can you work out an arrangement whereby your group is represented by one of the other groups involved?

As we noted previously, the costs of many dispute resolution processes are shared by the "protagonists." This means that a citizens' group will only have to shoulder a portion of the full cost. But your group will still have to find a way to cover the time of a senior spokesperson.

The creation of a resource pool—a "kitty" of money that the participants can spend as they need it—is essential. On the other hand, such a pool is not likely to be created until it is clear that negotiations are going to begin in earnest. Citizens' groups often have the most difficulty financing their involvement in the prenegotiation phase of a dispute resolution effort.

Obviously, a citizens' group contesting a proposed project does not want to accept money directly from the proponents of the project. The group's credibility would be suspect, and the legitimacy of the consensus-building process would be jeopardized. This is why it is often necessary to appoint an independent "resource pool manager." This person could be the convenor, or anyone else providing facilitation or mediation services. It could also be an entirely separate organization—such as the American Arbitration Association—that has no other involvement in the dispute resolution effort. In any case, all the participants must play a role in drafting the guidelines for the use of the funds in the resource pool. Once the funds are handed over to the resource pool manager, individual donors should have no special say about their allocation.

In the RiverEnd case, funds to support an independent technical assistance pool were provided by federal and state government. In the Harmon County sewage dispute, funds to support the mediation effort were channeled through the Office of Dispute Settlement at the state level. Funds to support joint fact finding in the fishing rights case came through the federal court to the mediator. In the social service block grant allocation case, funds to support technical staff to the mediator were provided by the Department of Social Services under a contract approved by all the parties. In other instances, public dispute resolution efforts have been funded by private foundations. In every case, citizens were able to benefit from the allocation of funds, some portion of which was provided by other stakeholders, without compromising their integrity or undermining the credibility of the consensus-building effort in the eyes of the community at large.

Can you present a united front? If your organization is badly split, you will probably be picked apart in the negotiations. Internal factions can make it impossible for your group to accept binding commitments. If you have no clear sense of what you stand for as a group, your influence and effectiveness at the bargaining table will be sorely limited.

Imagine that yours is a neighborhood group organized in response to a proposed development project, and that your organization includes several subgroups. One of the subgroups comprises the people who are opposed to any development at the proposed site; another group simply opposes the particular design that the developer has put forward. At the table, the developer will understandably be inclined to hear and accommodate the latter group. When he or she returns to the table with an improved design, your coalition will be in trouble. One faction within the coalition will be inclined to accept the offer; the other will remain inflexible. Of course, for strategic purposes, it is sometimes helpful to have members of a group play "hard" and "soft" roles to keep the other stakeholders honest; but if your group as a whole is truly split, you will find it extremely difficult to make and live up to any commitments.

This problem often results from putting too many groups into a massive coalition. Large coalitions are tempting ("in numbers there is strength"), but if your coalition encompasses too many factions you will actually be in a weaker position when it comes to striking practical deals. You are better off working with a smaller coalition, in which everyone shares a sense of the most desirable outcome.

Will it help your organization to participate? What does your group need most: new members or a negotiated settlement of a particular issue? In many cases, the health of an ad hoc citizens' group may derive directly from contesting a given proposal indefinitely. Sitting down to negotiate with the "enemy" simply lacks the drama of—for example—lying down in front of bulldozers. For some groups, continued and heated conflict generates financial contributions and attracts members. Negotiation may undercut these sources of organizational support.

Assess honestly what you are trying to accomplish. If your primary concern is building your organization rather than settling the dispute in question, then you may not have adequate incentive to seek a consensus. On the other hand, the most durable activist groups tend to be those that find a way to move from conflict to partnership with their adversaries. Indeed, the most effective organizations are those that have learned to continue developing while participating in consensus-building efforts. They realize that a call to negotiate is not necessarily a hidden threat to their long-term survival.

STRATEGY

Because of resource constraints, it is relatively uncommon for a citizen group to initiate a dispute resolution effort. If, however, your group finds itself in the position of proposing negotiations, and subsequently has to get the process off the ground, please refer to the strategies described for the public official—finding and employing a convenor, and so on. For the sake of brevity, we will assume that your group begins its involvement in a dispute resolution effort when you are contacted by a convenor.

During the prenegotiation phase, your primary concern should be building coalitions. Try to organize the largest possible number of groups and individuals with shared interests. Next, figure out the smallest number of representatives you need to send to the table. Work hard on the representation issue, clarifying your BATNA and aspirations, because a united front will give you additional bargaining power.

Work closely with the convenor to hire the most appropriate mediator. Members of your organization may need some evidence that the proposed consensus-building process is legitimate and will serve their interests—particularly if an adversary appears to be underwriting it. This is an appropriate opportunity to put such doubts to rest. Find an intermediary you can trust. Also, insist that the neutral possess excellent procedural know-how, substantial technical background, and an understanding of the dispute's political and organizational context.

If you think it might be useful, ask the mediator to organize a brief training session for your members, describing the process of dispute resolution and reviewing basic negotiation techniques. Be prepared—even eager—to undertake such a training session jointly with spokespersons for the other participating groups. If everyone has the same understanding of the most productive negotiating techniques, some of the time-consuming and destructive tactics that novice negotiators often employ can be avoided.

During the negotiation phase, make sure that your group and its spokespeople stay in close communication. It is extremely important that representatives not get too far ahead of their membership. Education and progress at the table must be matched by a growing understanding of the process on the part of all constituent stakeholders. If such parallel progress does not occur, ratification will be difficult.

For the citizen, the major strategic stance of the postnegotiation phase is to demand time. Once the draft agreement is hammered out, your negotiating partners are likely to insist upon prompt ratification. The public official and the business interest generally represent more unified (even monolithic) constituents; for them, ratification is relatively simple. For you, it is not. You need, therefore, to stretch out the time allowed for ratification. Never hesitate to demand the time you need—at this point, the other negotiating parties have a substantial investment in the draft agreement.

CONCERNS

As in the case of the public official, the citizen may encounter a number of additional concerns during the negotiations. Some of these are legitimate and require a careful response; other will resolve themselves.

One important concern is an extension of the strategic considerations stressed in the preceding section. Make sure that you, as a negotiator for a citizen or public interest group, have an effective means of checking back with your constituents. We present this as a concern because it is a task that may have to be repeated (and may require revised mechanisms) over the course of the negotiations.

You begin as the spokesperson for your group's interests. Gradually, as you gain an understanding of the other side's

interests, you become a spokesperson for the work of the group.
You may well realize that your group's initial aspirations were
unreasonable. But without help, your group will not grasp this.
The interactions between you and your membership that were
adequate at the beginning of the process may no longer suffice.
Consider additional meetings or periodic published reports to
your membership. Make sure they can easily reach you—to ask
questions or to express disappointment.

A second concern has to do with unequal technical capacity.
As a member of a citizen's group, you may well feel that government officials and business interests have scientific or technical
backgrounds—or access to such resources—that exceed yours.
This is not necessarily the case. The environmentalists in the
RiverEnd case, for example, certainly had no problem matching
wits with the technicians hired by the state and federal government.

Our experience suggests that you probably will not have to
cede much technical ground. Depending on the nature of the
dispute, you may have a surprising supply of firsthand knowledge, as well as access to sympathetic resource people. Search
hard within your membership for such resources, or look outside for sympathetic advocates who have technical backgrounds. Has a similar dispute occurred elsewhere? If so, which
technical people helped the citizens' cause? Can they help, or
at least refer you to someone else who can?

Compensation for technical services has to be considered. As
we have already pointed out, citizens' groups can sometimes
make the creation of a resource pool a precondition for joining
a consensus-building effort, especially if the outcome is likely to
hinge on technical argumentation. Such funds can be used to
balance access to technical resources. If you are unable to identify technical advisors willing to donate their services, demand
access to the resource pool.

Perhaps the most important concern for the citizen representative is power. This is a theme that we encounter constantly:

"They have resources, experience, and political clout that we can't hope to match," says the citizen. "How can we pretend to sit down as equals at the bargaining table?" The answer is necessarily complicated, but one fact stands out. Power, in negotiations, is fluid. You may well sit down at the table with a relatively small and seemingly inadequate measure of power. But that allocation is not fixed. The fact is that there are a number of things you can do to enhance your bargaining power.

You can enhance your bargaining power by improving your BATNA—that is, by developing a stronger and more convincing basis for your claim that you can do pretty well away from the table. The better your group can do in the absence of an agreement, the stronger you will be in the negotiations. Try to find a recent court ruling, for example, that is consistent with the outcome you would hope to achieve if you went to court. Similarly, you may be able to raise doubts in the minds of the other parties about what they are likely to get by acting unilaterally: "You thought you had the support of council member X," you might say to one of the other parties. "But we have a statement from that council member indicating her support for our group and promising that she will not help anyone until we have all made a good faith effort to reach an accord." In this same vein, if you can unearth information that undermines the validity of the claims made by others, it will strengthen your hand. This is especially true in public disputes, where legitimacy is as important as behind-the-scenes political clout.

You can also handle the actual negotiations in a way that enhances your bargaining power. For instance, try to come up with an ingenious way of meeting the concerns of the other participants while still achieving what you want for your group. This is often referred to as the "power of a good idea." Try to come up with "yes-able propositions"—proposals that the others can not possibly reject given their interests.

When you make statements, especially commitments, be sure you are prepared to back them up. A negotiator who reneges on even one promise is likely to lose leverage later on. Learn to disagree without being disagreeable. The other participants will be more likely to listen to what you have to say. Be prepared for each meeting. The negotiator who is not ready to report on his or her group's reaction to the last round of proposals will lose opportunities to shape the course of the negotiations.

Remember that in times of difficulty, the mediator is there to assist you. Use the neutral to underscore your concerns. If for strategic reasons you feel uncomfortable publicly enunciating a change in your group's negotiating stance, let the mediator relay this information to the other parties in private caucuses. If you feel that your interests are not being served, let the mediator announce this to the group as his or her observation.

Finally, regularly reexamine your coalition to see if it can be strengthened. David versus Goliath may be an unfair match; but thousands of Davids, acting in concert, may persuade Goliath to revise his estimate of his own power. The power of coalitions is enormous—provided, of course, that the members of the coalition share a commitment to the same outcome. Remember that coalitions may ebb and flow during a negotiation. You must constantly check to be certain that your coalition is holding together.

In summary, never think of your group as being powerless or alone. Even in isolation, you have considerable power. Your opponents have, after all, agreed to sit down and negotiate with you. Moreover, you may find other stakeholding groups with which to ally. You need not accept suggestions that you are underorganized simply because you are not formally incorporated, because you lack a legal department, or whatever. You and your neighbors will probably be around long after your opponents, whether they are governments or businesses, have changed leadership. You have a permanent stake in most distributional disputes, and you ought to be prepared to defend that stake. Continue to pursue all possible avenues to improve your BATNA, and to raise doubts in your adversaries' minds about their BATNAs. Conduct yourself in a manner that enhances your clout. If you are not certain which behavior will enhance your bargaining power, put yourself in the other person's shoes. Which behavior would convince you that the other person had power?

BUSINESS INTERESTS:
ANALYSIS, STRATEGY, AND CONCERNS

Like the public official and the citizen, the representative of business interests must first determine whether certain general prerequisites can be met before he or she should enter a consensus-building process. Will the right people be at the table? Will they be able to negotiate effectively? Can they avoid the traps that tend to sabotage consensus? (See the discussion of "prerequisites" earlier in this chapter.)

If you as a businessperson or head of an institution are involved in a public dispute, there is a reasonable chance you have provoked the conflict by proposing one sort of project or another. Citizens' groups are most often reactive, and public officials may lay out plans for things they would like to see done, but it is most often the business community that decides to take the risks involved in actually making things happen. Thus, you are likely to be on the defensive during the prenegotiation phase of most public dispute resolution efforts. You are also an easy target.

ANALYSIS

In addition to understanding the general prerequisites for a successful dispute resolution effort, the representatives of business interests must consider some additional prerequisites. Once again, we will present these as questions. If you, as a business representative cannot answer these questions in the affirmative, then you probably want to steer clear of consensus-building efforts.

Do you have the mandate to proceed? If your corporate structure is like most others, it is explicitly hierarchical. Therefore, you have to ask yourself whether you have the necessary mandate to enter into a consensus-building effort. If not, can you secure it by going to someone higher up the line? If you cannot get sufficient backing, do not start the conversation. If your hand is forced, and you must admit that you are not in a position to make the requisite commitments, the other participants will assume that your organization never intended to negotiate seriously. Under these circumstances, the chances for an amicable settlement will be greatly reduced.

Is there someone with relevant negotiating experience who can represent your organization? The businessperson who approaches a public dispute resolution effort as if it were a business transaction is in for a rude awakening. The businessperson regularly engaged in buying and selling may think he or she is on familiar territory. There are many similarities between consensus building and the processes that lead to satisfactory agreements in the business world. Most important is the emphasis, in both the public and private sectors, on satisfying informed self-interest. On the other hand, there is a significant difference between striking a business deal and settling a contentious distributional dispute.

On almost every score, the management of private business transactions is simpler than negotiations in the world of public disputes.[5] Consider some of the steps in consensus building as they apply in the private sector:

Getting started is generally not a problem. Business transactions are, for the most part, unassisted. One side expresses interest in buying or selling, and potential partners respond.

While no one wants to look too eager, an indication of a willingness to negotiate is not seen as a sign of weakness.

Representation presents no great challenge. Buyers and sellers represent themselves or appoint hired spokespeople. Each interaction usually begins with two parties—a buyer and a seller (although others may be added).

Agenda setting is perfunctory. Both sides approach the bargaining table with roughly the same agenda ("I want to sell it; you want to buy it"). There may be some incentive to link future deals, but such considerations remain secondary to the sale at hand. Bargaining protocols are tacitly understood and accepted.

Joint fact finding is negligible in a business transaction. Most often, each side does its homework before arriving at the table. If not, neither worries too much if the other is operating on bad information or faulty assumptions. Indeed, the seller may well be tempted to "hype" the product or service. The buyer probably expects this. Each keeps as much information confidential as possible.

Inventing and packaging options is, of course, a key step in making both private and public deals. But as with joint fact finding, the effort to create and combine options is tightly circumscribed in a business transaction. Again, in the simplest terms, the buyer's and seller's options are self-evident. Almost everything is reduced to equivalent dollar value, although the items traded may in fact take many forms.

Producing a written agreement may be time-consuming in a complicated corporate transaction, but the ground rules are clear. The negotiators follow the outline of a standard legal document, and lawyers subsequently use the rough agreement to produce a contract acceptable to both sides. It is also legally enforceable (if either party defaults, they will be sued), which solves the otherwise difficult problem of binding the parties to their commitments.

Monitoring and *renegotiation* are generally not significant issues in private situations. In some cases, the parties may include an arbitration clause in their final business agreement. This minimizes the difficulty of handling subsequent disagreements. Such procedures are common practice and are rarely invented anew in a business negotiation.

It might be desirable for more business negotiators to think about alternatives to the conventional approach to making deals as described here.[6] They might improve their negotiations by seeking to maximize joint gains, thereby leaving the parties in a better position to deal with each other in the future. In any case, it is clear that most business negotiators are experienced only in the give-and-take of positional bargaining. This puts a premium on certain strategic behavior, and ignores other considerations absolutely essential to the resolution of distributional disputes.

When your organization attempts to reach a negotiated settlement to a distributional dispute, therefore, you want to be represented by someone who has been involved in more than the simple buying and selling aspects of business. Your representative should be accustomed to dealing with the community and with political officials. Furthermore, he or she should be in close contact with the top echelons of corporate leadership.

Most large corporations, of course, recognize the need for effective community relations and have a department dedicated to that function—public affairs, external relations, or the like. But the individuals in those departments may not be your most effective negotiators. They may not, for instance, be familiar with the details of the project being proposed. Thus, it may be best to put together a negotiation team with the requisite skills and experience.

Can you be patient about deadlines? If you enter into assisted negotiations, you will find the going slow at the outset. In fact, you will be going very slowly, at least at first, and the process may seem hopeless—time-consuming, expensive, uncomfortable, and unproductive. This is the period when the two previous prerequisites (a mandate and prior experience) are most important. People within your organization will almost certainly seize upon the apparent shortcomings of the negotiations as the process drags on.

On the other hand, by working toward a consensus, you are trying to reduce the overall time and expense that would otherwise be involved in litigation or extended political negotiation. Like the public official, you have to look at the alternatives over the life of the project and beyond, and determine which approach is likely to generate a solution that can be implemented most efficiently.

If you decide upon a consensual approach, you will need patience. If you decide to move forward without first building consensus, you may find yourself in court, or locked in political battles. This is especially important for businesspeople to remember, because your calculations of your interests are usually time-sensitive. Most profitable ventures become unprofitable if delayed long enough. Paradoxically, it sometimes makes sense to "go slow to go fast."

Business interests have only three options when projects they propose turn out to be controversial. They can abandon them, attempt to implement them unilaterally and hope for the best, or enter into a consensus-building effort. The first course of action is "efficient," but produces nothing. The second may seem efficient and productive, but if it goes awry it may only generate years of controversy and legal wrangling. The third alternative—consensus building—initially seems inefficient and unproductive, but it may well present the best chance of generating a workable solution.

In summary, if you are not prepared to start slowly, do not start at all.

Do you intend to continue doing business in the same community? We have already raised this issue in our discussion of citizen group strategy. Some business organizations care a great deal about being perceived as a "good neighbor"; others do not. This decision is usually made on the basis of the company's sense of its likely future investment in the community. If your firm intends to work again in the region in which a particular dispute has arisen, that consideration must be part of your analysis of your options. A successful dispute resolution effort may well create a positive climate for future initiatives. At the very least, consensus should enhance long-term working relationships with citizens and political officials.

STRATEGY

As noted earlier, business interests are very likely to be the "cause" of public disputes. In other words, in many cases, the initiative comes from you and others must react to it. If your analysis leads you to conclude that consensus is possible, you may want to be the one to initiate assisted negotiations. Please refer to the section on prenegotiation advice for public officials regarding the best way to find and use a convenor, to hire a mediator or facilitator, and so on.

During the prenegotiation phase, when agenda setting begins, be prepared for pressure to frame the agenda as broadly as possible. This is important. The businessperson usually does not realize how many issues have to be put on the table in order for effective and mutually satisfying trades to be possible. The following scenario, for example, is played out again and again in the public arena.

The developer approaches the community group at the beginning of a consensus-building effort and says, "Here's my development plan." The community responds by saying, "We don't like it." The developer points out that the proposal is based on a great deal of prior research and expert advice, meets the letter of the law, and will produce valuable public benefits. The community indicates that it will find ways to block the project.

"Well, what do you want?" the developer finally asks with some exasperation. "You know that park on the other side of town?" the community responds. "We'd like you to fix it up for us." The developer is honestly astonished: "What? I can't do something way over there, off the site of my project!"

Businesspeople are only slightly less inclined than government officials to bristle at the prospect of off-site trades and other "extraneous demands." In some cases, public officials work under legal restrictions that preclude such linkages. But developers rarely do. You may find it useful, in fact, to think of this as a luxury. Because you are relatively unencumbered by such restrictions, you can afford to be very flexible with regard to the compensatory, in-kind, or mitigatory promises you make.

The dilemma for the business negotiator, of course, is how to avoid encouraging extortionate behavior. If the park across town is acceptable, why not day care for local children, a new roof for the public housing project, or anything anyone else wants? What is to stop the list from growing longer and longer?

The answer is to insist that each linked request meet the following three tests. First, anything that is requested must come from one of the participants in the negotiation, who must be prepared to make commensurate commitments in return. Second, the request must be accompanied by a convincing analysis of the cost or adverse impact that you are being asked to mitigate or compensate. (Would a noninvolved analyst confirm the reasonableness of the cost you are being asked to assume?) And, third, all the requests together must not exceed the value of the benefits of consensus (in other words, you must still do better than your BATNA). This means, by the way, that benefits to the community should be subtracted from the value of the adverse impacts to be compensated or mitigated.

The goal is not to encourage a wild trading spree. Rather, the intent should be to find a way to meet the underlying interests of each stakeholding group. The smart business negotiator lets it be known that he or she is willing to be "convinced on the merits" that compensation or mitigation is appropriate, but at the same time insists upon the three conditions listed here.

In any negotiating situation, the parties ought to prefer adversaries who are well prepared (that is, who know their BAT-NAs, are in close touch with their constituents, and understand the technical issues involved). Because most distributional disputes hinge, in part, on expert knowledge, it is important to verify that the public officials and citizens with whom you are dealing have access to the technical advice they need. In the example just cited, for instance, architects and engineers might be needed to determine whether a proposed development is technically feasible. A lawyer might be required to investigate pertinent zoning or deed restrictions, and what is legally allowed; and a financial expert might be called in to assess the economic feasibility of proposed alternatives.

You, as the developer, have a professional background in the field. You also have the financial resources to employ whatever consultants you need. The nearby residents have neither of these advantages and therefore cannot participate effectively—without help—in the negotiations. The presence of your lawyer, architect, or engineer will underscore this asymmetry in their eyes. What is the solution?

We argue that it is your responsibility to correct this imbalance of power. The other group or groups need to be given the resources to develop their technical expertise. Without such assistance, they will be unable to make informed judgments, and will therefore be reluctant to accept anything you say as an accurate portrayal of the situation.

It might seem unwise—or even suicidal!—to give aid and comfort to one's adversary in the context of a business transaction. Our experience suggests that in the long run of a distributional dispute, it is cheaper and more effective to do just that. Two points must be kept in mind. First, perceptions are as important as facts. Second, it is exactly the psychology of "ad-

versaries" that you and your negotiating partners need to overcome, particularly if you are trying to build consensus. You will
find it exceedingly difficult to operate in an atmosphere of distrust and hostility.

As the technological complexity of a dispute increases, the
likelihood that such suspicion and hostility will interfere with
the consensus-building process also increases. Thus, the more
technically complex the dispute, the more assistance the business community may have to provide in order to ensure that its
negotiating partners can deal wisely with all the issues.

Of course, financial assistance should not just be handed over.
The plans for the use of the funds donated to a resource pool
should be subject to the joint approval of all the participants.
Funds should be used for fact finding, not for the purchase of
"hired guns" to engage in a "battle of the print-out." Finally,
funds should probably be contributed in installments as the
consensus-building process passes certain milestones (although
the initial promise of funds should be for the whole amount).

Offering to share your technical support staff, by the way, is
an unsatisfactory alternative. Unless neutral experts, selected
jointly by all parties, are used, technical findings are likely to
be less than credible in the eyes of some of the participants.

Insist on a written agreement even if it memorializes an informal settlement that must still be incorporated into a formal
decision process, prior to implementation. Also, insist on the
creation of satisfactory enforcement mechanisms that will hold
citizens and public officials to their promises. In some ways,
yours is the most "responsible" organization at the table—
public officials may be turned out of office; citizen groups may
experience turnover in their membership or splinter into smaller
factions. If you invest months of time and substantial amounts
of money, you have every right to expect compliance with the
agreement.

This means, in turn, that you have a right and a responsibility
to be involved in the process of converting the informal agree-

ment to a formal one. Work hard on that issue, and be prepared to consider some unusual proposals suggesting how your company can be bound to an agreement. Keep in mind that just as you may continue to have suspicions about the other group ("They may splinter or disappear"), that group may well retain its suspicions about you ("Once the bulldozers go in, we'll have no more influence over this process"). The conversion from an informal to a formal agreement is a vital step in allaying these concerns. Hammer away on the theme that this is a shared priority: Everybody in the process wants to make sure that the agreement they have worked so hard on is codified.

CONCERNS

Most of the basic concerns of business interests have been suggested in the previous two sections. Before assisted negotiations begin, and even after they are under way, voices within the company are likely to raise fundamental objections to the process. "This is only going to make everything ten times harder," they will say. "Why don't we just make a deal with the mayor, behind closed doors, and let him sell it to the community?"

The answer, as emphasized in the early chapters of this book, is simple. You are less and less likely to get away with it. The political and business climates in America have changed, and will continue to change. The direction of all that change is away from deal making behind closed doors. Increasingly, private deals will tend to embarrass your company (and also the public officials involved) at some later point. Public negotiations are, indeed, big, messy, and time-consuming, but it is not clear that you have any real alternative, especially in the case of large-scale projects.

A second concern of the business interest representative is, "Can I trust these people? In the past, they haven't given me much reason to think so. I'm good for my word, but what about them?" The appropriate response to this concern was introduced earlier. Trust has very little to do with it. If you are negotiating with people you do not trust, keep insisting that they be explicit about how any proposed agreement can be ratified and enforced.

Finally, we raise an issue that should be a concern more often than it is. Can you get your organization to take this process seriously? Many businesspeople, unfortunately, look at the consensus-building alternative and say, "Well, we'll do it for public-relations reasons—but only if it doesn't take a lot of time and money. We're certainly not going to count on public negotiations to produce anything workable." The pitfall is obvious. With this attitude, your organization will only participate half-heartedly. A lack of commitment on your part will soon be obvious to the others, and may well scuttle the entire effort.

ADVANCES IN DISPUTE RESOLUTION

The aftermaths of the events that inspired the cases presented in this book are instructive. The Academy of Sciences in Metropolis informally spread the word about the session they organized to address the dioxin dispute. Other scientific groups soon volunteered to host similar sessions in their communities. Now, whenever the dioxin issue emerges—as it does regularly—so too does the notion of bringing the disputants together to work out a way of proceeding.

Judge Rollenkamp was pleased with the results of the mediation effort in the Harmon County sewage dispute. He subsequently discussed the process with numerous judges not only in his own state, but in other parts of the country as well. Since the Harmon County dispute was settled, more than a dozen other judges in several states have begun exploring the merits of using court-appointed special masters as mediators. As a result of the Chippewa fishing rights dispute, Judge Eastman, too, has become a strong advocate of mediated approaches to resolving complex cases.

RiverEnd was one of the earliest environmental dispute resolution efforts in the eastern United States. In the relatively few years since that negotiation was concluded, dozens of similar cases have been facilitated or mediated successfully. A report analyzing more than a hundred such efforts was published in 1985 by the prestigious Conservation Foundation in Washington, D.C.[7]

In explaining assisted negotiation, we imagined that the reader would be responsible for organizing a consensus-building process from scratch. We took this approach to show that there is nothing arcane or mysterious about the concept. In theory, having read and understood this book, you are now equipped to proceed.

Throughout this book, we have stressed the importance of putting yourself in the other person's shoes. Now, we will try to put ourselves in your place. Perhaps you are a regional transportation official, responsible for extending a rapid transit line into a suburban area that does not want the subway. Perhaps you are the head of an ad hoc citizens' group, organized to block the siting of a regional power plant or a halfway house. Or perhaps you are a developer trying to deal fairly with the environmentalists and historic preservationists who oppose your project. With this slim volume in hand, are you confident that you can generate consensus? Probably not.

Aside from the seeming intractability of the issues at hand, you may also be raising an obvious question. If these methods are so effective, why aren't they used routinely? The answer is that they are, in some cases. We can cite numerous instances at the local, state, and national level in which a consensus-building approach has been adopted, tested, and proven useful. More-

Taking Action

over, we can point to circumstances in which officials are now attempting to go beyond experimentation, to incorporate these processes into the everyday workings of government.

The following examples illustrate that individuals or groups using assisted negotiation are not indulging in wishful thinking. Since the mid-1970s, responsible leaders in the public and private sectors have been trying to find ways of using consensus building to supplement our legislative, administrative, and judicial processes.

AT THE LOCAL LEVEL

Many municipally supported dispute resolution programs have been created as alternatives to court. These have been established to help people work out their differences more rapidly, at lower cost, and without the trauma often associated with the judicial process. Most of these programs deal primarily with private disputes between neighbors, family members, and buyers and sellers. A few, however, offer assistance in distributional disputes. It is important to keep the distinction between the two types of local dispute resolution programs clear. For simplicity's sake, let us label court-connected programs that handle private disputes "alternative dispute resolution (ADR) centers." We will call free-standing centers that handle public disagreements "public dispute centers."

The ADR centers are the subject of substantial controversy.[8] Critics have charged that such alternatives to the court system offer little more than "second-class justice." We disagree; moreover, this charge has not been leveled at public dispute centers.

There are now free-standing public dispute centers in various parts of the country.[9] They are supported either by foundation grants or by fee-for-service contracts. The Mediation Institute in Seattle (with offices in Washington, D.C., Wisconsin, and California) was one of the first free-standing centers to offer dispute resolution services. The institute has been quite successful in helping to resolve environmental disputes. Similarly, the New England Environmental Mediation Center (with offices in Massachusetts, Connecticut, and Vermont) has played a key role in resolving various land use and environmental disputes throughout New England. In Virginia, the Institute for Environmental Mediation (based at the University of Virginia) has successfully mediated several site-specific disputes and helped resolve a number of regional and state-level policy disputes. The institute in Virginia has been supported primarily by foundation grants.

In New Mexico, the Western Network has provided mediation assistance in disputes over the allocation of water and land resources. In the Denver area, ACCORD Associates (formerly the Rocky Mountain Center on the Environment) and the Center for Dispute Resolution have played important roles in settling a wide range of distributional disputes, and have provided assistance in some significant policy negotiations, including the Denver Water Roundtable. The Forum on Community and Environment has taken a similar role in the San Francisco Bay Area.

Many of these centers were started with foundation grants and in subsequent years have been able to generate fee-for-service work as well as regular contributions from local supporters. They have worked hard to ensure balanced funding, with the goal of maintaining their independence. This is important: Centers that accept primarily industry support or government support may jeopardize their credibility as nonpartisan organizations.

For-profit centers (such as Interaction Associates in San Francisco, Boston, and Washington, D.C., and Endispute in Washington, D.C., Chicago, and Boston) have also been active as facilitators in a variety of public disputes, while simultaneously offering dispute resolution services to major corporations dealing with internal conflicts. Major organizations such as the Conservation Foundation (a nonprofit Washington-based research and policy center) and the Colorado-based Keystone Center have created highly regarded dispute resolution offices within their organizations. Consulting firms such as Boston's ERM-McGlennon offer public dispute resolution services, as well as other management and engineering consulting assistance.

The Neighborhood Boards Program in San Francisco is an interesting hybrid of an ADR center and a public dispute center.[10] It draws on existing community groups and offers neighborhood board members training in both private dispute resolution and settling distributional disputes at a neighborhood level. Boards such as these can serve as convenors in public disputes—or even as mediators, if all the parties are willing. In Honolulu, for example, elected neighborhood boards have played intermediary roles in local disputes.

Another exception to our distinction between the two types of centers is also in Honolulu: the Neighborhood Justice Center. It was established as a court-connected "alternative to court" for handling disputes between private parties; over the years, though, the center has also been quite active and quite successful in providing mediation services in local land use disputes.[11]

The techniques described in this book have proven effective in a wide variety of settings. Each of the more than fifty centers and organizations currently in operation has learned by trial and error that intervening in distributional disputes requires specialized knowledge of both the context and the conflict. One of the reasons that these centers have sprung up in every region of the country is that *local* connections are crucial for would-be intermediaries.

Some other preliminary efforts are under way which may lead to the institutionalization (or adoption by government) of assisted negotiation in ongoing municipal decision making. Many zoning appeals, for example, may soon be mediated routinely, because current pilot projects indicate that disputing parties tend to reach voluntary accords that are generally acceptable to zoning appeals boards. Other local administrative processes, involving the granting of permits, the siting of municipal facilities, the setting of budget priorities, and the formulation of growth management plans, may soon be mediated as a matter of course, before formal bodies are asked to make a judgment.

AT THE STATE LEVEL

Five states—Hawaii, New Jersey, Massachusetts, Minnesota, and Wisconsin—have created state offices to mediate distributional disputes.[12] With grants from the National Institute of Dispute Resolution in Washington, D.C., these offices are probably the most significant step thus far in the institutionalization of public dispute resolution. The primary role of these state offices is to match the parties in distributional disputes with appropriate intermediaries. In some instances, they also pay facilitators and mediators, usually when a dispute is of state-wide significance. The state offices are playing an important role in educating decision makers, both inside and outside government, about the advantages of consensual approaches to resolving distributional disputes.

The existence of state offices of mediation will help to overcome some of the chief obstacles to more widespread use of assisted negotiation. One advantage is in timeliness: These organizations can appear on the scene when a dispute is just beginning to smolder, and use the good offices of the governor or the state judiciary to bring the parties together. Moreover, they can foot the up-front costs of the prenegotiation phase, giving the parties time to see just how assisted negotiation works. They can also serve a screening function, maintaining a list of qualified intermediaries; in certain circumstances, they can manage resource pools, and serve as a conduit for paying mediator salaries out of funds contributed by the participants. Finally, they will undoubtedly play an important role in ensuring that careful evaluation and learning go on as case-by-case experience accumulates.

Even before the first state offices of mediation were created, a number of states had taken steps to employ assisted negotiation as a supplement to various administrative processes. Massachusetts, Wisconsin, and Rhode Island, for example, have adopted hazardous waste facility siting laws that presume mediation will precede formal siting decisions.[13] These laws are important for several reasons. First, they remove the obstacles to initiating consensus building. Second, they clarify what the protocols will be. Third, they make it easier to understand exactly how informally negotiated agreements can be formalized. The Massachusetts Siting Law, for example, spells out the steps involved in formalizing a negotiated agreement, and gives such agreements the force of law.

Other state efforts, some still embryonic, are quite encouraging. Several states have employed negotiated approaches to set electric utility rates.[14] Instead of relying on the typical adversarial model of rate setting (which pits utility companies against consumer advocates, with the rate commission as the final arbiter), these states have tried to bring together all the interested parties with a mediator to work out equitable rate increases. New York State is furthest along in its efforts to mediate utility rate disputes.

As was illustrated in the social service block grant case, states can use assisted negotiation to hammer out agreements on how to allocate their human service funds. This has happened recently in Connecticut, for example. Groups that were formerly adversaries (including providers of human services, state agency administrators, consumer and municipal representatives) were able to reach consensus on spending cuts and increases.[15]

It is clear that the states have taken the lead in developing consensual approaches to resolving distributional disputes. We can perceive an impending problem in the states' activities, however. Unless state laws explicitly authorize intermediaries to function in distributional disputes at both the state and local level, confusion and opposition is likely to arise whenever such approaches are proposed. In short, legislative action is needed to enable the widespread institutionalization of consensus building.

AT THE FEDERAL LEVEL

A number of interesting uses of consensus building have received attention at the federal level, particularly efforts to mediate the drafting of new regulations. The EPA, as well as the Federal Aviation Administration and the Occupational Safety and Health Administration, have been successful in bringing together the parties most likely to challenge proposed agency regulations, in order to draft consensual versions of the rules.

In the EPA's case, the agency has, on at least five occasions, sat at the table with more than twenty representatives of national environmental organizations and interest groups.[16] In the first case, the goal was to draft new regulations regarding financial penalties for truck engine manufacturers slow to meet the Clean Air Act's guidelines. In the second, the EPA sought to draft rules regarding the emergency circumstances under which certain new pesticides might be exempted from usual licensing procedures. Professional facilitators and mediators played a key role in the success of each of these efforts. The outcome in both cases were a set of proposed rules, which then went through the normal review and comment processes to guarantee that no parties who should have been involved had been overlooked. As it turned out, surprisingly few comments were received, and the draft rules were adopted without opposition. Given that in this period—1984—the EPA was defending in the courts almost 80 percent of the rules and regulations it proposed, these successes were quite noteworthy.

The EPA has also expressed serious interest in finding ways

to encourage negotiated settlements of Superfund cases. Clean Sites, Inc., a nonprofit organization established jointly by the major chemical companies and environmental organizations, is now involved as an intermediary at a number of sites. The creation of this sort of mediating institution is a precedent that may well inspire combatants in other public policy realms to form similar organizations.[17]

Not only is the EPA moving ahead with additional negotiated rule makings, but other agencies (including the Department of the Interior, the FTC and the Nuclear Regulatory Commission) have decided to mount similar efforts of their own. Over time, negotiated rule making may become the norm at the federal level, at least in instances when controversial rules are being promulgated.

Other federal agencies have explored additional uses of consensual approaches to resolving distributional disputes. Long-controversial questions are being reconsidered in light of these new tools. Which federal lands, for example, should be set aside as "forever wild"? Which parts of the continental shelf should be put out to bid for off-shore oil exploration? What new rules should govern the use of the national park system? The Corps of Engineers and the Department of the Interior—often lightning rods of environmentalists' discontent—are increasingly willing to try a consensus-building approach.

The federal courts may also provide an added impetus for the future institutionalization of consensus building. The success of the fishing rights mediation effort described in this book has encouraged federal courts to consider using mediation and non-binding arbitration in other complex distributional disputes—ones which the courts would prefer to have the parties settle on their own. The use of court-appointed special masters as mediators may also make it easier to get negotiations started, and help address the inability of certain parties to put up an equal share of the funds for a resource pool. In such cases, the court pays the mediator.

In conclusion, it may be useful to address what may seem to some to be a paradox: the institutionalization of ad hoc approaches to dispute resolution. After all, one might argue, the supreme virtue of an ad hoc approach is that it can be shaped to fit a given occasion. Will institutionalization cause the same kind of rigidity that led to the need for ad hoc approaches in the first place? We think not—as long as institutionalization means the creation of enabling statutes, funding arrangements, and procedural suggestions intended to encourage, rather than circumscribe, the case-by-case use of assisted negotiation.

SUMMARY

Consensual approaches to resolving distributional disputes are no longer new. On the other hand, neither are they so well understood that they have been generally adopted. Indeed, as we have stressed in earlier chapters, our various legislatures, agencies, and courts are in trouble today precisely because they have continued to use conventional dispute resolution mechanisms in situations where they are not appropriate.

As the merits of assisted negotiation become clearer, more and more attempts will be made to institutionalize these processes as supplements to existing mechanisms for resolving distributional disputes. At that point, the challenge will be to match each dispute with the most appropriate form of consensus building.

One way of thinking about the types of consensus building most appropriate to the types of disputes discussed in this book is outlined in figure 6.1. The vertical columns represent the three branches of government—legislative, executive, and judicial—and the horizontal rows represent the three levels of government: local, state, and federal. (For simplicity's sake, we have

FIGURE 6.1

Using Mediation and Other Forms of Assisted Negotiation

	Legislative	*Executive*	*Judicial*
Local	DIOXIN	JORDAN LANE	Housing court mediation
State	Coastal zone management legislation	RIVEREND	HARMON COUNTY
Federal		EPA-NEGOTIATED RULE MAKING	FISHING RIGHTS

omitted other levels, such as county government.) In all but one of the cells of this figure, we have cited a successful consensus-building effort. Those discussed previously are listed in capital letters; two additional cases are described briefly in the following paragraphs.

At the local level, the Navy Yard dioxin case indicates that a city council can use facilitation or mediation before it exercises its statutory authority. Similarly, the administrative agencies of local government can use facilitation or mediation to supplement their normal ways of handling licensing, permitting, and related efforts to enforce regulations. The zoning appeals board in Bexley was prepared to live with a negotiated agreement in the Jordan Lane case. In a great many other cities, site-specific development disputes have similarly been mediated and have yielded agreements that are being implemented through normal administrative processes.

"Housing Court Mediation" is the local/judicial cell in figure 6.1. In several cities, including Boston and New York, housing courts—accustomed to being burdened with hundreds of cases involving tenants and landlords—have sanctioned the use of mediation prior to scheduled trials. Although most of these are private disputes (and therefore distinct from the kinds of distributional disputes we have been discussing), some of the mediated cases have also involved broader housing policy disputes.[18]

At the state level, RiverEnd represents one of the many instances in which state regulatory bodies have used facilitation to supplement their normal administrative procedures. State agencies, as in the block grant case, can use outside mediators to help generate consensus on budget proposals. Similarly, requests to increase electric utility rates can be mediated prior to review by public utility commissions. In some ways, such a mediation would resemble current administrative hearings that produce stipulated agreements prior to board review. A key difference, though, is that the current adversarial hearings process could be replaced by joint problem solving.

Judge Rollenkamp was neither the first nor the last state judge to use a special master as a mediator to help settle a dispute pending before a court. State courts have expressed growing interest in the use of mediation and nonbinding arbitration, and their work with the new state offices of mediation is ample evidence of this.

Referring again to figure 6.1, "Coastal zone management legislation" is given as an example of a state level legislative effort. In Massachusetts, when new legislation was needed to respond to court-imposed requirements regarding the disposition of tidelands (the land between the high-water and low-water marks), a facilitated effort produced draft legislation that broke a serious deadlock, and produced agreement in a matter of weeks.[19]

The EPA has used both inside and outside facilitators to mediate rule-making negotiations. The convening process has been handled exclusively by outsiders. Other federal agencies including the Forest Service and the Department of Defense have used facilitated approaches to supplement normal grant-making procedures. Judge Eastman's use of mediated negotiation to settle the fishing rights case is just one of many instances in which federal district courts have used mediated negotiation to settle complex litigation. Several courts have also used nonbinding arbitration, including minitrials, to settle disputes involving thousands of litigants (such as the suits pending against the asbestos industry). And although Congress has yet to organize facilitated or mediated sessions to build consensus on policy questions, we expect that such efforts are not far off. In a sense, precedents already exist. Congress would only have to extend the bipartisan consensus-building efforts used to secure agreement on social security reform in the early 1980s—that is, to include other noncongressional representatives of relevant stakeholding groups in drafting legislative proposals—in order to engage in true consensus building.

There have even been successful intergovernmental mediation efforts. The Kettering Foundation, of Dayton, Ohio, has sponsored what they have called Negotiated Investment Strategy (NIS) dispute resolutions in several cities, including Columbus, Ohio; Gary, Indiana; and St. Paul, Minnesota.[20] These involved bringing together three teams—one representing local elected officials, another representing state elected and appointed officials, and a third representing the federal agencies with a stake in the long-term development of the cities involved. With the help of professional mediators, these teams were able to negotiate long-term public and private "investment strategies" that reconciled the conflicting priorities of the three levels of government. Given the recent emphasis on public-private partnerships, the Kettering Foundation's efforts provide us with an important clue about how to proceed on this crucial front.

If the disputants in a conflict situation are willing to work creatively to exploit their differences, and can keep in mind their common interests, negotiated approaches to dispute resolution can work. This means, though, that voluntary supplements to the conventional mechanisms used by our legislative, executive, and judicial branches must be devised. In particular, professional intermediaries—facilitators, mediators, and arbitrators—need to be included. And although numerous obstacles to consensus building exist (not the least of which is securing funding when disputing parties have an unequal ability to pay), these can be overcome. The cases presented in this book are only a small fraction of the evidence supporting this claim.

CHAPTER 7

Conclusion

As anyone who reads the daily papers knows, the complexity of public disputes can be daunting. Indeed, the pessimists among us have concluded that there is no choice but to "slug it out" in the political arena. We disagree. The strategies and techniques described in this book offer an alternative.

We have tried to show that it is possible to resolve public disputes fairly and efficiently, while incorporating the best technical and scientific advice available. Moreover, consensual outcomes arrived at in the fashion we have described are likely to be more stable than political compromises achieved through conventional means.

NEGOTIATED APPROACHES
TO CONSENSUS BUILDING

The parties in public disputes can, and should, satisfy their own interests. No apologies are necessary for pursuing selfish rather than altruistic goals. On the other hand, when individuals or groups must depend on support from others before they can take the actions they want, they must satisfy the needs of those other parties to achieve their own goals. Interdependence requires helping others in order to help ourselves.

In almost every public dispute, the contending parties have mixed motives. In the Middletown dispute, cited in the introduction, the parties wanted to solve the problem of the homeless and to do it in a way that was consistent with their own interests. The parties involved in Middletown had competitive aims as well as cooperative impulses. Unfortunately, they failed to take full advantage of these "dual" concerns, and in the process they made it even more difficult to work together in the future. Furthermore, they made no effort to gather information jointly or to develop forecasts collaboratively. It is no surprise that they could not agree on the best way to approach the problem.

The Middletown disputants failed to engage in even the most minimal form of brainstorming. They locked themselves into proposed solutions before even hearing the views of others. As the dispute wore on, the participants lost sight of their common interest and gave up the search for all-gain solutions.

They never tried to develop an informal written agreement. No one was asked to check back with his or her constituents to determine what the population at large really wanted done.

Those with the statutory authority to commit public resources and set policy in Middletown maintained complete control. They sought very little guidance from groups that might have been able to give them helpful advice. When they did seek input from others, they relied on public hearings that quickly deteriorated into nothing more than an opportunity to grand-stand for the media.

No joint monitoring process was established to keep track of what was working and what was not. No one accepted any responsibility for achieving specific objectives within a given time.

UNASSISTED AND ASSISTED NEGOTIATION

The disputants in Middletown thought they could work things out on their own. They would have been better off seeking outside assistance. By "assistance," we mean some form of procedural help.

The Jordan Lane case suggests that unassisted negotiations can succeed only when certain conditions are met. The Middle-town dispute involved too many complex issues for the parties to succeed on their own. In addition, the full range of stakehold-ers was not obvious; nor were all the key parties willing to engage in joint fact finding. Most important, each disputant's alternative to no agreement was not unattractive enough to bring them to the bargaining table.

Unfortunately, most public disputes do not meet these pre-conditions for success in unassisted negotiation. Large numbers of hard-to-identify parties are likely to be involved. The issues are typically complicated and numerous. And some of the par-ties are likely to view the lack of an agreement as an acceptable outcome. The RiverEnd, Harmon County, fishing rights, and social service block grant disputes illustrate these points quite nicely. The parties in many-issue, multiparty public disputes need neutral consensus-building assistance.

In such cases, intermediaries should be selected to fit the

specifics of the dispute. The backgrounds, affiliations, and reputations of the neutrals must be examined carefully by all the parties.

We have identified three forms of procedural assistance that can be helpful: facilitation, mediation, and nonbinding arbitration. Each involves a different level of intervention, although all leave the disputants as much control as possible. All three might have been tried in the Middletown dispute. Facilitation and mediation were effective in the major cases we presented.

Assuming that a dispute proves too difficult for the parties to handle, they might begin by engaging a facilitator to help with a variety of prenegotiation tasks, including stakeholder analysis, the formulation of ground rules to guide the interaction, and agenda setting. The facilitator, as we saw in the RiverEnd case, can provide "at-the-table" guidance and logistical support (arranging the time and place of meeting, taking and distributing minutes, and so on). The facilitator should only serve as long as all the parties are satisfied with his or her performance and the progress they are making.

The services of a mediator are typically required when caucuses or confidential between-meeting interaction is necessary, as in the Harmon County case. It is not inappropriate to ask a mediator to propose mutually advantageous "packages" when the parties have run out of ideas. In addition, the mediator should be empowered to "shuttle" back and forth when communication has broken down. To be effective, mediators need substantial grounding in the substance of the dispute. While they must maintain their nonpartisan stance at all times, this does not mean that they can be indifferent to the outcome of the dispute. As was the case in the fishing rights dispute, in particular, it is appropriate for a mediator to worry about the fairness, efficiency, stability, and wisdom of any agreements reached. This does not entitle the intermediary to steer the negotiations toward a particular outcome, but it does mean that the participants should expect the neutral to press them in ways that focus attention on the attributes of a good outcome. In the end, however, the agreement must still be consensual and must be "owned" by the participants.

Disputants can turn over more control (but still not total control) to an arbitrator who offers an opinion on how they should resolve their differences, but does not bind them. This is the last stop before the parties cross over into nonconsensual dispute resolution. By asking a mutually agreed-upon "judge" or panel to indicate how a court or a jury might settle a dispute, the stakeholders can gauge their aspirations more realistically. This often leads to voluntary resolution of private disputes, especially if one party has been holding out unrealistically.

LIMITS ON CONSENSUAL APPROACHES TO DISPUTE RESOLUTION

Why are the techniques described in this book still underutilized?

The most important reason seems to be a concern on the part of public officials that participating in consensual negotiations may constitute an abdication of legal responsibility. Such assumptions are misplaced. In almost every situation we have observed, including all the cases presented in this book, consensual approaches fit quite well within the constraints imposed by the laws governing the actions of elected and appointed officials. As long as the consensus-building process is conducted openly and all interested parties are invited to participate, there is no reason to worry about abdication of responsibility. Moreover, if the product of such negotiations is an informal written agreement that must still be ratified, all due process and equal protection requirements can be met.

Some public officials presume that consensus building means

giving up power. This is not true. Because informally negotiated agreements must be formally ratified by those in positions of authority, the status quo with regard to decision making will not change. Moreover, consensus means that all key participants—including the elected and appointed officials involved—must agree that an agreement serves their interests. Thus, no official who initiates or agrees to participate in a consensus-building process is giving up his or her power to veto an outcome.

We believe that public officials can increase their power by encouraging consensual approaches to dispute resolution. This is true because the public favors fairer, wiser, more stable, and more efficient resolution of distributional disputes.

From citizens and public interest advocates, we often encounter concerns about entering negotiations when resources and political power are unequally distributed. "Won't less powerful and less well-endowed parties be coopted or overwhelmed by more powerful adversaries?" they ask. "Isn't court the only place that the parties with less political power can be sure of getting fair treatment?"

In fact, conventional approaches to resolving distributional disputes place a heavy emphasis on political power and legal rights. Legislatures are particularly sensitive to the "clout" of lobbyists and interest groups. The courts, for their part, are primarily concerned with determining past facts rather than shaping future possibilities. This favors the innocent, not the less powerful. Moreover, the courts are singularly unconcerned about future relationships. The distributional cases that wind up in court are handled pretty much like criminal cases—winners and losers are identified—because that is what the courts are equipped to do.

Less powerful groups may have legitimate concerns about entering into consensus-building negotiations, but they should be wary as well about engaging in expensive court battles when distributional issues, rather than legal rights, are at stake.

Power and politics are essential ingredients in all public disputes, and they cannot be ignored. But consensus-building approaches to dispute resolution place a premium on problem solving rather than "settling" disputes. When the outcomes could be life-threatening, even the most politically powerful groups should be worried about the wisdom of the agreements reached. Indeed, in many public disputes a wise outcome is much more urgent than winning. When a powerful group commits to work for consensus, it tacitly agrees that raw political power is not a sufficient basis for resolving public disputes. This empowers those who are less politically powerful. On the other hand, it takes nothing away from those with more political power because all groups retain a veto.

In most negotiations, bargaining power (as opposed to political power) is fluid. The power of good ideas (that is, proposals that meet everyone's interests) is extremely important, and equally available to all the disputants. Cooptation is never inevitable, as any party can break off negotiations at any time.

One limit on the usefulness of consensus building is the time involved. The "average" negotiation varies between several months and a year or more. Both powerful and less powerful parties are often tempted to use other avenues that seem to offer a quick solution. The prospect of a speedy court ruling, for instance, is often difficult to resist. On the other hand, swift outcomes are most often a false hope. If disputes are not fully resolved to the satisfaction of all the parties, they merely shift to another arena. If public agencies, courts, and legislative bodies were able to act promptly, without the risk of subsequent challenge or reconsideration, consensus building would be much less attractive.

Without a doubt, the prenegotiation phase of a consensus-building effort can take a long time. All potential stakeholders must be contacted and briefed. Each group must choose a spokesperson. Appropriate intermediaries must be selected, ground rules set, and an agenda worked out. There may even be the need for extensive fact finding before problem solving can begin. In our view, however, these are good investments. As we have said before, it is often necessary to "go slow to go fast."

A major concern of both public officials and business interests is the possibility that splinter groups might emerge. We encounter this question frequently: "Doesn't the prospect of splinter groups severely limit the effectiveness and applicability of consensual approaches to dispute resolution in the public sector? Why invest significant amounts of time and money in a process that can be undermined at its conclusion by a runaway faction?"

There is no way to completely eliminate the threat of splinter groups. However, there are many ways to reduce the likelihood that they will form, and there are ways to blunt their impact if they do emerge. Issues of representation and ratification require special attention for just this reason. It is hard for a splinter group to gain the political credibility (and the money) that it needs to mount an attack if every possible effort was made to contact and include potential stakeholders, including those who emerged "in mid-stream."

If splinter groups form after an agreement has been ratified, it may still be possible to reassemble all the participants to consider concerns that were not addressed earlier. This should be up to the group as a whole. If renegotiation provisions have been included in the negotiated agreement, it is significantly easier to face and solve such problems.

Even if the negotiators cannot be reassembled, the agreement may withstand political challenges from splinter groups. "After all," the negotiators can argue truthfully, "they had their chance to raise issues during the negotiations. The final agreement was consensual—and at least until this splinter group arose, everyone willingly accepted it."

There is one more important point to keep in mind on the subject of splinter groups. Consensus-building approaches need only be as good as, or slightly better than, conventional approaches to resolving public disputes in order to justify their use. Conventional approaches, as we have seen, are always subject to challenge by groups unhappy with an outcome. Even when consensus building only forestalls some of these challenges—and we maintain that it can do far better—it presents clear advantages.

As we have tried to make clear throughout this book, the way to break the public disputes impasse is to *deal with differences* effectively. On the one hand, this means that we must find a way to cope with public disputes—to deal with them. On the other hand, and this is equally important, we should seek to settle distributional disputes by dealing or trading across issues that the parties value differently.

Skeptics suggest that, in reality, disputing parties will find very little to trade. In extreme cases, this may be true. If the parties can find nothing that they value differently, it may be impossible to "expand the pie" or design integrative agreements. On the other hand, even in a zero-sum bargaining situation, it can be advantageous for both parties to focus on the "rules of the game." How will they divide the pie if it cannot be expanded? This can be dealt with as a joint problem-solving task. Agreement on fair criteria for handling a zero-sum situation can enhance the prospects for successful implementation of whatever outcome is reached.

As it turns out, most public disputes are not of the zero-sum variety, even though they may be framed that way at the outset. All too often, disputants conclude that there is nothing to trade simply because they have not been thinking along these lines. In the Middletown dispute over the homeless, none of the targeted neighborhoods was offered compensation or a promise to mitigate adverse impacts. None was promised that an agreement to accept housing for the homeless could be traded off against future protection from other undesirable facilities.

In finding items to trade, it is important to range far afield.

All sorts of unconventional swaps are possible if the parties work to invent them. At the same time, there are ways to ensure that extortionate demands are not made.

THE PROMISE OF CONSENSUAL NEGOTIATION

One view of social reform in the United States is that all ideas like consensus building are fads—that they emerge from time to time, have their brief vogue, and fade away. From a conservative perspective, almost all social reforms create more problems than they solve—especially when the government is involved.

As a tool for resolving distributional disputes, consensus building does not depend on government intervention. Public agencies must be involved, of course, but in most cases both public and private institutions are involved. Consensus building can be proposed by any party. No abdication of private responsibility is involved. In fact, individual initiative is a critical component of the negotiated approaches to consensus building described in this book.

Our view of why social reforms often fail is that they are imposed from above. In effect, the government attempts to instill new values. But a stubborn fact of human nature tends to intervene. Very few people can be convinced to change their underlying sense of right and wrong—of what ought to happen and what ought not to happen—in response to a governmental edict. Thus, reforms emerge, and may even be institutionalized, but they nonetheless fail because human nature is resistant. If the vehicle of reform fails to address such underlying motivations, it is doomed.

One of the most exciting aspects of consensual approaches to dispute resolution is that once people use them, and find that they work, those people become advocates. The act of participation, and especially the fruits of success, changes their sense of how best to proceed. Thus, the idea of consensus building will be promulgated by the most effective advocates imaginable: those who have tried it and seen it work. Unlike most reforms, consensus building has the great advantage of built-in learning.[1] The "reformed" become the reformers.

We contend that it is precisely this kind of learning that allows a reform to take root and endure.[2] As a result, we are confident that consensual approaches to dispute resolution will thrive. As they do, it will be easier to avoid or break whatever impasses emerge. Consensual approaches to the resolution of public disputes will increasingly offer an opportunity to demonstrate that democratic institutions can work effectively.

Further
Reading

INTRODUCTION

For an overview of the positive functions that conflict can play,
see Louis Coser's *The Functions of Social Conflict* (New York:
Free Press, 1964).

Roger Fisher and William Ury's *Getting To YES: Negotiating
Agreement Without Giving In* (Boston: Houghton Mifflin, 1981)
provides an excellent introduction to the key elements of a
consensual approach to negotiation.

THEORY AND PRACTICE OF
DISPUTE RESOLUTION

Two of the most important books in the negotiation field are
Thomas Schelling's *The Strategy of Conflict* (Cambridge,
Mass.: Harvard University Press, 1960) and Howard Raiffa's
The Art and Science of Negotiation (Cambridge: Harvard University
Press, 1982). These provide a general theory of negotiation.
Stephen Goldberg, Eric Green, and Frank Sander, *Dispute
Resolution* (Boston: Little, Brown & Co., 1985), offers a collection
of readings that review the full range of dispute resolution
techniques and strategies. Another useful collection, upon
which we drew heavily, is the special issue of the *American
Behavioral Scientist* 17, 135 (1983), which was devoted entirely
to articles on negotiation.

SOURCES OF DIFFICULTY

Jane Mansbridge's *Beyond Adversary Democracy* (Chicago:
University of Chicago Press, 1983) provides numerous insights
into the conventional workings of democracy, as does Joshua
Cohen's *On Democracy* (New York: Penguin, 1983). Richard
Walton and Robert McKersie's classic *A Behavioral Theory of
Labor Relations* (New York: McGraw-Hill, 1965) presents the
basic concept of "mixed motive bargaining." Dean Pruitt and
Jeffrey Rubin's *Social Conflict* (New York: Random House,
1985) summarizes the literature on traps and escalation.

UNASSISTED NEGOTIATION

Gerald Williams's *Legal Negotiation and Settlement* (St. Paul: West, 1983) presents important evidence on the success and failure of cooperative and competitive approaches to negotiation. Lawrence Bacow and Michael Wheeler's *Environmental Dispute Resolution* (New York: Plenum, 1983) analyzes a number of other public disputes that were settled without outside assistance. Roy Lewicki and Joseph Litterer's *Negotiation* (Homewood, Ill.: Richard Irwin, 1985) contains an excellent review of the research that has been done on integrative bargaining.

MEDIATION AND OTHER FORMS
OF ASSISTED NEGOTIATION

Many books look at facilitation, mediation, and nonbinding arbitration. Several of the most relevant to people interested in public disputes are Michael Doyle and David Straus, *Making Meetings Work* (New York: Playboy Press, 1976); Jacob Bercovitch, *Social Conflict and Third Parties: Strategies of Conflict Resolution* (Boulder, Colo.: Westview Press, 1984); Jay Folberg and Ann Taylor, *Mediation: A Comprehensive Guide to Resolving Conflict Without Litigation* (San Francisco: Jossey-Bass, 1984); and Timothy Sullivan's *Resolving Development Disputes Through Negotiation* (New York: Plenum, 1984). For a detailed review of public disputes in which mediation has played an important role see Gail Bingham's *Resolving Environmental Disputes: A Decade of Experience* (Washington, D.C.: Conservation Foundation, 1985), and Lawrence Susskind, Lawrence Bacow, and Michael Wheeler, *Resolving Environmental*

Regulatory Disputes (Cambridge, Mass.: Schenckman, 1983). For a summary of research on mediation see the special issue of the journal *Social Issues* 41, 2 (1985).

TAKING ACTION

For a review of the community dispute resolution movement, see Richard Abel's *The Politics of Informal Justice: The American Experience* (New York: Academic Press, 1982), and Roman Tomasic and Malcolm Feeley, *Neighborhood Justice: Assessment of an Emerging Idea* (New York: Longman, 1982). For more information on the ways in which public officials view consensus building, see Nancy Huelsberg and William Lincoln's *Successful Negotiating in Local Government* (Washington, D.C.: International City Management Association, 1985), and Carl Moore and Chris Carlson, *Public Decision Making: Using the Negotiated Investment Strategy* (Dayton, Ohio: Kettering Foundation, 1984). For a detailed look at the views of business executives, we recommend David Lax and Jim Sebenius, *The Manager as Negotiator* (New York: Free Press, 1986), as well as Max Bazerman and Roy Lewicki, *Negotiating in Organizations* (Beverly Hills, Calif.: Sage, 1983). For more on the ways that citizen action groups view negotiation, see Lawrence Susskind and Michael Elliott, *Paternalism, Conflict, and Co-Production: Learning from Citizen Action and Citizen Participation in Western Europe* (New York: Plenum, 1983), and Manuel Castells, *The Grass Roots and the City* (Berkeley: University of California Press, 1985).

CONCLUSION

Robert Axelrod's *The Evolution of Cooperation* (New York: Basic Books, 1984) provides important insights into the nature of zero-sum bargaining over time. See also Kenneth Boulding, "Conflict Management as a Learning Process," in Anthony deReuck and Julie Knight, eds., *Conflict in Society* (Boston: Little, Brown & Co., 1966). Donald Schon's *Beyond the Stable State* (New York: Norton, 1971) offers further evidence on the importance on built-in institutional learning as a key to social reform.

Notes

CHAPTER 1. Introduction

1. Michael O'Hare, Lawrence Bacow, and Debra Sanderson, *Facility Siting and Public Opposition* (New York: Van Nostrand, 1983).

2. Lawrence Susskind and Laura Van Dam, "Squaring off at the Table, Not in the Courts," *Technology Review* (July 1986): 36–44.

3. For an overview of the problem of homelessness in America, see John Erickson and Charles Wilheim, eds., *Housing the Homeless* (New Brunswick, N.J.: Rutgers Center for Urban Policy Research, 1986).

4. A great many authors have made this point. See, for example, Sheila Jasanoff and Dorothy Nelkin, "Science, Technology, and the Limits of Judicial Competence," *Science* 214 (December 11, 1981):1211–1215, and Lon Fuller, "The Forms and Limits of Adjudication," *Harvard Law Review* 92 (1962):353–409.

5. For a general description of the problems inherent in the administrative process, see Richard Stewart, "The Reformation of American Administrative Law," *Harvard Law Review* 88 (1978): 1667–1813.

CHAPTER 2. Theory and Practice of Dispute Resolution

1. For an overview of the field of dispute resolution, see Stephen Goldberg, Eric Green, and Frank Sander, *Dispute Resolution* (Boston: Little, Brown & Co., 1985). For more on the debate regarding the problems associated with the informality of "alternative dispute resolution," see Jay Folberg and Alison Taylor, *Mediation: A Comprehensive Guide to Resolving Conflicts Without Litigation* (San Francisco: Jossey-Bass, 1984), chapter 3.

2. The concepts of efficiency and elegant trades are best explained in Howard Raiffa, *The Art and Science of Negotiation* (Cambridge: Harvard University Press, 1982).

3. The concept of prospective hindsight is explained in Michael Wheeler, "Prospective Hindsight," *Negotiation Journal* 3 (January 1987):7–10.

4. The debate over the proposed Attleboro Mall in Sweden's Swamp was covered by the *Boston Globe* in front-page stories on 6 March 1986, and 14 May 1986. The *New York Times* also described the dispute in a section 2 story on 14 May 1986.

5. For a summary of what scientists do and do not know about wetlands, see Orville T. Magoon, ed., *Coastal Zone '83: Proceedings of the Third Symposium on Coastal and Ocean Resource Management* (New York: American Society of Civil Engineers, 1984), vols. 1–3.

6. The pitfalls of advocacy science are further explained in Connie Ozawa and Lawrence Susskind, "Mediating Science-intensive Policy Disputes," *Journal of Policy Analysis and Management* 5, 1 (1985):23–39, and J. D. Nyhart and Milton Carrow, eds., *Law and Science in Collaboration* (Lexington, Mass.: Lexington Press, 1983).

7. The importance of realistic commitments is explained further in Roger Fisher and William Ury, *Getting To YES: Negotiating Agreement Without Giving In* (Boston: Houghton Mifflin, 1981).

8. The most important aspects of a good working relationship are described in Fisher and Ury, *Getting To YES*.

9. The concept of packaging is outlined further in Raiffa, *The Art and Science of Negotiation*.

10. The notion of "dual concerns" or "mixed motives" in negotiation was first presented by Richard Walton and Robert McKersie, *A Behavioral Theory of Labor Negotiations* (New York: McGraw-Hill, 1965), and further elaborated in Dean Pruitt, *Negotiation Behavior* (New York: Academic Press, 1981).

Notes

CHAPTER 3. Sources of Difficulty

1. For a general discussion of negotiated rule making see Philip Harter, "Negotiating Regulations: A Cure for the Malaise," *Georgetown Law Journal* 71 (1982): 1–117.

2. Lawrence Susskind and Gerard McMahon, "The Theory and Practice of Negotiated Rulemaking," *Yale Journal of Regulation* 3, 1 (1985): 133–165.

3. The dynamic of "agency capture" is described in Paul Sabatier, "Social Movements and Regulatory Agencies: Toward a More Adequate View of Clientele Capture," *Policy Sciences* 6 (September 1975):301–342.

4. The RiverEnd case draws in part on materials presented in Lawrence Susskind, "Citizen Participation and Consensus Building in Land Use Planning: A Case Study," in Judith deNeufville, ed., *The Land Use Debate in the United States* (New York: Plenum, 1980).

5. For an overview of the synfuels program, see Richard H. K. Vietor, *Energy Policy in America Since 1945* (Cambridge, Engl.: Cambridge University Press, 1984). The demise of the program is reviewed by E. Marshall in *Science* 25, 4662 (10 August 1984):604–605.

6. For a technical summary of the Superfund program's origins, see Frederick R. Anderson, "Negotiation and Informal Agency Action: The Case of Superfund," *Duke Law Journal* 86, 2 (1985):261–380.

7. Ezra Vogel, *Japan as Number One: Lessons for America* (Cambridge: Harvard University Press, 1979).

8. This case draws in part on materials presented in *Reports from the Mediator,* a newsletter published between December 1984 and May 1986 by the Partnership Forum for Social Service Priorities, Program on Negotiation at Harvard Law School, Cambridge, Massachusetts.

9. The best description of lobbying in America and our ambivalent attitudes toward it are in Grant McConnell's *Private Power in American Democracy* (New York: Knopf, 1966).

10. This case draws in part on materials presented in Lawrence Susskind, "Court-Appointed Masters as Mediators," *Negotiation Journal* (October 1985):295–300.

11. For a brief review of the attitudes of the various interest groups toward the Superfund program, see *Sierra Magazine* (November–December 1984).

12. This case draws in part on materials presented in Connie Ozawa and Lawrence Susskind, "Mediating Science-intensive Policy Disputes," *Journal of Policy Analysis and Management* 5, 1 (1985):23–39.

13. Whether or not America is an unduly litigious society is an open question. See, for example, William Felstiner, Richard Abel, and Austin Sarat, "The Emergence and Transformation of Disputes: Naming, Blaming, and Claiming," *Law and Society Review* 15 (1980–81):631–654, and Marc Galanter, "Reading the Landscape of Disputes: What We Know and Don't Know (and Think We Know) About Our Allegedly Contentious and Litigious Society," *UCLA Law Review* 31, 4 (1983).

14. This discussion of court procedure draws on Lawrence Susskind and Alan Weinstein, "Toward a Theory of Environmental Dispute Resolution," *Boston College Environmental Affairs Law Review* 9, 2 (1980):143–196.

15. Much of this case is based on "The Lake Wasota Fishing Rights Game" (Case no. 20004), published by the Clearinghouse of the Program on Negotiation at Harvard Law School, Cambridge, Massachusetts. See *Clearinghouse Catalog*, 2d ed. (November 1986):45–46.

CHAPTER 4. Unassisted Negotiation

1. The concept of BATNA was originated by Roger Fisher and William Ury in *Getting To YES: Negotiating Agreement Without Giving In* (Boston: Houghton Mifflin, 1981).

2. The calculation of expected value in a negotiation context is explained by Howard Raiffa, *The Art and Science of Negotiation* (Cambridge: Harvard University Press, 1982).

3. The BATNA estimation techniques are presented in Raiffa, *The Art and Science of Negotiation.*

4. The distinction between these two types of bargaining is nicely explained in Roy Lewicki and Joseph Litterer, *Negotiation* (Homewood, Ill.: Richard Irwin, 1985).

5. For an excellent presentation of the "anchoring" process, see chapter 2 of Raiffa, *The Art and Science of Negotiation.*

6. Extensive research on the "dollar auction" is presented in Allan Teger, *Too Much Invested To Quit* (New York: Pergamon, 1980).

7. Jeffrey Z. Rubin, "Psychological Traps," *Psychology Today* (March 1981):52–63.

8. J. Brockner and Jeffrey Rubin, *Entrapment in Escalating Conflicts* (New York: Springer-Verlag, 1985).

9. This case is based in part on material presented in the "Neighborhood Care, Inc. Game" (Case no. 20005.1), published by the Clearinghouse of

the Program on Negotiation at Harvard Law School, Cambridge, Massachusetts. See *Clearinghouse Catalog,* 2d ed. (November 1986): 88.

10. Some of the problems of achieving effective representation are discussed further in Lawrence Susskind, "Power and Power Imbalances in Dispute Resolution," in *Removing the Barriers to the Use of Alternative Methods of Dispute Resolution* (South Royalton, Vt.: Vermont Law School Dispute Resolution Project, 1984).

11. The details of how to complete a conflict assessment are discussed in Susan L. Carpenter and W. J. D. Kennedy, *Managing Public Disputes: A Practical Guide to Reaching Agreements* (San Francisco: Jossey-Bass, forthcoming).

12. The strengths and weaknesses of this strategy are spelled out in Thomas Schelling's "An Essay on Bargaining" in *The Strategy of Conflict* (Cambridge, Mass.: Harvard University Press, 1960).

13. The distinction between interests and positions is explained further in Fisher and Ury, *Getting To YES.*

14. This is a phrase coined by Fisher and Ury, *Getting To YES.*

15. William J. Gordon, *Synectics* (New York: Harper and Row, 1961).

16. The single negotiating text procedure is elaborated in Roger Fisher and William Ury, *International Mediation: A Working Guide* (Cambridge: Harvard Negotiation Project at Harvard Law School, 1978).

17. Malcolm Rivkin, *Negotiated Development: A Breakthrough in Environmental Controversies* (Washington, D.C.: Conservation Foundation, 1977).

18. See, for example, Roger Fisher, "Negotiating Power: Getting and Using Influence," *American Behavioral Scientist* 27, 2 (November–December, 1985):149–166.

CHAPTER 5. Mediation and Other Forms of Assisted Negotiation

1. The debate on the role of the mediator is presented in Joseph B. Stulberg, *Taking Charge/Managing Conflict,* (Lexington, Massachusetts: Lexington, 1987).

2. The details of how the EPA's resource pool worked are reviewed in Lawrence Susskind and Gerard McMahon, "The Theory and Practice of Negotiated Rulemaking," *Yale Journal of Regulation* 3, 1 (1985):133–165.

3. For more on minitrials, see Eric Green, "The CPR Mini-Trial Handbook," in *Corporate Dispute Management* (New York: Matthew Bender, 1982).

4. David Lax and James Sebenius, *The Manager as Negotiator* (New York: Free Press, 1986).

5. Gerald Williams, *Legal Negotiation and Settlement* (St. Paul, Minn.: West, 1983).

6. This point is explained further by Jacob Bercovitch, *Social Conflicts and Third Parties: Strategies of Conflict Resolution* (Boulder, Colo.: Westview, 1984).

CHAPTER 6. Taking Action

1. This point is made convincingly by Roger Fisher and William Ury, *Getting To YES: Negotiating Agreement Without Giving In* (Boston: Houghton Mifflin, 1981).

2. These constraints are detailed in Lawrence Susskind and Allan Morgan, "Improving Negotiations in the Regulatory Process," *Electric Perspectives* (Spring 1986):22–31.

3. See chapter 4 of Lawrence Bacow and Michael Wheeler, *Environmental Dispute Resolution* (New York: Plenum, 1984), for an inventory of the creative ways in which legal contracts can be used.

4. The decide-announce-defend syndrome is described in Dennis Ducsik, "Citizen Participation in Power Plant Siting: Aladdin's Lamp or Pandora's Box?" in Robert Lake, ed., *Locational Conflict* (New Brunswick, N.J.: Rutgers Center for Urban Policy Research, 1987).

5. For a review of the way private business negotiations are usually handled, see David Lax and James Sebenius, *The Manager as Negotiator* (New York: Free Press, 1986).

6. This applies especially to real estate developers. See Lawrence Susskind, "Negotiating Better Development Agreements," *Negotiation Journal* 3 (January 1987):11–15.

7. Gail Bingham, *Resolving Environmental Disputes: A Decade of Experience* (Washington, D.C.: Conservation Foundation, 1985).

8. Roman Tomasic and Malcolm Feeley, eds., *Neighborhood Justice: Assessment of an Emerging Idea* (New York: Longman, 1982).

9. For a fairly complete listing of public dispute centers, see the *Dispute Resolution Resource Directory* (Washington, D.C.: National Institute for Dispute Resolution, 1984).

10. For a more detailed discussion of the various designs of local dispute resolution programs, see Daniel McGillis, *Community Dispute Resolution*

Programs and Public Policy (Washington, D.C.: U.S. Department of Justice, National Institute of Justice, 1986).

11. For a report on the Hawaii center's success in handling local land use disputes, see Tom Dinell's "Patterns of Resource Disputes in Hawaii," in *Proceedings: Seminar on Conflict Resolution for Energy Siting and Land Use* (Honolulu: Hawaii Department of Planning and Economic Development, 1986).

12. For a review of the state offices of mediation, see Lawrence Susskind, "NIDR's State Office of Mediation Experiment," *Negotiation Journal* 2 (October 1986):323-327.

13. Lawrence Bacow and James Milkey, "Overcoming Local Opposition to Local Hazardous Waste Facilities: The Massachusetts Approach," *Harvard Environmental Law Review* 6 (1982):265-304. Gail Bingham and Daniel Miller, "Prospects for Resolving Hazardous Waste Siting Disputes Through Negotiation," *Natural Resources Lawyer* 17 (Fall 1984):473-489.

14. Three of these attempts are described in Lawrence Susskind and Allan Morgan, *The Uses of Mediation in Electric Utility Regulatory Negotiation: The Results of Three Demonstrations,* report prepared for the Edison Electric Institute by the Public Disputes Program of the Program on Negotiation at Harvard Law School, Cambridge, Mass., May 1986.

15. For a summary of Connecticut's effort to negotiate spending cuts and increases, see Lawrence Susskind and Connie Ozawa, "Mediated Negotiation in the Public Sector," *American Behavioral Scientist* 27, 2 (December 1983):255-275.

16. Lawrence Susskind and Laura Van Dam, "Squaring off at the Table, Not in the Courts," *Technology Review* (July 1986):36-44.

17. For a description of the mediation efforts of Clean Sites, Inc., see Jonathan Marks and Lawrence Susskind, *Negotiating Better Superfund Settlements—Lessons from Experience and Recommendations for the Future,* prepared for the Environmental Protection Agency, Washington, D.C., 1986.

18. Daniel McGillis, "Neighborhood Justice Centers and the Mediation of Housing-Related Disputes," *Urban Law Annual* 17 (1979):245-269, and S. Gillers, "New Faces in the Neighborhood: Mediating the Forest Hills Housing Dispute," in R. B. Goldman, ed., *Roundtable Justice* (Boulder, Colo.: Westview, 1980):59-85.

19. Lawrence Susskind and Scott McCreary, "Techniques for Resolving Coastal Resource Management Disputes," *Journal of the American Planning Association* 51 (Summer 1985):365–374.

20. Carl Moore and Chris Carlson, *Public Decision Making: Using the Negotiated Investment Strategy* (Dayton, Ohio: Kettering Foundation, 1984).

CHAPTER 7. Conclusion

1. An example of such a built-in learning process is presented in Lawrence Susskind and Charles Perry, "The Dynamics of Growth Policy Formulation and Implementation: A Massachusetts Case Study," *Law and Contemporary Problems* 43 (Spring 1979):144–196.

2. This argument was originally presented by Donald Schon, *Beyond the Stable State* (New York: Norton, 1971).

Index

abortion, 17
ACCORD Associates, 226
accountability, 11, 21, 36, 107
acid rain, 16
activist judiciary, 40
ad hoc: approach, 76–79, 103, 188, 232; representatives, 105
administrative agencies, 10; action by, 130; "capture," 37–38, 257n3; and control, 138; and impasse, 8, 10, 255n5; judicial review of, 71–73; negotiations by staff in, 129; and power of majority, 39–40; procedures of, 35–36; regulations of, 198; rule-making in, 35–36; use of dispute resolution by, 229–30, 234–35

adversary system, 71
advocacy science, 29–30, 37, 256n6; vs. joint fact finding, 115–16
affirmative action, 17
agenda setting, 110–13, 119, 215, 218; and intermediaries, 142, 144, 167, 180
agreements, 238; anchoring, 88, 258n5; binding, 11, 123, 125–26, 143, 148, 177, 191, 200, 206, 222; business interests and, 215, 221–22; fairness of, 25; formalization of, 130–31, 143, 148–49, 198–99, 221–22, 229, 241; and intermediaries, 143, 147–49, 163–64, 167, 170–71, 240–41; legality of, 124,

consensus-building *(continued)*
intermediary's tasks in, 142–43;
limits on, 241–46; organizing,
223; prerequisites for, 188–92,
204–7, 213–14; public officials
and, 193–204; summary of, 237–
41; three phases of, 93–94, 95,
140–50; unassisted, 94–135; usefulness of, 13–15; use of, 224–36
Conservation Foundation, 224,
226–27
constitutional disputes, 17, 18–19,
76, 77, 192
consumer advocacy groups, 17, 187
contingencies, 56, 124–25, 129
contract: intermediary's, 139–40,
141, 144; legal, 130, 198, 260*n*3
convenor, 195–97, 204, 208, 218,
227, 234–35
cooperation: and bargaining position, 88–89; and clustering, 202;
vs. competition, 33–34, 86, 88–
89; as negotiating style, 181–82
cooptation, 25, 243
corporations, 17, 187; with internal
disputes, 226; and minitrials,
177–78; *see also* business interests
Corps of Engineers, 231
costs: allocation of, 73, 168–70; and
benefits, 23–24, 146, 170–72, 219;
and citizen groups, 205–6; of
consensus building, 13, 78; of
court-appointed mediators, 231;
and public officials, 202–4; state
offices of mediation and, 228; and
time, 180; of trades, 219; of unilateral action, 202–3; *see also* resource pool

courts, 4, 8, 9, 17–18, 35–36, 38, 40,
70–73, 82, 211, 243, 258*n*14; dispute resolution programs, 225,
231, 234, 235; and power imbalances, 242–43; splinter groups
and, 201
creating vs. claiming, 180–81, 182
creationism, 17
creative thinking, 135, 199
credibility, 103, 150

dam proposals, 110, 116, 117
deadlines, 191–92, 204, 216–17
"decide-announce-defend"
approach, 202–4, 260*n*4
decision making, 11, 20, 57, 227–28
delay, 37, 58, 72, 190–91, 203
demands: and agenda, 111–12; extortionate or excessive, 117–19, 180,
181, 182, 219–20
democracy, 13, 38–39, 76–77, 250
Denver Water Roundtable, 226
Department of Defense, 235
Department of the Interior, 231
developers, 12, 28–29, 41–47, 86–87,
126, 154–55, 169, 187, 190–91, 199,
206–7, 233, 260*n*6; strategy for,
218–19
dioxin dispute, 66–70, 132, 152, 157–
61, 223, 233
direct action, 135
disabled, 53
disagreement, 161, 212
discretion, 37
disorganized groups, 56–57

Index

Index

public dispute centers, 225–27, 260n9

public interest groups, 18, 187, 242

public officials, 12, 13, 128, 252; accountability of, 11; analysis by, 193–95; authority of, 18–19, 184–85, 200, 241–42; concerns of, 184–85, 199–204, 214–42, 244, 252; and control, 138; defined, 186–87; at impasse, 3, 8–9; and implementation, 209; intermediaries and, 193–94; and offers to cooperate, 88–89; negotiation by staff, 129, 193; strategy of, 195–99

public opinion, 19, 103, 154

public policy disputes: advances in resolution of, 223–36; analysis of, 187; business interests and, 213–23; citizens and, 204–13; difficulty of resolving, 8–10; distributional vs. constitutional, 17–19; examples of, 12–13; further reading on, 251–52; implementing consensus building in, 186–236; key players in, 186–87; and need for assisted negotiation, 136–37, 239–41; negotiation strategies, appropriate, 187; new consensus building approach to, 10–15, 237–41, 244–47; numerous recent, 16–17; prerequisites for negotiation of, 188–92; public officials and, 193–204

public postures, 137–38, 140–41, 162–63; see also positions

"pyramiding interests," 202

radioactive waste dumps, 16

ratification: difficulties, 123, 127–29, 194, 200, 209, 223, 244; and intermediaries, 143, 148; time needed for, 209

rebutting best-case summaries, 177

reciprocity, 188–89

record-keeping, 107–8, 119, 201

referendums, 4, 10, 19, 57–58

reframing dispute, 170, 192, 204

regulations, 35–36

Rehnquist, Justice William, 72

relationships: improving societal, 10; in negotiating group, 183, 256n8; stability dependent upon, 32–33

renegotiation: of agenda, 113; in business transactions vs. consensual approaches, 216; and intermediaries, 143, 149, 167; provisions, 32–33, 132–33; and splinter groups, 244

representation: and accountability, 21; ad-hoc, vs. general purpose, 33, 78; alternating or rotating, 105–6; for business interests, 214–16; choosing, 101–8, 208; for citizen groups, 209–10; clustering and, 201–2; controversies over, 106–7; difficulties, 136; "figurehead," 106; finding legitimate, 191, 244; and group commitment, 104–5, 148, 200; intermediaries and, 141–44, 148; of less powerful groups, 14, 102–3; and public official, 197–98; and ratification difficulties, 127–29; size of group, 104; and technical issues,

representation *(continued)*
106; in unassisted negotiations, 101–8
reputation, of potential intermediary, 139
residential neighborhoods, 86–87
resource pool, 145, 205–6, 231, 259*n*2; business interests and, 221; citizen groups and, 210; manager, 205–6, 228
resource recovery dispute, 65–70, 132
Rhode Island, 229
rights: basic, 192; to die, 17; to walk away, 96
risk: and BATNAs, 82–83; business interests and, 213; of first meeting, 96; and trades, 180
RiverEnd mass transit dispute, 41–47, 57, 82, 127–28, 152, 153–57, 189, 201–2, 206, 210, 224, 234, 239, 257*n*4
Robert's Rules of Order, 108
Rocky Mountain Center on the Environment, 226
role playing, 154–55
rotation of spokespeople, 105
rule(s): changing, 21–22; intermediaries and, 144; -making process, 35, 234–35, 257*n*1; *see also* protocols

satisfaction, 22, 80
school desegregation, 17
selective perception, 92, 115
self-enforcing agreements, 125–26, 199

"self-fulfilling prophecies," 91–92
"self-help," 84–85
sequencing: of agenda items, 113; of agreements, 171–72; of reciprocal actions, 125–26
severability clause, 32
sewage dispute, *see* Harmon County sewage dispute
side-by-side problem solving, 26–27
Sierra Club, 187
"single-text procedure," 124, 147–48, 259*n*16
site-specific disputes, 226, 233
siting decisions, 13, 16, 17, 18, 102, 228
slogans, 64
"snowballing," 202
social reforms, 246–47, 253
social security, 235
social service block grant dispute, 49–55, 101–2, 109, 165, 172–75, 206, 229, 239
social service providers' wage issue, 52, 172, 173–74
special master, 61–63, 73, 224, 231, 234
splinter groups, 105, 127–28, 200–201, 202, 221, 222, 244–45
spokespeople, 102, 105–6, 191, 204, 105–6; *see also* representation
stability, 31–33, 39–40, 79, 80
stakeholders, 11, 13; attitudes and perceptions of, 25; choosing form of assistance by, 151; clarifying BATNAs of, 81–85; gauging satisfaction of, 80–81; given adequate chance to participate, 21; identifying, 11, 103–4, 133, 136,